NATION
FORMATION
AND
SOCIAL
COHESION

This research project was supported by:

FRIEDRICH EBERT STIFTUNG

South Africa Office

Irish Aid
Government of Ireland
Rialtas na hÉireann

NASPERS

NATION FORMATION AND SOCIAL COHESION

An Enquiry into the Hopes and Aspirations of South Africa

MAPUNGUBWE
INSTITUTE FOR STRATEGIC REFLECTION (MISTRA)

MAPUNGUBWE
INSTITUTE FOR STRATEGIC REFLECTION (MISTRA)

Mapungubwe Institute for Strategic Reflection (MISTRA)
First floor, Cypress Place North
Woodmead Business Park
142 Western Service Road
Woodmead 2191
Johannesburg

First published August 2014

© MISTRA

ISBN 978-1-920655-85-3

Published by Real African Publishers
on behalf of the Mapungubwe Institute for Strategic Reflection
(MISTRA)

First floor, The Mills
66 Carr Street
REAL AFRICAN PUBLISHERS   Newtown, Johannesburg 2001

Copy editor: Angela McClelland
Indexer: Tanya Barben

MAPUNGUBWE INSTITUTE (MISTRA)
[A NON-PROFIT COMPANY][104-474-NPO]
REGISTRATION NUMBER 2010/002262/08
["THE INSTITUTE"]

CONTENTS

FOREWORD

Among the vexed questions in the evolution of humanity's systems of social organisation are issues of nation formation and social cohesion. Nations, widely understood, date back centuries and have reflected different forms in various parts of the world and in different historical epochs. More strictly organised as nation states, nations and their geographic configurations are associated with the industrial era and the emergence of the capitalist mode of production.

The organisation of humanity into nations provides a functional utility to human relations. Yet, the notions of nation states, nationhood, and citizenship – conferring a sense of belonging and exclusion, representing organisational forms around which endowments are appropriated, and reflecting markers of collective identities – do evoke much emotion. Indeed, in most parts of the world, blood was shed in building nations and in asserting their rights in relation to other nations.

This is even more acutely manifest in postcolonial polities, straddling the very acts of conquest and dispossession, imposition of geographic entities, enforcement of discriminatory policies, mobilisation for national emancipation, and building of new societies.

Contained within these processes are ebbs and flows in self-definition and the evolution of identities. While mobilisation for a sense of nationhood contains within it a homogenising tendency, pride in the roots from which a variety of identities originate, and the ordering of social status within a nation, can have a centrifugal effect.

It is from this perspective that this treatise on nation formation and social cohesion in South Africa is approached. Drawing from literature that defines nations as, among others, political, cultural, economic, and territorial constructs, the study seeks to assess the extent to which South Africa satisfies the theoretical prerequisites to be a nation. This forms the foundation of the report's assessment of progress that has been made since the attainment of democracy.

In doing so, a hornet's nest is necessarily stirred. Besides geography, as well as economic and political systems, to what extent do South Africa's people constitute a nation? Do the erstwhile colonial settlers – who, unlike in most other parts of the postcolonial world, have decided in large numbers to make the country their permanent home – deserve equal recognition as members of the emergent nation? Given the many languages, sets of culture, the legacy of racism and socio-economic deprivation, and varying political interests, how strong are the centripetal impulses; how have they played themselves out in the past twenty years; and what are the prospects for the future? In other words, the many complexities that characterise the challenge of nation formation find acute expression in South Africa.

Against this background, two issues arise which have informed the texture of this study. First, the various attributes that are identified to define a nation are inadequate: they have to be combined with the more recent and somewhat diffuse notion of social cohesion, which also embraces people's dignity and welfare and the legitimacy of the State. Second, nation formation and social cohesion can be theorised and assessed at a generic level, but the lived experience of 'ordinary citizens' does add the kind of flavour that macro-indicators can hardly capture. Thus an 'actor-orientated approach' was adopted, represented in the case studies that are outlined in the report.

The concept of 'nation formation' is used to emphasise the fact that, unlike with the more popular notion of 'nation building', the emergence of nations is a process that does not lend itself to artificial homogenising impositions. Yet the role of agency – from the State to civil society and individual citizens – is not underestimated. This understanding informs the recommendations in the concluding chapter.

The researchers themselves will be the first to admit that there are many gaps in the report. MISTRA did not set out to pen the final word on this matter. Rather it aims to add another drop to the fountain of ideas, debate and knowledge on the 'national question' as experienced in post-apartheid South Africa. We do hope that through its insights and inadequacies this report has met that modest objective.

Our profound thanks to the project team: from the thought leaders and the field workers to the administrators, whose labours gave life to this undertaking. MISTRA is also indebted to the funders of this project, and to the Institute as a whole, whose generosity has afforded our minds the space to wander so South African society can continue its journey to discover and nurture its humanity.

Joel Netshitenzhe
Executive Director

CONTRIBUTORS

Yacoob Abba Omar is MISTRA's director of operations and was formerly South African Ambassador to the United Arab Emirates and the Ambassador to Oman respectively. Abba Omar has held several corporate and public sector positions: Director of Public Affairs at Meropa Communications, Chief Facilitator of the Presidency's Scenarios, General Manager of Corporate Communications at Armscor, Deputy Chief Executive of the Government Communication and Information System (GCIS). He is currently reading for a Ph.D. on 'Sovereignty and National Identity' at the University of the Witwatersrand and holds an M.Phil. in South African Political Economy (Nelson Mandela Metropolitan University).

Leslie Dikeni is a senior researcher at MISTRA in the faculty Humanity. He has an MSc in Rural Sociology (University of Wageningen, the Netherlands) and was a doctoral candidate at the École Pratique des Hautes Études en Sciences Sociales (School for Advanced Studies in the Social Sciences). Dikeni is a visiting research fellow at the School of Public and Development Management (University of the Witwatersrand) and a research associate at the University of Pretoria. Dikeni has co-edited with William Gumede *The Poverty of Ideas: The Retreat of Intellectuals in New Democracies* and is the author of *South African Development Perspectives in Question*.

Robert Gallagher is an activist who has worked in a variety of non-governmental organisations (NGOs) on development issues in the Eastern and Western Cape provinces. He was formerly an executive trustee of the Bethelsdorp Development Trust (BDT) in the Eastern Cape. Gallagher currently runs a small environmental NGO, Penviro, that deals with coastal waste management in the Western Cape. Gallagher holds a BA Degree in Social Sciences (University of the Western Cape).

Feizel Mamdoo has a rich background in the movement for democracy and development in South Africa. His particular interest in arts and culture includes community heritage reclamation. He is a founding director of the award-winning Fietas Festival, a community cultural initiative to reclaim the heritage of his birthplace, Fietas. Mamdoo has worked in a variety of state organisations and NGOs dealing with issues of arts and culture and has been involved in film production. He has also served as editor for various community publications. He currently runs his own company called Journey, Home and Treasure: Feizel Mamdoo Creative Enterprises. He holds an MA in the Sociology of Development (University of Essex, UK).

Shepi Mati is a journalist who previously worked for the Institute for Alternative Democracy (IDASA) as a researcher. Formerly a national president of the Congress of South African Students (COSAS) he has also worked for various civil society organisations in various parts of the country. Mati holds an M.Phil. degree in Journalism (University of Stellenbosch) and an Advanced Diploma in Institution Development (Manchester University).

Joel Netshitenzhe is the Executive Director and Board Vice-Chairperson of the Mapungubwe Institute for Strategic Reflection (MISTRA). He is a member of the National Planning Commission, the ANC National Executive Committee, a board member of the Nedbank Group and Life Healthcare Group, and a Champion within Programme Pioneer of the Nelson Mandela Foundation and Life College Association.

Netshitenzhe was Head of Communication in President Nelson Mandela's office before joining the Government Communication and Information System (GCIS) as CEO in 1998. From 2001 he jointly ran the GCIS and headed the Policy Co-ordination and Advisory Services (PCAS) in The Presidency. From 2006 he headed the PCAS on a full-time basis until his retirement in 2009.

Netshitenzhe has a Master of Science (MSc) degree in Financial Economics, a post-graduate diploma in Economic Principles (University of London, SOAS), and a diploma in Political Science (Institute of Social Sciences, Moscow).

Andries Oliphant is a writer, publisher, academic, literary arts and culture theorist and policy developer. He was educated at the Universities of the Western Cape (UWC) and Oregon, USA as a Fulbright Scholar in Comparative Literature. He is currently Head of Theory of Literature at Unisa. Oliphant has been involved in independent publishing in South Africa – a literary editor for Ravan Press and *Staffrider* magazine, and general editor at the publishing house of the Congress of South African Writers (COSAW). He has served on various panels dealing with the development of South Africa's arts and culture heritage discourse.

ACKNOWLEDGEMENTS

The research into *Nation Formation and Social Cohesion* has spanned some three years involving a large team of researchers, writers, and project team members coming from academia, CBOs, as well as the private and public sectors.

The objective of *Nation Formation and Social Cohesion: An Enquiry into the Hopes and Aspirations of South Africans,* one of MISTRA's priority research projects, is to attempt to peel the skin off the proverbial onion to examine different interpretations and meanings attached to the concept of nation formation and social cohesion. Through different case studies in the different provinces of South Africa, the researchers provide us with interesting narratives on the experiences of a variety of local actors' experiences on the concept of nation formation and social cohesion. The collaboration has brought to the fore a body of work that has informed and shaped this publication. We would like to extend our gratitude to the following:

Core Team

Andries Oliphant (lead writer), Yacoob Abba Omar (who joined the team in 2013), Shepi Mati (field researcher in Western Cape), Vincent Williams (field researcher in Western Cape), Robert Gallagher (field researcher in Northern Cape), Feizel Mamdoo (field researcher in Gauteng), and Sandile Ngidi (field researcher in KwaZulu-Natal).

MISTRA also wishes to acknowledge the guidance of Fébé Gqubule Potgieter, project team leader, and Leslie Dikeni, project co-ordinator and senior researcher at MISTRA. Our thanks equally go to the two peer reviewers who provided detailed feedback on earlier drafts of this report.

Editorial Team

Joel Netshitenzhe, Yacoob Abba Omar, Leslie Dikeni and Rachel Browne

MISTRA Staff

Gail Smith, Thabang Moerane, Hope Prince, Thabiso Chiloane

Project Funders
Friedrich-Ebert-Stiftung (South Africa), Irish Aid and Naspers

MISTRA Funders and Donors

SA Corporates
- ABSA*
- ACSA
- Adcorp
- African Bank
- Ahanang Hardware and Construction
- Anglo American*
- Anglo Platinum*
- Aspen Pharmacare
- Baswa
- Batho Batho Trust*
- Brimstone
- Chancellor House
- De Beers Consolidated Mines Ltd
- Discovery
- Impala Platinum
- Liberty Life
- MMI Group
- MTN Group Ltd*
- Multichoice
- Mvelaphanda Management Services*
- Nedbank*
- Peu Group
- SAB Ltd*
- Safika Holdings
- Shanduka Group*
- Simeka Group*
- Standard Bank*
- Tiso Foundation
- Xstrata*
- Yellowwoods*

Local Foundations
- Graduate School of Development Policy and Practice (GSDPP) at the University of Cape Town
- National Lotteries Board
- NECSA
- Sexwale Family Foundation
- South African Post Office
- Transnet Foundation*
- Wiphold

International Agencies
- Chinese Embassy
- Friedrich-Ebert-Stiftung South Africa
- Olof Palme International Center

Individuals
- Jean-Marie Julienne
- Jackie Mphafudi
- Mathews Phosa*
- Cyril Ramaphosa
- Peter Vundla

* Contributed R500 000 or more

CHAPTER ONE

INTRODUCTION

This research report is the outcome of one of the priority projects of the Mapungubwe Institute for Strategic Reflection (MISTRA) publicly launched in 2011. It focuses on the processes of nation formation and social cohesion in postcolonial and post-apartheid South Africa. It dwells on the challenges and the advances made with respect to these political and social developments since 1994.

The report invariably engages with history, as well as with social and political theory, in relation to the prospect of developing a politically stable, socially inclusive and integrated society capable of meeting the needs of all its citizens and other members in a rapidly changing local, regional and global environment.

While processes of nation formation and social cohesion are by definition inward-looking, in so far as they pertain to local and national developments in a particular country, in this case South Africa, they nevertheless also relate and respond to global developments. This is so since societies across the globe, no matter how insular, are never completely cut off, and thus quarantined, from regional and global forces and developments. Hence, the project links theories of nation formation and social cohesion to actual practises, both focused on the attainment of a just society founded on the irreducible equality of all its members on the one hand, and the factors militating against achieving this, on the other. While its focus is South Africa, its history and its local and national challenges and choices, it draws on contemporary theoretical and critical perspectives pertinent to South African society and the path it set out on since 1994.

In the context of fixed and predetermined historical outcomes, nationalist discourses inevitably draw on nationalist projects, close to home and further afield, in an effort to avoid errors made elsewhere. While this is unavoidable, it should be expected that apparently successful social and political processes related to the construction of a national and sub-national cohesive society will come up against specific local and national conditions that would require context-specific strategies and solutions forged in the sweep of unfolding developments and actualities. In other words, there is no master plan available than can be transferred unmodified from elsewhere. Even if it could be presumed such a plan were available, it would be defeated by the historical experiences and contextual conditions and forces of societies.

Accordingly, this study proceeds by interrogating the theoretical suppositions of nation formation and social cohesion with South Africa in mind. This serves as a starting point for a thorough reflection on these two processes, with the aim of arriving not at a synthesis but at a conceptual position where their interdependence, specifically for postcolonial societies and South Africa in particular, could be interrogated effectively and critically.

This constitutes a break with conventional conceptual practises that treat nation formation and social cohesion not only as distinctive, but also as separate and even divergent. It investigates and attempts to rethink theories of nationalism as grand overarching projects concerned first and foremost with attaining national liberation, followed by the construction and consolidation of a unitary national state.

Viewed thus, it quickly becomes evident that, far from being a grand national historical project, it can only succeed in all its phases under local conditions of popular support and solidarity, manifested at all levels across a given nationally-designated territory. This applies to both armed and negotiated forms of liberation. As such, it is a popular historical event based on the participation of a decisive national majority. It, on the other hand, can be a settlement arrived at among contesting elites, usually foreign and native, which not infrequently results in a mere transfer of power and privileges from foreign to national elites.

This study conceives of nation formation as a political project that does not begin after national liberation but well before in the struggles to defeat national oppression. As has been the case in South Africa and other colonised societies, these struggles involved protracted efforts to construct a united front of people of diverse cultures and classes capable of defeating either external or internal minority domination.

While struggles for the attainment of national sovereignty, especially in instances of foreign domination, accrue to themselves multiple dimensions ranging from economics to language, religion and culture, these are enlisted and function in the service of a primary national political goal: national liberation and the attainment of nationhood. While carried out under specific historical conditions, and thus varying so greatly that no single theory or model can fully account for the specific form and content of every instance of nation building, nevertheless, everywhere, these struggles centre on attaining and maintaining *maximum inclusion* and cohesion among the majority of the population in a given territory. In terms of exclusive forms of nationalism, as in the case of ethnic nationalism, such unity may be sought among minorities. South Africa is familiar with both forms.

In turn, social cohesion, in current theory, is generally conceived as a post-nationalist project in established nation states where either sections of the national majority or historical and new immigrant minorities find themselves excluded and marginalised. In a certain sense, while social cohesion signifies a process related to nation formation based on optimal inclusion and solidarity, it is in fact more concerned with addressing the *negative effects* of economic, social, cultural and other forms of exclusion that develop in highly unequal and stratified societies, or in ones where sections of the population, local or immigrant, are subject to systemic exclusions in different spheres of social life. Theories of social cohesion take their bearings from problems and experiences in recent developments in Western European and North American societies; but are applicable to all nation states where class, gender, generational, disability, cultural and social exclusions are prevalent.

In the case of South Africa, the struggle for national emancipation – while constructed on a multi-class and cross-cultural basis, attainment of formal political and juridical independence and principles of equality, justice and redress – did not bring about the full inclusion of the majority of the population, economically or otherwise, in the post-apartheid society. Rather, it can be argued that it perpetuated elements of old forms of mass exclusion, or produced new ones on such vast scales that the process of nation formation could be said to have been left inadequately attended, with the construction of a non-racial national bourgeoisie and middle strata at the expense of the urban and rural poor having assumed prominence.

These developments and their negative impact on nation formation and social cohesion are examined in this report. The report abandons the discrete treatment of 'nation formation' as a process struggled for, attained and concluded with the advent of national liberation. On the other hand, it questions the notion of 'social cohesion', conceived as formal national unity without broad-based inclusion and participation, as a questionable strategy for preserving the established order. Instead, the post-apartheid national democratic state, as a political and juridical entity in South Africa, seeking to undo and 'overcome the divisions of the past', as the Preamble of the Constitution of 1996 puts it, is a state which is constitutionally committed to a society 'united in our diversity' pledged to 'address the injustices of the past'. This, premised as it is on cultural inclusiveness and equality, logically and necessarily brings nation formation and social cohesion processes together in a way that enables the interface and combination of national and subnational programmes and initiatives centred on nation formation and social cohesion.

The report consists of eight interrelated chapters, variously authored. Chapter One is written by Andries Oliphant and Leslie Dikeni, and discusses the theoretical and methodological aspects that underpin, inform and guide the research. Chapters Two and Four are written by Andries Oliphant.

Chapter Two investigates the two main aspects of the study, namely the theories and processes of nation formation. The term 'nation formation' is used in the place of the term 'nation building' to avoid the coercive associations the latter term has acquired, and to suggest an ongoing, gradual and perhaps never finalised process. The third chapter by Yacoob Abba Omar contextualises past and present debates on the national question in South Africa. Joel Netshitenzhe is the author of the annexure to Chapter Three, a paper produced in the early years of South Africa's democracy. Chapter Four discusses social cohesion and links it with processes of nation formation in national and subnational constellations.

A unique and creative element of this project was to examine the lived experiences of communities in various parts of the country – the actor-oriented approach – among others, to establish how communities interface with one another in their diversity; how they relate to institutions of authority, and how these institutions advance or hinder both nation formation and social cohesion. Chapters Five, Six and Seven by Shepi Mati, Feizel Mamdoo, Robert Gallagher and Leslie Dikeni respectively, consist of the four field reports conducted at sites in the Western Cape, Gauteng, the Northern Cape and KwaZulu-Natal. These reports vary in content and scope as a consequence of the varied conditions under which they were conducted.

The final chapter concludes the study by drawing on the findings to outline some possible interventions aimed at enhancing the processes of nation formation and social cohesion in South Africa.

In addition to the chapter authors, MISTRA would like to acknowledge the contributions made by Fébé Potgieter Gqubule, the project research leader; in Gauteng: Nqobile Zulu, Angelita Mills, Vusimuzi Khumalo and Lucas Spiropoulos; and in the Western Cape, Vincent Williams.

The second and the fourth chapters relate partly to research produced by members of the MISTRA research team for the Diagnostic Report of the National Planning Commission (2011) and the National Strategy for Nation Building and Social Cohesion of the Department of Arts and Culture (2012).

METHODOLOGICAL FRAMEWORK AND RESEARCH PROCESS

This section outlines the methodological and conceptual underpinnings of the research methodology. It deals with the research methods and concepts by interweaving the theoretical, methodological, and data collection aspects arising from, and directed towards, engaging with the interrelated processes of nation formation and social cohesion. It further provides a framework for investigating how the various social actors, organisations and parties organise themselves and participate in challenges related to nation building and social cohesion in South Africa as a national, provincial and local project directed towards overcoming inequalities and divisions spawned in the colonial era.

Based on this, a four-fold strategy is pursued: 1) Critical examination of public declarations and commitments made at all levels of government to work towards building a new inclusive, non-racial society and the proposed plans on how to achieve this; 2) Probing how the nation building and social cohesion objectives of this task are implemented; 3) Identification of the obstacles confronted along the way, and the extent to which they were, or were not, overcome; 4) Examination of public perceptions of the extent to which the State succeeded or failed in achieving the objective of building an inclusive society, united in its diversity.

The point of all this is to establish how diverse social actors, individually, collectively, and grouped in public institutions with different and more often than not conflicting interests, negotiate, or fail to negotiate, the challenges encountered by post-apartheid South Africa's attempts to construct an inclusive and stable nation state; and at the same time achieve a sufficient degree of social cohesion among diverse peoples and cultures in a dynamic and open political and social culture based on equality. This, as in other postcolonial African societies, cannot be attained on the basis of the homogenous nation states of antiquity and the Western-style nationalisms of modernity. It has to be directed towards negotiating diverse social traditions and diverse cultures in response to both old and new South African complexities arising from a society working towards forging shared values and principles of equality and inclusiveness. As a comparative and critical exercise, it is ultimately concerned with what seems to be the withering prospects of nationalism in a time of globalisation amid persistent internal contradictions and social divides.

This calls for investigations into how the State proposes and engages in practises designed to deal with institutional weaknesses that are found to hamper nation formation and social cohesion processes in everyday interactions and contestations between, and among, different social actors. This is important, especially at the level of how social actors organise their livelihoods and harness their respective resources to construct their own conceptions; and organise projects in local community settings that interface in a variety of ways, ranging from partnering with, as well as opposing, formal state interventions. Such interventions are treated as ongoing social processes, shaped and reshaped by complex and often contradictory internal and external dynamics, as well as by the specific local conditions in which these interventions unfold. Accordingly, it is highly problematic to assume that all instances of nation formation are nothing more than identical processes, regardless of the specific contexts; or that all modern nationalism projects are basically enactments in different localities of a basic unchanging form shaped by ineluctable logic, and by even coercive centripetal and homogenising forces associated with forms of nationalism predicated on monolithic principles. Although nationalism is now recognised as the universal process that underpins and shapes struggles for national liberation and sovereignty, it necessarily assumes diverse incarnations and differing trajectories relative to the specificities of time and place.

A key concern of this study is to investigate the extent to which homogenising and generalising theories and conceptions of social cohesion, in combination with monolithic concepts of national unity cast in stone, impact negatively on social expectations at different levels of social life – national, regional and local – against the background of a long history which sought, but failed, to achieve complete subjugation; and despite systematic and sustained social fracturing along ethnic, religious, cultural, linguistic, and spatial lines. Thus, the divergent interpretations that different social actors attach to the concepts of nation formation and social cohesion are material to this study. These divergent interpretations are critical in the history of coercive practises and impositions that have infected many nationalist movements and wrecked nation formation and social cohesion processes in culturally heterogeneous postcolonial societies – even in ones with negligible degrees of diversity but with histories of acute domination and inequality.

To approach this complex and complicated field, the actor-oriented approach will thus be applied. It entails studying state interventions based on individual and shared opinions of how social, political, material and other resources are allocated and applied by the State for the benefit of inhabitants in specific localities, and the impact of this on nation formation and social cohesion. It involves the historical knowledge of local actors in different localities engaged in past struggles against national oppression and social exclusion, and how this informs attitudes and shapes current participation in processes and projects aimed at fostering national, regional and local practises of equality, inclusion and solidarity within and across diverse social groupings.

In this regard, attention is focused on economic and social inequalities and exclusions, persistent spatial divisions and changing spatial dynamics, shifts in personal, ethnic and national identities, old and new forms of prejudice and discrimination, as well as a range of other factors which relate to and impinge on everyday life.

For this purpose, the case study methodology was decided on since it provides opportunities to highlight and analyse the processes by which social actors conduct their daily social interactions, and how they manage their social world in resolving problematic developments. The cases are not treated as representative samples in the sense of illustrating the basic principles of any given social structure. Nor are they necessarily always locality-based, since the project, while involving communities, is strictly speaking not a 'community studies' project.

While interviews are a basic tool of fieldwork, the field reports are not based solely on the method of gathering information, views and attitudes from key informants and respondents. Of equal importance is the observation of a variety of social situations involving various persons. Case studies can reveal either the fragility or the robustness of the existing order, and social patterns of legitimacy or otherwise. A series of case studies can also shed light on processes of social reproduction and change, and on where interventions are called for.

Informed by the twin subjects of the research project, namely nation formation and social cohesion, cases were selected which the research team postulated variously had potential to reveal, among others, the following:

- How individuals and groups devise their own strategies for improving their social circumstances in local conditions where there is a competition for resources.

- How intermediate personnel such as government technocrats attempt to deal with the pressure on them from local people and the national government; how they interpret their tasks and relate their formal obligations to personal career or political aspirations.

- How individuals and groups deal with interventions by public authorities such as political parties using 'race' and ethnicity to foster divisions, exclusions and conflict.

- How in some instances the South African government responds or reacts to international developments, in particular within the United Nations, to deal with inequality, prejudice and discrimination.

- How individual economic or political careers and family-based enterprises are developed over time as alternatives to broad-based economic transformation.

- How political, economic, social and cultural change, initiated by public authorities or by individuals and civic organisations, is viewed in relation to building bridges between, and solidarity among, diverse communities.

A fieldwork method was decided on to ensure that researchers go to where people live to conduct investigations. The method, as Spradly (1979) has it, is the touchstone of intimate, first-hand social enquiry at close quarters. Originally practised by cultural anthropologists, it has been applied in this project to encourage the immersion of outsiders into the lives of communities for some duration. This facilitates a familiarisation with local conditions, personalities and the social dynamics, and allows for observations of, and insights into, both the staged and off-stage moments of community life.

It therefore requires asking situational questions related to the rhythms and rituals of everyday life in processes where research becomes a reciprocal process of learning. At its most effective, it requires necessary and sometimes both necessary and sufficient levels of mutual respect and trust to allow both the fieldworker and her or his interlocutors to get below the surfaces of social life as presented in existing empirical data. To this end, four sites in the Western Cape, the Northern Cape, KwaZulu-Natal and Gauteng were selected for fieldwork focused on nation formation and social cohesion.

This study also sought to construct theoretical concepts, strategies and programmes that can help shape society differently.

The ideas for conceiving the methodological framework adopted in this study began in project team workshop discussions and continued in formal and informal settings. This led to much experimentation during the course of the research aimed at unearthing unique insights that would contribute to policy and societal discourse on the themes of nation formation and social cohesion.

CHAPTER TWO

CONCEPTUALISING NATION FORMATION

Introduction

This chapter provides a general theorisation of the phenomenon historically known as 'nation building' as practised by a variety of countries across the globe in the course of the modern era[1]. The era coincided with the internal consolidations and outward expansion of several countries in post-renaissance Europe. This being the case, it should, however, be kept in mind that processes of gathering people with a shared ancestry and history, as well as diverse peoples into a geopolitical order of state formation in what is today known as a nation, has a long pre-history in Africa and other parts of the world. It could, in fact, be argued that many modern forms of nationalism often appeal to the ancient collective memories and geographical location of a group of people for the historical legitimation of established, as well as new and emerging, nation states.

Even so, the term 'nation building', according to Hroch (2006), has recently fallen into disfavour. This is due to the coercive history and top-down engineering approach associated with it, especially during the nineteenth and twentieth centuries in countries such as Germany and Italy.

Twentieth century aberrations of nationalisms in Europe, Asia, Africa and the Americas, Vincent (2002) reminds us, engendered in many instances a profound 'discomfort' and 'abhorrence' (p.5) to nationalism as violent, intolerant of diversity and inherently repressive or given to forced and

---

1. Parts of this chapter are based on previously published essays by Andries Walter Oliphant: 'Fabrications and the Question of a National South African Literature' in the *Journal of Literary Studies Volume 20,* June 2004, pp.5–24; and the *Diagnostic Report on Nation Formation and Social Cohesion* commissioned by the National Planning Commission.

prescriptive assimilation, prejudice, discrimination and exclusion. Nationalism of the ruling bloc in South Africa under colonialism and apartheid is a case in point.

In this regard, while modern nationalism is presented by theorists and historians, such as John Plamenatz (1976), Hans Kohn (1964) and others, as a social and historical process driven by rationality and freedom, it has a dark side to it. Accordingly, Chatterjee (1986) points out that the 'origin' of nationalism is 'coval with the birth of universal history and its development; is part of the same historical process which saw the rise of industrialism and democracy. In its essential aspects, nationalism therefore represents the attempt to actualise in political terms the universal urge for liberty and progress. And yet, the evidence was undeniable that it could also give rise to mindless chauvinism and xenophobia, and serve as a justification for organised violence and tyranny. Seen as part of the story of liberty, nationalism could be defined as a rational ideological framework for the realisation of rational, and highly laudable, political ends. But that was not how nationalism made its presence felt in much of recent history. It has been the cause of the most destructive wars ever seen; it justified the brutality of Nazism and Fascism; it has become the ideology of racial hatred in the colonies and has given birth to some of the most irrational revivalist movements as well as to the most repressive regimes in the contemporary world' (p.20).

Given the above, Margaret Moore (2006) reassures that political philosophers presently 'almost unanimously assert that policies of coercive assimilation are unacceptable' (p.98). However, according to her there is also 'increasing recognition that the creation of a unified national community will not occur naturally ... as a corollary of 'modernisation'. Nation formation is, after all, a political and social project advanced by political movements and promoted by states, hence its critical importance for the long-term stability of any given society.

In light of this, the term 'nation building', in this study, is replaced by the concept of 'nation formation'. It is consequently conceived as a modernising, multi-causal and dynamic process based on non-coercive political and social consensus. While goal-directed, it is an ongoing open-ended process of making and remaking under changing conditions and new challenges.

DISCOURSE ON NATION FORMATION

The discourse on nation formation in South Africa has found expression in discussions, debates, stratagems, and programmes, especially during the period shaped by the protracted struggles against the colonial dispensation established with the permanent settlement of Europeans at the Cape in 1652. It should, however, be noted that processes of nation formation and social cohesion predate the colonial era in South Africa as the dynamics of fusion and fission described in the 2013 MISTRA study on the rise and decline of the Mapungubwe state[2], and other historical records of state formation in southern Africa, make clear. As Chapter Three demonstrates, in the more recent era this discourse assumed a particular intensity during the twentieth century in South Africa and across the colonised world. It has continued in the postcolonial period after 1994, in relation to the challenges of constructing and consolidating, from the fragments of a previously divided society, a sovereign state, founded on a unitary principle which accords citizenship and equality to all members and communities of its diverse population.

As such, discourse on nation formation should not be treated as a recent phenomenon, but as something both archaic and contemporary in so far as it pertains to social bonds, whether actual or imaginary. These bonds, rooted in history, link together human beings and discrete, yet entangled family units and larger collectives, communities and associations as a geographically situated and distinctive people who see themselves as, and declare themselves a nation. Politically, this is the basis for claims to the inalienable right of self-determination, however narrowly or broadly conceived. It is a discourse that runs through the ages. In South Africa, its specific anti-colonial contours and dynamics, viewed in combination with precolonial developments, constitute the historical range of this discourse.

It can be stated that, while the process of state formation on a national scale was constitutionally attained in 1994, the development of an inclusive society, in which the rights accorded to all citizens have been translated into social and economic reality, is not patently discernible. At the same time, in other parts of the world, what once served as models of the nation state founded on principles of sovereignty and homogeneity have recently come under new fracturing pressures of cultural heterogeneity, economic differentiation, and globalisation, which combine to weaken, and even destabalise, older nation states.

---

2. *Mapungubwe Reconsidered: Exploring beyond the rise and decline of the Maupungubwe state*, MISTRA, 2013.

In this context, nation formation has been accorded different interpretations by different social actors at various times and at different levels of the evolution of the State. The concept is frequently used to either divide the diverse members of society into distinct, fixed and static collectives, or to lump them together in a manner that the nation is treated as the equivalent of the State, and even of the country, as a geographical entity.

Of critical importance here are the implications of the colonial legacy with its baneful and discredited strategies of ethnic differentiation. In a different mode, and as a counter to this, are the discursive obliterations of diversity, and the proclamation of an abstract homogeneity in the drive to forge a South African national identity. This has resulted in practises that perpetuate old divisions and foster new cleavages by promoting a variety of forms of national chauvinism to fuel intergroup hostilities and even xenophobia. As a consequence, the mechanical application of the concept of nation formation (or more accurately nation building) contains the dangers of being alienating to many South Africans who see its invocation as a potentially homogenising strategy designed for new forms of domination and exclusion.

Accordingly, it is necessary to determine whether the current period constitutes a regression of the liberating ideas, principles, values and practises wrought in the struggle against racial domination and division in South Africa. Allied to this is the need to assess to what extent this historical ensemble of what might be called the emancipatory social and political heritage of South Africa is still relevant to the present and the future. This chapter, then, seeks to trace the theoretical and conceptual parameters of nation formation as preliminary steps towards investigating the history of the national project, its current status, and its future prospects.

WHAT IS NATION FORMATION?

The process of nation formation poses a series of questions, the first being: What is a nation? Other interrogations issuing from this question and related to 'nationalism' and the 'nation state' follow in the wake of this and lead to the underlying governing questions, however conceived: Is South Africa a nation state? Is it a nation? If it is, how has it been constituted? If it is not, why not? Alternatively, is South Africa a nation state in the making? If so, where is it situated along the trajectory of such a process? These questions are addressed conceptually and temporally, that is, in both their theoretical and historical guises. A first elementary step in this regard is to home in on the etymological adventure of the word 'nation'.

In respect of what a nation is, Oliphant (2004, p.10) cites Greenfeld (2001, pp.251–252), who traces the semantic evolution of the term and argues that the modern concept 'nation' has a long history. According to Greenfeld, the modern meaning of the concept is a product of a series of semantic changes over time in relation to social and political changes in Europe. Derived from the Latin word *natio*, meaning 'something born', it signifies *origin* in the general sense of birth, and in the particular sense of place of birth.

In ancient Rome, it designated communities of foreigners who lived in the city state as aliens without the rights and privileges of Roman citizens. The political meaning of 'citizenship', often confused with nationality, carried forth across the ages, and still pertains to rights accorded to persons at birth or through naturalisation in a bounded space whose national territories are cities or places, not merely of residence, but localities of birth. Thus, in Rome, communities of foreigners constituted 'nations', while persons of Roman birth enjoyed the status of 'citizens'. This points to a practise in which foreigners either possessed, or were ascribed, 'national identities' distinct from Roman citizens.

In this cultural practise, the term 'nation' had a derogatory, inferior, and non-Roman connotation. Since the Roman polity was based on the city state, being a member of a nation, rather than a citizen of a city state, placed foreigners below Romans in terms of civic status. 'Nations' were denied the rights of citizens. Under such circumstances, national affiliation could hardly have been deemed positively since, according to Greenfeld '[i]t marked the extent to which the community of foreigners did not belong to the larger defining community of Romans' (ibid. p.252).

Oliphant (2004), following Greenfeld (2001, p.252), points out that during the Middle Ages, roughly demarcated as spanning the period from 300 CE to 1300 CE, the term 'nation' underwent a radical semantic change. Then it 'was applied to the communities of students in medieval universities, who were rarely born where the university was situated' (ibid.). Since medieval universities were open to everyone across the Christian world, students from different geographical regions were housed together in quarters shared with their professors. This, evidently, is in accordance with the Roman usage of the word, invoked and applied to set foreigners apart from local inhabitants.

In the course of their academic life, students, along with their professors, participated in debates and in the process came to be associated with the intellectual positions they held, expounded and defended. The result was that every community of students and professors came to be identified with a particular set of ideas which differentiated them from other 'nations'.

This, Greenfeld said, changed the Roman meaning of nation as 'a community of foreigners' (2001, p.252) to signify a 'community of opinion' with a shared origin. In the universities the new meaning did not completely supersede the earlier one. In restricting it to communities within the university, the term no longer bore the derogatory connotation it was given in Roman discourse, even though its application was still exclusionary: only foreign students constituted nations.

Upon completion of their studies, students lost their 'national identity' and were assimilated into the clergy. In this historical phase, the word 'nation' attached to itself the meaning of a special group, even an elite one. Hence, in the course of the Middle Ages, this meaning of a 'nation' as a distinctive or even exceptional group began to be applied to the various representatives within the Christian republics with religious, cultural and political authority, but not to the population of these geo-religious formations.

The term, according to Greenfeld, acquired its modern meaning in sixteenth-century England. In a dramatic transformation it came to signify 'the people' (ibid.). From its ancient biogeographical semantics marking origin, identity, and exclusion from the rights of citizens, this term, once reserved for outsiders, and later for special groups, was given an inclusive meaning to encompass a population. From ascriptions first to marginal, then to special, groups, it came to signify a people as a whole. Thus the significance of birth in a specific geographical space, as well as the attribution of exceptionality associated with earlier meanings given to the term, was extended to the population of England as a whole. Concerning this, Greenfeld writes:

> *The magnitude of this conceptual revolution can be fully appreciated only if we consider the change that occurred simultaneously in the meaning of the word "people". In English, French, German and Russian discourse, among others, before it was made the synonym of "nation", the word meant "rabble" or "plebs"; the general referent of the "people" was the so-called "lower" classes. It should be pointed out here that the concept of nation as signifier of people has parallels in southern African languages in the words such as 'Sizwe' which basically refers to the people*

of a given territory as a whole and may be treated as equivalent terms to those of nation (2001, p.252).

Thus, designating the *people* as the 'nation', the populace, long despised and excluded from the privileges of Roman citizenry and feudal society everywhere, divested the concept of its derogatory and restrictive or elitist meanings. Infused with immense prestige, it was redefined to signify loyalty and political solidarity among diverse peoples gathered in a bounded territory under a sovereign ruler. Consequently, Greenfeld concludes 'a major transformation was effected in the image of the social order: defined as a nation, the community, inclusive of all classes' (ibid.), was construed as sovereign and as a community of equals. From here it is a short distance to the modern usage of the term.

In this regard, Guibernau (1996) writes that in modern political discourse 'nation' refers 'to a human group conscious of forming a community, sharing a common culture, attached to a clearly demarcated territory, having a common past and a common project for the future and claiming the right to rule itself' (p.47). This leads Oliphant to point out (2004, p.11) that, although the matter of birth and territory and the right to rule itself serve to mark the group as indigenous, the master trope for this kind of collectivity is what is held in 'common'. This commonality, while serving as a signifier for what is shared within the group, also serves to mark it as different from other groups. This conjures up a chain of real or imagined identities and differences, suggesting that the axis along which the signifier 'nation' operates is fraught with instability, tension and the danger of disintegration by internal contradictions and external threats. What, then, is a nation?

Anthony Smith's (1991, p.22) list of attributes of a nation can be supplemented with Guy Michaud's (1992, p.112) theory of collective identities, which are expanded by Oliphant (2004, p.12) to generate the following attributes that define the nation as a social collective with:

- a shared consciousness of forming a homogenous group;
- a shared descent or origin;
- a shared and recognised demarcated territory;
- a mass public culture disseminated to all through a shared public education system;
- a shared indigenous language;
- a shared indigenous or nativised religion;

- a shared national political dispensation;
- a shared legal system;
- a single economic system, and
- equal political, civil, and economic rights for its citizens.

This conception, presented as an abstract typology, and not as an actual historical phenomenon, circulates in discourses on modern nationalism in various forms. These commonalities are frequently considered, if not as a precondition for nation formation, then at the very least as the guiding political objective of the nation formation project. This rubric of commonality is considered not as an absolute precondition for nation formation, or even as an objective of such a project. This set of attributes, premised as it is on the desire for homogeneity, is frequently considered a prerequisite for the construction of nations.

In this regard, it is instructive to recall the debates that shaped the discourse of nationalism in the wake of the October Revolution in the early twentieth century when the Bolsheviks were faced with the challenge of dealing with the diverse cultures of Russia on the eve of the overthrow of the Russian empire. To this end, Lenin's thesis on 'The Socialist Revolution and the Right of Nations to Self Determination' (1917, p.157–168) asserts that autonomy, including the right to secede, is a precondition for the formation of a democratic union or federation of socialist states. It is a precondition for socialism since the conquered peoples of pre-revolutionary Russia were incorporated as subordinates to the empire. Some years before this, in 1913, Stalin had produced a pamphlet, *Marxism and the National and Colonial Question*, in which he produced a list of characteristics resembling the above typology. According to Stalin, a nation which is neither a tribal nor racial phenomenon consists of five characteristics, namely: a stable community of people, a common language, a clearly demarcated historical territory, a coherent national economy, and a distinct social and cultural area (1954, pp.303–313). This would eventually be mechanically applied, regardless of specific conditions and contexts, in such a way that it obscured the fact that societies with diverse cultures can, and have, constructed autonomous national states which include different groups. South Africa, as it will become clear in Chapter Three, is nevertheless a historical example of this. For this reason the typology above should in no way be construed as a prerequisite for nation formation, since it would foreclose the multiple and diverse ways in which a nation state can, and has been, constructed.

However, the very idea of unity and homogenisation suggests overcoming pre-existing or existing divisions, disunity and differences. Why otherwise bother to embark on the arduous and often violent project of nation formation if a people, unexpectedly divided by conquering invaders since time immemorial, constituted the kind of singularity and unity of the modern nation modelled on modern European projects of unification, uncritically and undifferentiatedly universalised? Since primordial unity is a myth, Oliphant argues (2004, p.12) that the coming-into-being of a nation, politically and culturally, is invariably a project involving, with varying degrees of intensity, the coercive fusion of diverse and previously divided peoples into a linguistic, cultural, territorial and political unity, not once and for all, but under specific historical conditions. This unity in identity, if it is achieved, is not immune to fissure under changing internal and external conditions.

Propelled by internal rivalries and contestations, or by external threats, whether real or imagined, projects of nation formation are often driven by both liberatory and repressive agendas. Where this occurs in linguistically homogenous societies it always involves either the voluntary sublimation of difference or its suppression. In linguistically diverse societies such putative unity is often achieved by the elevation of a dominant language or the dominant rise of various related languages, including variants of a language into a national language, and the construction of a culture in which selective debris of the defeated are modified and incorporated into the new emergent or self-proclaimed triumphant national culture. This marks the process of nation formation in the very narrative it lays claim to, as a site of power, prejudice, intolerance, and violence, masquerading as the topos, if not the paragon of benevolent inclusivity. Hence the bloody trail left in the wake of nations (2004, p.12).

Oliphant observes (ibid.) that some qualifications are needed at this point. Not all the features listed above are necessarily present in all groups who regard themselves, or are referred to, as nations. Linguistic, cultural and religious diversity has not prevented Belgium, Canada, Nigeria, and many countries in Latin America, from referring to themselves as nations, nor from being viewed as such.

This prompts Oliphant (ibid.) to conclude that a nation is not just a linguistic, cultural, religious, and economic grouping or 'formation', but it is 'also, and crucially, a political entity' (ibid.) based on a collective decision to form a nation, of which the 'rallying cry is that of popular sovereignty and unfettered self-rule. It issues from within the group with regard to its rights to autonomy within the boundaries defined as the national territory'. It is frequently, and perhaps always, a radical response to forms of foreign domination. Accordingly, it is quite possible to construct a nation state not made up of a single or homogenous people who claim to be a nation made up of indigenes, as well as those who have come to identify with the cause of national autonomy.

Oliphant (2004, p.12) mentions that referring 'to heterogeneous societies as nations' compounds the problem set out to be clarified in the chapter. 'It is salutary to reflect that what is often meant when "nationhood" is invoked, is not the actual linguistic and cultural homogeneity of the people, but rather the territory of political sovereignty, no matter how fragmented or tenuous. It is this divergence from the meanings of the term "nation" that renders the term and societies either living under its banner, or aspiring to do so, unstable. The extremes of these divergences are the definition of a "nation as signifying a homogenous people on the one hand, and on the other hand" its application "to a politically sovereign and centralised state with a diversity of cultures and peoples" (p.13).' This volatility, Oliphant (2004) argues, issues from the invocation of the concept of the national as a 'self-defining term, beyond critical examination' (ibid.).

In the light of this, the abstract meaning reserved for the term 'nation' here is that of a social formation with a common language, culture and history, conscious of constituting a community of interests and values residing in a geographically defined and unified sovereign state. This is the putative model nation state which is applicable to only a limited number of states, however improvised or borrowed. 'Whether such societies – larger than kinship clusters of comparatively localised communities – exist or ever existed is open to question. The nation, in the sense of singularity, in all respects would seem to be an ideological construction with little purchase in "reality". In this regard, that the actual multiplicity of everyday experiences and differences contradict assumptions of cultural continuity and commonality, to say the least, frustrates abstract assertion of homogeneity (ibid.).'

It is for this reason that for the long-term stability and survival of any state, its people must share, or believe they share, a common identity, past and future. In the absence of this, societies, whether homogenous or heterogeneous, will be plagued by social tensions, conflicts, prospects of secession and even disintegration.

The populace in a nation state must further subscribe to a set of shared values, symbols and institutions. This does not require that all its members have to be culturally identical in every respect. Such homogeneity, by the way, is only possible in relatively small ethnic (and perhaps really only in sub-ethnic) groups. Where such homogeneity exists in larger heterogeneous nation formations, cultural, linguistic, and other differences are either suppressed or submerged or eradicated. This is the case even with putative homogenous states such as Japan, Finland, Botswana and Lesotho, all of which at some point in history consisted of diverse clusters of people with regional and local identities and allegiances, who, over time, are incorporated and bound together in a national state in which pre-national diversities are attenuated.

In other words, cultural homogeneity is not an absolute precondition or requirement for every possible case of nation formation. This is so since diversity and difference can be accommodated in federal or various other inclusive political and social arrangements designed for coexistence on the basis of equality.

However, what is indispensable for a nation to coalesce is that there should be general consensus on what constitutes the geographical and political legitimacy of a particular society. This constitutes the basis of the social contract on which the nation is endorsed and founded by its subjects: that is the people as agents, and creators, of the nation.

In this regard, Margaret Moore (2006) reasons that where it is impossible to create a culturally homogenous nation state, the ethical imperative requires that the State negotiates and constructs a political order that is inclusive of the established and legitimate diversity of the society. This is precisely what informs the architecture of the postcolonial South African state.

One could thus conclude that a nation is not essentially a linguistic, cultural or religious formation, even though nations approximating this do exist. It is crucially, and perhaps irreducibly, always a political entity in the first place. In the South African context, its rallying call is national sovereignty, self-rule and democratic accountability. It issues from within the social group, whether homogenous or heterogeneous, assembled to assert its rights to autonomy within the geographical boundaries claimed as the national territory.

The above, understood as nationalism in the thinking of Fanon, Cabral, Biko, Mandela, Mbeki, and a host of other African nationalists, is the subjective and historical agency of the nation, ushered into objective social and historical existence. Such history may have its roots, as with most African states, in the arbitrary geographic divisions imposed by the General Act of the 1884 Berlin Conference. It moves over time through three interlinked phases, which Hroch (1985 and 2000) identifies as an initial intellectual and elitist interest, followed by patriotic anti-colonial agitation, to culminate in a mass national movement.

This temporal development serves to popularise and democratise the form and content of the nation as both real and constructed to its historical and social context. Accordingly, it is eminently possible to have a nation state without a homogenous population or people that can nonetheless claim to be a nation consisting of indigenes, as well as settlers and immigrants, all of whom have come to identify with the cause and objectives of national autonomy.

SOME CONSTRUCTS OF NATION FORMATION

Since the construction of nation states cannot be reduced to a single unchanging form, it is advisable to consider a range of possible constructs. With respect to African nationalism, Clarke (2001), Hardt and Negri (2001) and Neuberger (2006) trace the roots of African nationalism to both the Americas and Africa. The founding figures include: Toussaint L'Ouverture of Haiti; the Jamaicans Edward Blyden and Marcus Garvey; Henry Sylvester Williams and George Padmore from Trinidad; Frantz Fanon and Aimé Césaire from Martinique; and W. E. B. Du Bois from the United States; as well as early African nationalists such as Cheikh Anta Diop from Senegal; Kwame Nkrumah from Ghana; Jomo Kenyatta from Kenya; Nnamdi Azikwe from Nigeria; Julius Nyerere from Tanzania; and Abdullah Abdurahman, Pixley ka Isaka Seme, Solomon Plaatje, John Dube, John Tego Jabavu, Josiah Gumede, James la Guma and Mahatma Gandhi from South Africa.

A political construct constitutes the population as a unified nation in a common territory with shared political institutions, a political history, common economic, legal and educational systems, as well as equal rights for all its members.

A cultural/ethnic construct constitutes a diverse population as a unified nation on the basis of a common origin, language, religion, traditions, customs, mores, political, legal and economic systems, and a high degree of consciousness of forming a distinctive ethnic nation.

A religious construct constitutes the population as a unified nation on the basis of a common religion.

An economic construct constitutes diverse peoples as a nation on the grounds of common economic and political systems and equality for all its members.

A territorial construct constitutes a unified nation state in a common territory, with shared economic, legal and political systems, but with separate educational, cultural and religious, public and civic institutions.

A multinational construct constitutes a single territory with a federal political system consisting of a diversity of semi-autonomous national communities residing in ancestral regions.

A disintegrative misconstruct is the failure to constitute a unified nation in culturally homogeneous or culturally heterogeneous populations resulting in national implosion and sometimes even disintegration.

Specifically devised for this diagnosis, the list of 'ideal' attributes or features of a nation set out elsewhere in this chapter, and the typologies above, can now be used in three diagnostic ways and they are as follows. First, they can be used as a checklist for the typologies to establish the specific content and profile of each construction or typology. By determining the number of attributes specific to each construct, the relative stability and long-term viability of each can be theoretically determined as a potentiality. Second, by adding up the number of attributes found in a particular social formation, and by establishing which of the attributes are most prevalent, the main 'anchors' for nation formation of a particular society can be identified and consolidated in practise. Third, the significance of the attributes that are missing from a particular society, and their importance for national cohesion, will assist in deciding on strategies and programmes to develop weak or absent attributes if deemed critical and necessary for the durability of the construct.

For example, South Africa possesses seven of the ten shared attributes listed above. This is a very high score. It lacks three shared attributes insofar as it does not possess a common language, religion and culture. This is a relatively low score when compared to the seven attributes it does have.

This would suggest that in theory South Africa has a relatively good prospect of developing into a viable national formation, provided it harnesses its linguistic, cultural, and religious diversity as a source of strength, and as touchstones for an inclusive non-racial democracy as spelt out in the Constitution of the Republic of South Africa (1996).

Furthermore, identifying which of the attributes South Africa possesses are weak or problematic, such as for instance a 'shared economy' with its present stark imbalances, strategies aimed at eradicating all forms of economic exclusion become imperative. This equally applies to education, land, and everything else.

How then, Oliphant (2004) asks, do these 'imaginary constructs' become real? The answer is through the process of nationalism as the social, political, and cultural forces which produce the nation. In this regard, nationalism is 'the ideology which produces the awareness and the consent of being': to be, to want to be, and to become a nation. 'This is done by mobilising populations to work in support of the political institutionalisation of the nation' (p.13). Nationalism, furthermore, is defined by Guibernau (1996) as the 'sentiment of belonging to a community whose members identify with a set of symbols, beliefs, and a way of life, and have the will to decide about their common political destiny' (p.47).

Oliphant (2004) points out that 'sentiment here suggests an emotive affiliation or an affective' sense of belonging. As such, it is 'something one subscribes' and consents to 'rather than the assertion of any empirical fact' (p.13). This is not to be dismissed out of hand, irrationally. Such sentiment of a conscious sense of belonging is the expression of a social desire to be part of a unified collective. As such, it 'asserts a specific national identity as different from other national identities' (p.13).

In the fervour of nationalism, that is, its insistence on peculiarity, it of course makes far too much of difference. To this extent, far from decentring the so-called bourgeois subject, understood as the mythical free individual, it emerges with its double, in which bondage and freedom are indistinguishable. In this, nationalism responds to specific historical challenges by appealing to the past. So, Ernest Renan writes:

> [a] nation is a soul, a spiritual principle. Two things, which are in truth one, constitute this soul or spiritual principle. One lies in the past, one in the present. One is the possession of a legacy of rich memories; the other is the present-day consent, the desire to live together, the will to perpetuate the value of the heritage that one has received in an undivided form.... The nation, like the individual, is the culmination of a long past of endeavours, sacrifice, and devotion. Of all cults, that of the

ancestors is the most legitimate, for the ancestors have made us what we are. A heroic past, great men, glory (by which I understand genuine glory), this is the social capital upon which one based the national idea. To have common glories in the past and to have a common will in the present; to have performed great deeds together, to wish to perform still more, these are the essential conditions for being a people. One loves in proportion to the sacrifices to which one has consented, in proportion to the ills one has suffered. One loves the house one has built and handed down. The Spartan song – "We are what we were; we will be what we are" – is, in its simplicity, the abridged hymn of every patrie (Renan 1995, p.19).

Based on the above, Oliphant (2004) argues that nationalism is the collective expression, necessarily of diverse peoples, to become or to be part of a larger social formation called the nation.

While nationalism draws on patriotism, that is, love for the fatherland, with all the patriarchal implications of this affection, its political aspirations are territorial sovereignty and its values, and the equality of its members. Its cultural content is a shared language, common symbols, customs and values. Its physical, or nativist, element is birth in a geographically specified territory. Nationalism, then, is the ideological force that rallies and binds together different peoples by appealing to the idea of a common origin and a shared culture, regardless of their differences. Its objective is to constitute a state in which those who agree that they belong together may govern themselves with the promise of a free life and as equal citizens.

Its central thrust, therefore, is to subsume all differences in a larger all-embracing structure. Historically, this has frequently implied the solidarity of a diversity of peoples who consider themselves native to a territory in the face of what is experienced, and opposed, as foreign domination. Thus, internal differences are suspended while a divide is projected outwards to mark a line of division between the indigene and the foreign invader.

Still, how does nationalism account for the existence or the coming-into-being of a nation? Some theory, that is some explanatory intervention on how the various forms of nationalism account for phenomena they produce, is called for here. An interrogation yields two governing explanatory thrusts: one is essentialist, the other relativist. While there are many varieties of each of these two types, for brevity, focus here is only on the main forms of each.

The essentialist view on the origins of a nation is based on the belief that the distinguishing qualities of the nation are inherent to it and to the people who constitute it. The nation, in these terms, is considered a self-evident and necessary truth. These qualities, which are exclusive to the nation, render it a unique and admirable phenomenon. The essentialist view conceives of the nation as the expression of a primordial identity. In the words of Hans Kohn (1961), it is merely the latest and most manifest 'expression of the oldest and most primitive feelings in man' (p.4). The two main forms that this view has advanced claim that the nation is a natural, or a divine, phenomenon.

The divine theory is associated with Friedrich Schleiermacher (1768–1834). According to Schleiermacher, the nation is:

> a natural division of the human race, endowed by God with its own character. Every nationality is destined through its peculiar organization and its place in the world to represent a certain side of the divine image, for it is God who directly assigns to each nationality its definite task on earth and inspires it with a definite spirit in order to glorify Himself through each one in a particular manner (Schleiermacher, quoted by Kedourie, 1974, p.58).

The nation, according to this view, is the instrument of a people chosen by God for them. This, obviously, is an extension of the divine discourse on which medieval monarchy was based, now carried over into the realm of one form of eighteenth-century German nationalism. It follows from this that the language, literature and culture of each nation will be seen as divine attributes and will be used to express and reflect the God-given identity of the nation.

According to Oliphant (2004), '[t]he natural explanation is represented in the ideas of Johann Gottfried von Herder (1744–1803). His view also roots the origin of nations in a sacred source, but in his case it is a natural manifestation. He conceives of humanity, grouped into nations, as the highest form of divine perfection' (p.15). Von Herder asserts that 'every human perfection is national ... and every nationality bears in itself the standard of its perfection, totally independent of all comparison, with every nation as an organic unit with each branch of its culture as an organic part of a larger unit. It is a "natural plant", a "national animal". The biological, that is the natural processes of birth, growth, maturity and decay as well as the ties of blood, are the origin and history of a nation' (Von Herder, quoted in Ergang, 1996, pp.169, 324). 'A nation', he writes, 'is as natural as a plant, as a family, only with more branches' (ibid. p.84–85).

According to Oliphant (2004), Guibernau (1996, p.49) calls this a 'socio-biological' view that combines the image of a plant and the concept of a family to construct a metaphor for the family. This discourse has ethnic and racial overtones since it conceives of the nation, its culture, language and literature as organic products of a naturally given identity.

'This discourse on nationality has overt ethnic and racial overtones. It regards the nation, its language, its literature, and its culture as organic products of a naturally given ethnic identity. In both the divine and the natural accounts, the nation is conceived as a necessary, absolute, and immutable entity. It is a phenomenon beyond human agency, historical circumstance, and any other contingency (p.16).'

The relativist or constructivist view, which stands in diametrical contrast to the essentialist view, considers the nation not as something sacred and absolute, but as a product relative to its historical circumstances and context and to its relationship to a variety of other factors. It is not immutable but subject to change. While national identity is viewed as part of the broader imperative of individual and group identity, it is posited that no identity is inevitable or necessary. Like all identity, the nation is a social, cultural and political construct or invention. Here, too, two main explanations can be identified. The first is an economic account, and the second, a psychological explanation.

Ernest Gellner (1983) is a leading proponent of the economic theory of the origin of nations. He argues that the nation originated from forms of divisions of labour associated with complex and rapidly changing modern industrial society. The dislocations and mobility resulting from this, in time, engenders forms of egalitarianism. In contrast to pre-industrial societies where social roles were fixed and stable, and the barriers of rank were rigidly cast, the conditions of production in industrial societies, he argues, while still based on stratification, are less rigid and more fluid and therefore disruptive.

Oliphant (2004) picks up on Gellner's point that this, along with new centralised and standardised institutions of education, mechanised production, regulated working hours, production rates, quality controls and transportation schedules, a degree of homogeneity is produced in the lives and culture/s of a population mobilised for national unity in the service of capitalist interests.

The process of national homogenisation of a population, uprooted from the micro-groups of local life and enlisted, most often, in military-like fashion by capital as disposable labour, insisted on 'the people', the much-loved phrase, as an undifferentiated and pliable populace.

Gellner asserts: 'It is nationalism which engenders nations, and not the other way round (1983, p.55).' In other words, it is not nations which give rise to nationalism, as is sometimes thought; although once formed, nations ensure that survival by means of every form of nationalism it calculates will secure the nation. In the process of constructing nations, nationalism selectively draws on pre-existing and historically inherited cultures, including languages and literatures, transforming them to both reflect the aspirations of the people and to meet the requirements of industrial society.

Oliphant (2004) also identifies for particular attention the psychological theory of nation formulated by Benedict Anderson (1983). Like Gellner, he places the emergence of the nation in industrial society, but where Gellner emphasises the conditions of production in industrialised societies, Anderson singles out the role of public education:

> ... public education for everyone within its reach and mass market communications (first books, then newspapers, radio and television) which together appeared to make sense of modern life and to create the illusion of vast new "citizen" communities (Anderson 1991, p. 615).

Thus, people who had never met each other were imagining themselves to be part of the same community. It was, however, the role of the printing press in disseminating literature in the vernacular in Europe which rapidly came to be associated with the broader social lives of the people within a specific language territory. So the seeds of what would eventually become national languages were sown.

Anderson (1991) claims that the languages which circulated in print facilitated the emergence of national consciousness by creating uniform patterns of communication and exchange in which large numbers of people participated. In the process, the language spoken by the majority of the people was, for the first time, also the language of power, public administration, and discourse.

Nationalisms, whether essentialist or relativist, Oliphant (2004) argues, rely on fabrication. They construct commonalities by piecing together disparate peoples into a trans-ethnic formation in which differences are elided in what is held as a shared heritage. The nation is fabricated because, even in its non-pejorative sense, it is an assemblage of language, culture, religion, land, history, and whatever else, and is forged into a single entity, not at whim, but from the contingencies of power and in the furnaces of history.

If this commonality is always geo-specific and proper to people living under their own rule, then the structure within which this sovereignty is actualised is the nation state. *The Concise Oxford English Dictionary* defines state as 'the organised political community under one government'. It is the institutionalised political authority governing a community within a specific territory. In this sense, a 'nation state' is the political authority of a homogenous people with a shared language, culture, religion, and other symbols, values and traditions held in common.

As Guibernau (1996) asserts, the relation and difference between a nation and a nation state is that while the members of a nation are conscious of forming a community, the nation state seeks to create a nation and develop a sense of community stemming from it. While the nation has a common culture, values and symbols, the nation state as an expression of nationalism has as an objective – the creation of a common culture, symbols and values. The members of a nation can look back on a common past: if the members of a nation state do likewise, they may be confronted with a blank picture – because the nation state simply did not exist in the past – or with a fragmented and diversified one, because they belonged to different ethno-nations.

In the light of this, Oliphant (2004) asserts: 'The nation state then, politically, institutionalises the identity posited by seldom-produced nationalism (p.18).' However successful in the short- and medium-term the repressions, marginalisations and exclusions invariably produced by nationalist projects, being interventions aimed at achieving unity advanced as singular and monolithic in the long-term, and during unpredictable currents of internal and global changes, are nothing more than what they actually are: contingent, vulnerable, fragile, and even explosive formations.

STRANDS OF NATIONALISM IN SOUTH AFRICA

In light of the above, various strands of nationalism can be identified in South Africa: in the precolonial state there were formations of pastoral and other settlements, and at the time of the Union of South Africa, British imperialism, after defeating a nascent Afrikaner nationalism, tried to promote a form of white settler unity as a way of ruling South Africa. This nationalism was driven by economic imperatives. It failed as Afrikaner nationalism came to dominate political discourse in South Africa, promoting its ideology of ethnic nationalism. It was driven by essentialist ideas of racial purity and divine destiny. By the same token, white incursions and domination before and during the Union of South Africa served as a catalyst for a nascent African nationalism rooted in territorial and historical claims and demands for equality. The ascendency of Afrikaner nationalism and apartheid in turn gave rise to a national liberation struggle with a non-racial and trans-ethnic ideology. Each of these variants of nationalism produced its own literary articulations, the strongest of which are perhaps the articulations of Afrikaner nationalism, African nationalism, and the non-racial national liberation discourse.

It is clear, however, that while present-day South Africa could be said to consist of a single state, the territory designated the Republic of South Africa is made up of a diversity of cultural and linguistic groups. These range across African, Asian and European traditions, all of which are internally differentiated. This fragmentation and diversity, upheld and fostered under colonialism and apartheid, represents an impasse to the emergence of a single nation with a common language, culture and religion. However, the establishment of a single unitary South African state, which is the product of the struggle by the majority of the population against both foreign and minority settler domination, is based on the principle of sovereign rule by all its people, all of whom are equal before the law. It can even be termed a democratic state without a nation.

States without nations, Guibernau (1996) mentions, are typical of situations where a single, territorially bounded state is made up of a diversity of cultural and linguistic groups. Such polyethnic and territorially based states are common in Africa, having been constructed within the arbitrary territorial boundaries pegged out by colonial occupation, rather than out of protracted internal processes. Such nation states are actually in the majority because, as pointed to earlier, mono-ethnic states are rare.

Hence, in a country such as South Africa, made up of diverse linguistic and cultural communities, the immediate and even long-term prospects of a single monolithic nation seem remote, given a constitution which recognises cultural and religious diversity and accords equality to eleven languages and extends constitutional recognition and support to a variety of other languages. In the absence of cultural and linguistic homogeneity, the constitutional framework of equality in diversity serves as the basis for a considerable degree of political stability and coherence. This relative stability and coherence must, however, not be confused with unity in the sense of singularity: the oneness of undifferentiated uniformity. It marks what might be termed the 'post-nationalist' state, in which diversity, if not celebrated, is no longer suppressed or placed under erasure by homogenising nationalism but is accepted as a social and cultural reality that cannot be wished away or violently eradicated.

This notwithstanding, the proclivities of nationalism, even in what presently is considered a post-nationalist epoch of globalisation and erosion of nation states, mean that, speculatively at least, there cannot be an absolute impasse to unity and social cohesion. This applies even in situations in which multiplicity, diversity and difference take precedence over modernist impulses towards singularity, in which the many nationalisms of the world were forged. In the light of this, it becomes necessary to rethink the process of nation formation in South Africa.

Whatever form it takes, this invented narrative, to rephrase Bhabha (1990), will have to configure the 'many' cultures not into 'one' and into what the Constitution of South Africa enjoins: 'We, the people of South Africa, believe that South Africa belongs to all who live in it united in our diversity.'[3] This calls for the development of strategies and programmes that will foster social solidarity and unity in diversity, as opposed to some fictional homogeneity.

South African nationalisms, evidently, are products of the various strands of African, Asian and European nationalisms. This flows from the diverse composition of the population and the respective histories of its constituent members.

While its precolonial African forms were agrarian and involved contestations over land, especially against advancing colonialism, its modern forms can be traced to the third quarter of the second half of the nineteenth century. Its modern trajectory, Pallo Jordan points out, 'transcends the narrative of one movement (2005, p.87).'

If nationalism is understood in the terms of Fanon (1990), Cabral (1980), Nkrumah (1976), Hodgkins (1956) and others as organised opposition and resistance by indigenous peoples to foreign rule, nationalism in South Africa goes back to the early phases of colonial rule. The main types of nationalism in South Africa and their genealogies are outlined below in thumbnail profiles.

---

3. The Preamble to the Constitution of the Republic of South Africa Act 108, 1996. http: www.gov.za/documents/constitution/1996/a108 Accessed 21/02/2014.

Afrikaner nationalism was more systematically precipitated by mass Afrikaner exodus from the Cape in the 1830s after the abolition of slavery by the British. Based on European forms of ethnic nationalism, the ethnic group, conceived as the *volk*, is posited as the primordial national unit. This word is often mistranslated into English as the 'people'. There are other equivalent terms in Afrikaans, Dutch, and German for the English word 'people'. *Volk* literally signifies an ethnic community or tribal folk. Its objective was Afrikaner self-rule in an own national territory. This eventually developed into the ideology and political system of apartheid, which captured state power in 1948 until it was defeated in 1994.

White English liberal nationalism emphasised individual freedom and human rights for whites and was loyal to, and sought to pursue, the interests of British imperialism to the exclusion of blacks. It clashed with Afrikaner nationalism during the nineteenth and early twentieth centuries. After 1910, with the formation of the Union of South Africa, Afrikaner and English nationalisms found common cause in maintaining white rule, and coexisted.

African nationalism, according to Neuberger (2006)[4], assumed at least eight distinct and interrelated forms in the period after colonial intrusion. Also manifest in South Africa, a ninth form, namely diaspora nationalism, is added here:

- **Primary Resistance** involved localised uprisings and territorial conflicts in opposition to colonial advancement and conquest. It spans the period from the second half of the 1600s to the beginning of the nineteenth century.
- **Proto-nationalism** marked the formation of the first African nationalist organisations which petitioned settler and imperial authorities with demands for equal rights with the colonists. It covers the late 1800s to the 1920s.
- **Cultural Nationalism** envisaged African political, social, and cultural renewals and restoration in opposition to colonial denigration. It runs from the earlier 1900s, through the 1970s and the present.
- **Liberal Nationalism** is based on liberal democratic ideas of trans-ethnic human rights, national self-determination, and modernisation. It waxed and waned from 1910 and informs aspects of the South African constitutional dispensation adopted in 1994.
-

---

4. pp.515–524.

Socialist and Communist Anti-colonialism is based on the link Lenin established in 1917 between capitalism and colonialism: it shaped nationalist discourse in South Africa from the early 1920s onwards. The Communist Party of South Africa, in alliance with the African National Congress, diagnosed South Africa as 'a colony of a special type' and supported the strategies and objectives of the 'national democratic revolution'.

- **Radical Nationalism** developed in southern Africa where colonial rulers resisted the decolonisation process in other parts of Africa. Repressed, it sought the defeat of colonialism by political, economic, diplomatic, and military means. Emerging in the late 1950s, it achieved its objectives, in the end, through negotiation.

- **Pan-Africanist Nationalism** is constructed on the common historical experiences of colonialism by Africans across the continent, and Africans in the Diaspora, in the early twentieth century, during which a series of Pan-African conferences were held in 1900, 1919, 1921, 1923, 1927, 1930, and 1947. This includes the First Congress of African Independent States convened in Ghana in 1958, which informed discourse on continental unity.

- **Territorial Nationalism** is constructed by virtue of the fact that postcolonial states in Africa, with a few quasi-exceptions such as Botswana, Swaziland, and Lesotho, are primarily multi-ethnic. As states without homogeneous nations, the main basis for national sovereignty is the 'national territory' as partitioned during colonial rule.

- **Diaspora Nationalism** involves the struggles of emigrant populations displaced from place of origin through slavery and other forms of indentured labour practised during the era of colonisation, which saw the importation through slavery of African, Indonesian, Indian, and Chinese labourers into the Americas and South Africa.

Some qualification is called for in relation to the 'nation' constructs outlined above. It should be borne in mind that constructs, like the typology of the attributes of a nation outlined earlier, are conceptual entities, and that in practise, hybridisation or mixed constructions are frequently found. For example, all nation formations, as mentioned, are in the first and final instance political constructs. This is so regardless of whether they are predominantly cultural, territorial, economic or religious in character. Furthermore, since it is not possible to achieve national cohesion on the basis of a single static national attribute or feature, nation formation involves a complex combination of a number of attributes which are strategically organised to coalesce under specific social, historical, political, economic and cultural conditions specific to each society. As such, no mechanistic formula can account for its various manifestations.

Nation formation, as mentioned at the outset, is a multi-causal, layered and complex phenomenon which, more often than not, must negotiate a multiplicity of identities, classes and conflicting interests. Nations are formed under specific historical conditions and are dynamically developed in response to changing conditions. Every viable national formation, therefore, is a particular configuration of a number of elements designed to achieve and maintain the greatest possible degree of unity in a world of diversity and centrifugal forces.

Even a cultural construct of a homogenous ethnic group is seldom, if ever, a monolith. Cultural convergence within an ethnic group, for instance, does not presuppose the absence of political, regional, class, gender, language, and other differences, as Afrikaner and other ethnic nationalisms in South Africa and elsewhere have demonstrated.

In this regard, South Africa can be construed as, and in fact is, a trans-ethnic and **multiracial and culturally diverse political construct** with a firmly established national territory, and a legitimate political dispensation based on non-racial democratic principles and human rights values. It has single economic, legal and educational systems. The high degree of support for this dispensation is evident in the consistently high electoral participation shown by South Africans since 1994. Against this stands the gaping and searing economic, land and educational divisions which make for a torn and tattered social fabric. This suggests that the political settlement on which democratic South Africa was founded has not been able to overcome the history of social and economic divisions inherited from the past. One of the aims of this study is to establish the extent to which cultural diversity has moved beyond the axiology of racial division and domination towards the shared sense of unity and equality – at least among culturally diverse social groups – which informs the society politically inaugurated in 1994 and constitutionally grounded in 1996.

Two questions arise: First, how divided or how united are South Africans at present, and what degree of social and political coalescence is required for the long-term stability of a nation in the making? Second, at the level of nation formation theory, does national liberation, that is, overcoming invasive domination, regardless of the composition of the population, signify the attainment of nationhood in the full sense of the word, or merely the crucial but limited attainment of political independence and sovereignty? These questions are dealt with in the next chapter where the historical and current debates related to the construction of an inclusive national state are traced.

CHAPTER THREE

AN AFRICAN WISH: CONTEXTUALISING DEBATES ON 'THE NATIONAL QUESTION' IN SOUTH AFRICA

Introduction

This chapter traces the debates generated within the anti-apartheid movement on the question of the South African nation and the strategies for its construction. It ends with a brief treatment of how the South African nation is seen in the National Development Plan (NDP)[5] and the declaration which emerged from the Nation Building and Social Cohesion Summit of 2012.

From the beginning of the twentieth century, debates around how a South African nation can be created have revolved around many propositions. The actual labels may not necessarily reflect watertight epistemological categories, and they are used here in their popular designations in historical political discourse. Some of the main ones are:

- The 'Black Republic' thesis, which, it shall be argued, in asserting the rise of a black-led independent state embodied the modernist impulses of the time.
- The Colonialism of a Special Type (CST) theory, which constructed the notion of a colonising nation and a colonised nation residing in the same

5. http://www.npconline.co.za/medialib/downloads/home/NPC%20National%20Development%20Plan%20Vision%202030%20-lo-res.pdf

territory.

- The narrow Africanist approach, which is seen as reflective of the ethnic-based school of which there are several strains. In the South African context it has been promoted by the Pan-Africanist Congress and counterposed the principle of non-racialism.
- The majoritarian Africanist approach found within the ANC, which recognises the numerical superiority of indigenous Africans in South Africa as the most oppressed and exploited members of society. The ANC accordingly places a special emphasis on African leadership, as well as prioritising addressing the conditions of African people.
- The multiple identities or 'rainbow nation' notions, which could be seen as instances of a postmodernist approach.

Two important themes have run through the different positions in the century-long discourse on South Africa's nationhood. The first theme, that of unity of all South Africans, was captured by Thabo Mbeki in his opening address to the National Conference on Racism (Conference Report, 2000) when he quoted Nokukhanya Luthuli, the 90-year-old widow of Chief A. J. Luthuli, who expressed 'this simple but profoundly humanist and African wish: My wish before I die, is to see blacks and whites living harmoniously in a united South Africa' (p.45). The second theme is the creation of democracy. From the very early days of the founding of the South African National Native Congress through the National Conference on Racism (NCR) of 2000, to the NDP of 2012, the issue of representivity has seized the attention of most leaders.

As shown in Chapter Two, dealing with theoretical approaches among the major schools that have dominated thinking on national identity are the modernists and the ethno-symbolists. Two further schools which have had an influence are the postmodernist and the postcolonial schools.

The modernists have argued that the emergence of nations represented a move away from antiquity and towards modernity. Nations were a functional response to the movement of society from the agrarian age to the industrial age. The school is represented by writers like Ernest Gellner, Benedict Anderson, Eric Hobsbawm and Liah Greenfeld, as well as most schools of Marxism. The ethno-symbolist, or essentialist school, emphasised the ethnic root of nations. Nations were a community of common descent, often relying on traditions and customs in their constitution. Anthony D. Smith, who argued that a nation is a 'community of common descent', is the best exponent of the ethno-symbolist school.

Reacting to what Homi Bhabha (1990, p.293) referred to as the 'historical certainty and settled nature', with which modernist thinking imbued the concept of nations, the postmodernist school prefers seeing nation as formed and transformed continuously. 'Nation' is seen as a product of narration and an ongoing tension between 'master-narrative' and 'counter-narratives'. The postcolonial school has its roots in the anti-colonial movement of the mid-twentieth century. The emphasis of anti-colonial thinking was on modernisation, or catching up with the West. This philosophy was rooted on the nation state as the means for uplifting decolonised peoples through education and ambitious development projects.

In tracing the roots of postcolonial theory, Partha Chatterjee (1986) argues that post World War Two decolonisation made the nation state the universally accepted form of the modern state. The strand in the postcolonial approach which best focused on repression and resistance is that of the Subaltern Studies approach, which was organised around the Subaltern Studies journal launched in 1982 under the editorship of Ranajit Guha in India. Nationalist elite politics was recognisable by its legalism, constitutionalism and adaptation of colonial and precolonial institutions. The politics of the subaltern, on the other hand, were based on traditional structures of kinship, territoriality or class associations, and was relatively more violent. According to Guha: 'The co-existence of these two domains or streams indicated "the *failure* of the Indian bourgeoisie to speak for the *nation*" (1988, pp.41–42).' However, Guha continues, the 'braiding together' of the two strands saw the mobilised masses 'put the characteristic imprints of popular politics on campaigns initiated by the upper classes' (ibid.).

As democratic South Africa enters the third decade of its existence, there is a discernible emergence of ascriptive ties becoming the basis of political and economic networks, as well as the growing distance between the well-off and the poor. This growing inequality and the new, at times divisive, identities have welded the concerns on nation formation and social cohesion ever so firmly. This is explored below in the context of the NDP and the Declaration on Social Cohesion.

NATIONAL INDEPENDENCE FOR SOUTH AFRICA

The Black Republic thesis is discussed as an example of a programme that reflected the totalising approach of the modernist era. Ernest Gellner (1983), in spelling out his modernist approach to nation formation, argued that nations should be seen in terms of will, culture and political units. Greenfeld has argued that nationalism helped achieve 'the grand social transformation from the old order to modernity' (1992, p.487). This modernist approach comes to the fore when looking at how the ANC at its inception, and the Communist Party in the 1920s, defined the struggle for national liberation in South Africa, especially through the prism of the end of the wars of dispossession.

The end of the nineteenth century saw the defeat of indigenous resistance to colonial domination and the beginning of exclusivist centralised state formation leading to the creation of the Union of South Africa in 1910. The Union of South Africa represented the incorporation into the new state of diverse people in a differentiated manner. According to Greenstein, the creation of Union shifted the locus of resistance to 'struggles for political rights within the framework of white-dominated state structures' (1995, p.3). In this climate the South African Native Congress was created in 1912, expressing loyalty to the empire and seeking to extend the limited franchise of the Cape to other provinces and 'intelligent natives' who were willing to help preserve peace and security among the ignorant 'mass of the people' (Odendaal, 1984).

Meli (1988) cites the formation of independent African churches, the discovery of diamonds and gold, and the subsequent emergence of an African working class as equally important factors in shaping African nationalism. He traces the roots of African nationalism to the 1882 formation of Imbumba Yama Africa (Union of Africans). At the same time, the rise of the Ethiopian churches reflected, as Odendaal (1984) points out, a growing interest in African administrative and doctrinal independence from white control and 'to go and teach our own people by ourselves' (pp.23–29). Greenstein observes that: 'the Ethiopian churches generally were open to all Africans, regardless of their ethnic and tribal origins (1995, p.6).' The construction of the 'other' at that point in time emerges from Greenstein's explanation that: 'The crucial defining features of "natives" in official eyes were not their ancestry, colour, or residence as such, but rather their presumed links to the pre-colonial past in terms of land claims, ethno-linguistic identifications, and supposed allegiance to traditional political institutions (ibid.).'

The proclamation of the Union in 1910, despite appeals to the British crown to extend the qualified franchise, spurred attempts at unity among the

African elite. Underlining the importance of this, Meli writes that: 'ethnic divisions were seen as a hindrance to the development and emergence of a broad African nationalism. In fact, there was a view that the defeat in the resistance wars had been caused by the fact the Africans were fighting separately and independently of each other. With the enactment of the Act of Union in 1910, the African people confronted the continued racism entrenched in the constitution; Britain had granted independence to white South Africa and the conditions of black South Africa remained the same in 1910. Black South Africa, instead of being a colony of Britain, became a colony of white South Africa (1988, p.68).'

Developments in the 1910s could, according to Rotberg, be characterised as the 'awakening phase' (1972, p.73) in the rise of national consciousness. This phase culminated in 1912 with the founding conference of the South African Native National Congress (SANNC, renamed the African National Congress in 1925) with delegates from all four provinces of the South Africa of the time. Pixley ka Isaka Seme, in his now well-known call, urged putting an end to 'the demon of racialism, the aberration of the Xhosa-Fingo Feud, the animosity that exists between Zulus and the Tongas, between the Basuthos and every other Native' (Karis and Carter, 1972, p.73). Karis and Carter point out that he emphasised that since all Africans were one people, the Congress was to be 'a National Society or Union for all the Natives of South Africa' (ibid). The draft constitution of the SANNC had as its goals 'the promotion of unity and mutual co-operation between the Government and the Abantu Races of South Africa' (Karis and Carter, 1972, vol. 1, p.73). Greenstein (1995, p.8) observes that the Congress sets its sights on representing indigenous people without laying claims to political power, which was seen as a white institution. A council of chiefs, created with the aim of avoiding ethnic differences, had an advisory role.

According to Meli, the narrow outlook of white workers and the limited size of the African working class did not allow for more radical tactics to be used. Two factors helped change this in the 1920s: the creation of the Industrial and Commercial Workers' Union in 1919, which saw African workers being organised into unions, and the emergence of the socialist movement within the white working class. 'The carriers of these new socialist ideas were white immigrants from mainly Europe, particularly Eastern Europeans who had fled religious and political persecution (1988, p.69).'

In this context, the Communist Party of South Africa (CPSA) had an early influence on the course of nationalist discourse. Nyawuza (1990) points out that until the Sixth Congress of the Comintern in 1928, the CPSA's programme strove for a united front of black and white workers fighting for a socialist South Africa. Simons and Simons point out that 'the concept of African power was so far removed from current ideologies and apartheid realities, however, that even veteran communists doubted whether it was sound' (1969, p.338). Ivan Izosimovich Potekhin, who made a name for himself as the father of the African Studies Institute in the USSR, later insisted that the early ANC was an organisation of comprador chiefs. The Simonses have argued, however, that he 'did not adequately examine the process of amalgamating scores of formerly independent and often antagonistic societies into a single nation' (1969, p.235), thus not realising the revolutionary step being taken with the creation of the SANNC. Bunting concludes that this oversight of the CPSA to develop a correct policy to the national movement 'was at least in part due to the failure of the national movement ... to reveal its full potential' (1992, p.68).

THE INDEPENDENT BLACK REPUBLIC

Sidney Percival Bunting, who had opposed the Black Republic slogan, addressed the Comintern in 1928 on this issue. He was quoted approvingly by Brian Bunting: 'The CPSA is itself the actual or potential leader of the Native National Movement; it makes all the national demands that the national body makes, and of course much more, and it can "control" nationalism with a view to developing its maximum fighting strength. It can and will respond to the entire struggle of all the oppressed of South Africa, natives in particular (1992, p.69).' Thus, according to Simons and Simons (1969), by 1927 the 'Brussels Congress of the League against Imperialism' was beginning to raise the notion of a democratic, independent Native Republic. Nyawuza noted that in the same year the Comintern recognised that 'the socio-economic and political divisions which hinder the process of the emancipation of the South African proletariat from bourgeois-nationalist ideology has divided the South African working class into workers of the colonizing, ruling nation and those of the oppressed, disenfranchised indigenous nation' (1990, p.54–55).

There was initially little enthusiasm for the 'Black Republic' slogan proposed by the Comintern. Douglas and Molly Wolton were the ones in favour at the Central Executive Committee level, with the former arguing that 'eventually blacks must predominate in this country, a Black Republic must be realized' (Nyawuza, 1990, p.45). Opposition was based on fears that the slogan would be used by chiefs in the ANC for narrow, ethnic objectives, or that it would encourage anti-white attitudes. Jordan, while describing the debate around the Black Republic thesis as 'the most controversial chapter in South African Marxism', saw it representing a 'quantum leap for Marxist theory in South Africa, and for the CPSA' (1988, p.123). As a result of the approach, 'the land question, the national question and capitalist power were integrally linked. It projected a bourgeois-democratic alliance under the leadership of the working class. As Moses Kotane explained, "the independent Native Republic, which in essence means a bourgeois republic ... must necessarily pre-suppose a democratic workers' and peasants' republic ..." (ibid.).'

Slovo points out that this thesis itself came to reflect Stalin's definition of the nation as a community of language, culture, territory and economy. By 1932, the Comintern was calling for 'complete and immediate national independence for the people of South Africa: for the right of the Zulu, Basuto, etc. nations to form their own independent republics; for the voluntary uniting of the African nations in a Federation of Independent Native Republics; the establishment of a workers' and peasants' government. Full guarantee of the rights of all national minorities, for the Coloured, Indian, and white toiling masses' (ibid. p.143).

Comparing this against a 1997 ANC position paper, Filatova points out that though the Black Republic approach was subsequently dropped 'it must have left a deep trace in the hearts of many Communists for it successfully mingled their nationalist and socialist aspirations. The words "native South African Republic" may be seen as incorporating Africanism in general, and "African hegemony" in particular, and the mention of "equal rights for all national minorities" takes care of the context of multicultural and non-racial society' (1997, p.50). The debate around the position paper referred to by Filatova is dealt with in greater detail below, viewed through the lens of the ANC's 1997 debate.

DEFEAT OF THE MODERNISING FORCE

The Native Administration Act of 1927, which Jordan described as the 'earliest attempt to create a comprehensive legal framework for racial oppression' (1997, p.9), provided for a Supreme Chief in the form of the Governor-General. The latter post had been created through the South

Africa Act of 1909. Marks (cited in Greenstein) points out that 'although chiefs were subsidized by the state, and therefore were not independent, at a deeper level tribal sentiments signified a rejection of white colonial rule rather than an attempt to find a place within it' (1995, p.9). Jordan was less charitable when he described this move as the 'institutional incorporation of "traditional leaders" through a corruption of pre-colonial legal traditions and merely as extensions of racial domination by proxy' (1997, p.9).

Greenstein (1995, p.9) argues that concerns about land were widespread, but such concerns manifested themselves in localised forms, relating to 'specific territories rather than to indigenous rights in the abstract. As a result, rural causes were infrequently taken up by urban-based political organisations and their potential remained untapped, at least until the late 50s'. Paralleling the more nationalist political activity of the ANC, 'people in rural areas frequently adhered to tribal, ethnic and regional identities, leaderships and organisations with a pronounced pre-colonial bent ... It is important to note that ... (t)raditional symbols frequently joined new identities and organisations to provide legitimation for defiance politics' (1995, p.10).

Greenstein cites the Bulhoek Massacre of 200 unarmed believers of the Eastern Cape Israelite movement who had refused to move from their camping grounds and to pay taxes. This represented 'strong rejectionist sentiments, opposing white domination and state authority in a mixture of indigenous and Christian prophetic symbolism' (1995, p.10). Such popular uprisings, as witnessed for example in 1906 when the Bambatha Rebellion occurred in Natal, or the peasant uprising of the 1960s in Pondoland, can be seen as examples of the subaltern that Guha and Chatterjee were writing about. Jordan points out that the latter revolt was 'directed against both the newly installed "Bantu authorities" and their paymasters in Pretoria. That revolt was inevitably led by commoners who identified with the modern liberation movement and whose assemblies adopted the Freedom Charter as their programme' (1997, p.11).

However, Jordan cannot gloss over the real distance between the nationalist movements and the rural masses. On one hand, such localised, rural resistance was unable to assume national proportions while the use of English by national political movements widened the gap between rural and urban-based politics. As Greenstein explains: 'The latter advanced notions of a comprehensive trans-ethnic African identity which continued to face competition from localized identities (1995, p.12).' Furthermore, in the mines and factories the organisation of work teams and shifts, as well as hostel arrangements, was ethnic or tribal based – further strengthening such identities. This inability to bridge the gap continues to haunt the ANC to this day as it tries to work out a dispensation to include traditional authorities in the system of local government.

Greenstein (1995) cites Cobley (1990, pp.82–83), arguing that 'ethnicity was not necessarily obstructive to nationalism (despite the ANC leadership's concerns). It provided building blocks for the construction of a comprehensive African identity, promoting pride in African history within the context of regeneration of tradition on new foundations ... Only when ethnicity was constructed as a direct alternative to nationalism (as happened with apartheid policies) did a clash between the two become inevitable'.

At a point in the history of South Africa, when the modernist impulse from a new colony to an independent republic should have prevailed by creating a new national identity, it was destroyed by a more powerful force – the all-white alliance reflected in the Union of South Africa. One can discern at the turn of the twentieth century the beginning of a fusion of will and culture (to use Gellner's terms), but the polity was weak. This awakening can, as Greenfeld has suggested, 'be traced to the structural contradictions of the society' (1992, p.587) – in this case the struggle between the coloniser and the colonised.

IMAGINED COMMUNITIES

The approach of Colonialism of a Special Type (CST), where South Africa is seen as a country of two nations, is examined in this section as an example of an imagined community. It begins by considering the concept of national democracies and then looks at how the CST approach arose, what the criticisms of this approach are, and the notion of two nations as enunciated by Mbeki (1998). This approach to nation formation – where nations are seen as imagined social constructs – is attributable to Anderson (1993), Hobsbawm (1994), as well as Gellner (1983). Gellner, for example, had argued that nationalism creates nations where they do not exist. Anderson, in *Imagined Communities* (1993), emphasised the nation being imagined as a community with the attendant emphasis on a 'deep, horizontal comradeship'.

To appreciate the CST thesis and the way a nation is constructed within the thesis, it would be useful to look at the concept 'national democracy'. Hudson (1986) points out that the possibility of 'transitional social structures', which reflect the 'interests not of any one particular class, but of the widest strata of population of the newly-free nations' (p.18), led to the concept of 'national democracy' being introduced in the Marxist-Leninist world. It was meant to fill a significant conceptual breach and was formally introduced via the declaration of the meeting of eighty-one Communist and Workers' parties in 1960. It meant 'to designate that category of ex-colonial (and dependent) countries which could be identified as engaged on a non-capitalist path of development in opposition to imperialism and towards national autonomy' (Hudson, 1986, p.18).

This was a remarkable step given the shifts in Marxist thinking, such as debates on the efficacy of Popular Fronts. These shifts in thinking had concrete expression in the relationship between the ANC and the SACP. The 1960 declaration was the culmination of thinking which I. I. Potekhin (1996), who was to become the Africa expert in the USSR, had introduced. He had argued in 1949 that: 'in a struggle against imperialist enslavement, the interests of the bourgeoisie coincide with these of the entire people. The leading role in the national liberation movement in most of the colonies of Tropical and South Africa is now performed by the national bourgeoisie and the national intelligentsia (p.15).'

THE CST APPROACH

The development of the notion of national democracies, combined with the debate on the Black Republic thesis, led to the depiction of South Africa as a case of Colonialism of a Special Type (CST). Edward Roux described this at an early stage when he argued at the Sixth Congress of the Comintern in 1928 that:

- Comintern should integrate the phenomena of the emergent African working class and anti-colonial resistance in Africa into the international movement against imperialism.
- There should be cognisance of 'two imperialisms'. There was the white 'local Afrikaner imperialism with its headquarters in the Union of South Africa (and) ... the broader imperialism with its headquarters in Europe' (1990, p.54–55).

Nyawuza suggests that this helped pave the way for the CST theory. By this he meant 'the situation where the colonizer and the colonized reside "side by side" in the same territory, which has been the case since 1910 when Britain granted political power to the whites in South Africa who used it to further oppress the black majority' (1990, p.48). Jordan combined the Black Republic and the CST theses in a neat rendering of the national question, which he described as 'centred on three sets of problems: those of national oppression (of minorities or majorities) within a single political unit; of colonial oppression; and of the unification of the disparate sections of potential nations' (1988, p.110). He pointed out that the ANC position 'posits that in South Africa, the national and colonial questions are synonymous; it asserts that the creation of democratic institutions in South Africa is the only means of resolving the national and colonial question; and it argues that the people of South Africa today constitute two antagonistic blocks (one being the coloniser; the other the colonised) and that the only means of unifying them and dissolving the antagonism is through democracy. Thus, in South Africa, the three sets of problems that the national question sought to resolve are interpenetrating' (ibid.).

As pointed out earlier, the unity of all South Africans is seen as a *sine qua non* for the creation of a South African nation. At the core of this is an imagined community which is the South African nation. For Jordan, the resolution of colonial antagonisms among South Africans is through the prevalence of democracy. In the 1997 debate on the national question, Jordan argued that the material basis of this unity lies in 'the homogenising effect of urbanisation on the whole society (which) expanded the area of shared values among Africans, Coloureds, Indians and Whites as members of a common society. The Black African, Coloured and Indian leadership that grew within these circumstances accepted the modern world because they recognised its liberatory potential in opening up new vistas for themselves and their people. They were modernists' (1997, p.6).

Neville Alexander also contributed to the theme of constructed identities and inventions when he argued that 'nations are the mode of existence of virtually all capitalist and socialist formations. They are the "mould"...' (1986, p.66). However, he also points out that 'because the nation has to be constructed ideologically and politically on the basis of developing, i.e. ... also changing capitalist forces and relations of production, each of the antagonistic classes in the social formation, generally speaking, conceives of the nation differently in accordance with its class ideology' (1986. p.68). In answering the question why the national liberation struggle is 'the inescapable form of the class struggle' (ibid.) he cites Therborn, who writes: 'It is, then natural – and not an aberration of underdeveloped consciousness – that class ideologies co-exist with inclusive-historical ideologies, constituting the subjects of the contradictory totality of an exploitative mode of production and/or social formation (1982, p. 27).'

Jeremy Cronin described the relationship between national liberation and socialism as follows: 'The national aspects of the current struggle are encompassed within the goals of building national unity and national independence … the democratic aspect embraces the struggle for basic democratic rights.' While an alliance of social forces was necessary, the following 'sufficient conditions' had to be met for 'substantial transformation' (1986, pp.75–76).

- Working class involvement in 'all fronts of the national democratic struggle – on the shop floor, in rural areas, on the civic front, and in education'.
- The deepening and extension of mass-based democracy.
- The use of a 'scientific approach to struggle' (in other words, a Marxist-Leninist approach).
- 'An internationalist perspective' within the national democratic struggle itself (ibid.).

CRITICISMS OF THE CST

Hudson argued against the CST, writing that 'prima facie South Africa is not a colonial society' (1986, p.24). The CST 'assumes the fact of "colonial domination" and then uses this assumption to prove the validity of its conclusions' (ibid.) that the path towards socialism is through an initial stage of national democratic revolution. Probably imposing Amilcar Cabral's more mechanical depiction of the stages of a revolution on the CST, Hudson rejects the 'two-stage' theory on the following grounds:

- 'The material requisite for socialism exists in South Africa – there is a certain level of industrialisation, the presence of socio-economic contradictions and the existence of a strong enough working class.
- The nature of national oppression in South Africa does not necessarily result in the dominance of racial/national (and not class) subjectivity. He

cites the work of Chantal Mouffe and Ernesto Laclau in trying to develop a theory of social identity which underlines "the impossibility of deriving from an agent's place in the relations of production his dominant 'subject-position'… if social agents in South Africa identify themselves in racial terms, this cannot be attributed to an experience of racial subjectivity, itself the product of ideological struggles" (1986, p.32).'

Hudson concludes that 'national/racial identity has not been shown by the CST analysis to enjoy an inevitable primacy in South Africa. In fact a much wider range of political identities can and does exist in South Africa than is able to be acknowledged by the CST analysis' (ibid.).

Alexander (1986) argued that 'it is simply a fallacy to claim that black workers are faced with two autonomous but intersecting systems of domination, viz. a system of "racial domination" and a system of "class domination…" what happens in practice is that the workers, like other class agents, are confronted with a range of actual and possible identities … from which they select those which they consider appropriate to their situation. Which of these identities will be selected is a question of practical politics' (p.71). This argument is re-examined in the discussion on multiple identities.

Fine and Davis find common cause with Hudson when they argue that there are four problems with the popular front approach characteristic of the national democratic revolution thesis:

- *The bourgeoisie in South Africa have proven to be unreliable opponents of apartheid.*
- *Upholding the sanctity of capitalist private property in a free-market or mixed economy neglects the need … of workers to advocate methods and goals, which go beyond the norms of capitalist private property.*
- *Taking worker support for granted may mean losing support.*
- *Restraining working class struggles to maintain broader unity 'may weaken the liberation movement as a whole'* (1988, p.282).

Another important critique of the CST came from those who subscribed to the racial capitalism approach, in essence arguing that the system of apartheid was but one of many manifestations of capitalism. This view finds contemporary expressions, as Soske, *et al.* (2012) point out, among a diverse group of scholars such as Hein Marais, Patrick Bond, William Gumede,

Neville Alexander and John Saul who 'concentrate on the domestic and international conjuncture of the 1980s to early 1990s and the structural continuities within South Africa's unique system of racial capitalism ... their interventions challenge the idea that liberation has been achieved in any straightforward sense: core aspirations of the anti-apartheid struggle, like social equality, economic democracy, the redistribution of land, and the transformation of the country's racist urban infrastructure have largely been deferred, if not abandoned outright' (p.43).

Notwithstanding the critique, the CST thesis continued to exert a powerful influence on how the South African nation was understood by the ruling ANC. For example, in his speech in the parliamentary debate on reconciliation and nation building on 25 May 1998, Mbeki raised the question of two nations, arguing that the attainment of formal democracy had not changed the material conditions spawned by the colonial system. He said: 'A major component part of the issue of reconciliation and nation building is defined by and derives from the material conditions in our society which have divided our country into two nations, the one black and the other white. We therefore make bold to say that South Africa is a country of two nations. One of these nations is white, relatively prosperous, regardless of gender or geographical dispersal. It has ready access to a developed economic, physical, educational, communication and other infrastructure ... the second and larger nation of South Africa is black and poor, with the worst affected being women in the rural areas, the black rural population in general, and the disabled. This nation lives under conditions of a grossly underdeveloped economic, physical, educational, communication and other infrastructure. It has virtually no possibility to exercise what in reality amounts to a theoretical right to equal opportunity, with that right being equal within this black nation only to the extent that it is equally incapable of realisation (1998, p.8).'

Mbeki traced the root of the existence of the two nations to the colonial period, arguing: 'This reality of two nations, underwritten by the perpetuation of the racial, gender and spatial disparities born of a very long period of colonial and apartheid white minority domination, constitutes the material base which reinforces the notion that, indeed, we are not one nation, but two nations. And neither are we becoming one nation. Consequently, also, the objective of national reconciliation is not being realized (ibid.).'

Many of the positions outlined above are guilty of Greenstein's charge that 'one can study ideologies within a class-analytic framework, dismissing identity as a theoretical factor' (1994, p.644). This is probably one of the key weaknesses of the CST approach: it does not adequately address the issue of what identity is engendered by the colonial situation. Greenstein warns against taking 'identification in group terms for granted rather than analysing it historically ... all Africans were excluded from power, not because of their class origins or subversive politics, but because of their common African identity, regardless of their diverse social affiliations and relations to the process of production' (ibid. p.656). In other words, they were the easily identifiably colonised 'other'. This leads into a consideration of the construction of an Africanist identity – that is the identity asserted by the colonised.

AFRICANISM AND THE AFRICAN RENAISSANCE

The debate around 'Africanism' in the ANC brings to the fore the ethno-historical approach advocated by Anthony Smith (2006). The thesis will investigate Africanism in two senses:

- The Pan-African level, which strove to rise above ethnic, and even national, identities.
- The sense of assertion of African leadership in the struggle against apartheid and now in the leadership of government. This is due to the predominant size of the African population as well as it occupying the rung of the most oppressed and exploited section of South African society.

The Africanist strand is a clear manifestation of Smith's ethnic-based approach, which sees nations being based on 'ethnic cores' that have been shaped into a national identity. There were two key movements when this strand emerged strongly: in the late 1950s leading to the eventual breakaway of the PAC from the ANC, and in 1997 when the issue of non-African representation was debated in the ANC's structures.

THE ROOTS OF PAN-AFRICANISM

As discussed above, the question of Pan-African unity has been a key theme in nationalist discourse in South Africa and on the continent. Overcoming the ethnic divisions which had been fostered by the colonisers was a major challenge for nationalist leaders. How Africanism has been resorted to, to achieve the strategic goal of unity of the African people, is pertinent here.

An example of early Pan-African mobilisation is that of Henry Sylvester Williams, who was responsible for the first Pan-African conference in London in 1900 where Du Bois declared: 'The problem of the twentieth century is the problem of the colour line – the relation of the darker to the lighter races of men in Asia and Africa, in America and the islands of the sea (1992, p.94).' According to Lemelle (1992), Du Bois saw the problems of Diasporan Black Africans as part of an international struggle of oppressed people for freedom and justice. Marcus Garvey (Du Bois' contemporary), on the other hand, saw the problem in cultural, economic and psychological terms. He believed the basic problem was that blacks lacked knowledge and pride in their African ancestry and therefore could not counter white racism. The ultimate solution was returning to Africa and building their own state.

The debates within South Africa's liberation politics tended to divide along these lines as well. But Greenstein has argued: 'The relations between Pan-African and more circumscribed identities were never thought through. The adherence to a global identity did not make other bases for identity disappear (1995, p.11).'

An instance of the persistence of other identities Greenstein refers to is the complaint by Sol Plaatje in 1931 that the 'failure of our race to unite is due to the failure of its leaders to unite. The demon of tribalism is the great stumbling block to our unity ...' (1995, p.12). More recent examples of this were the use of ethnic mobilisation by Bantustan leaders supported by the apartheid government to counter the project of national unity advanced by the liberation movements generally, and the ANC, specifically.

AFRICANIST THINKING WITHIN THE ANC

The campaign against the abolition of the Cape franchise for African males in the 1940s foregrounded narrow Africanist thinking within the ANC. The All African Convention (AAC) condemned the bills legislating disenfranchisement and called for common citizenship for Africans. It argued, as Karis and Carter record, for a policy of political identity so that a South African nation is created 'in which, while various racial groups may develop on their own lines, socially and culturally, they will be bound together by the pursuit of common political objectives' (1972, p.31).

This is a profoundly modernist approach which ran counter to the more primordial emphasis on Africanness which emerged at the time. The Ten Point Programme adopted in 1943 at a joint meeting of the AAC and the Anti-Coloured Affairs Department (Anti-CAD) became the programme of the Non-European Unity Movement. Similar demands were contained in *African Claims in South Africa* adopted by the ANC at its 16 December 1943 conference. It proclaimed that 'the African people in the Union of South Africa urgently demand the granting of full citizenship rights such as are enjoyed by all Europeans in South Africa' (Ebrahim, 1999, p.398).

The 1944 Manifesto of the ANC Youth League's Africanist emphasis contrasted with the ANC's approach. The Manifesto could be regarded as the first avowedly Africanist document produced by a mainstream nationalist organisation. The Manifesto, according to Williams, saw the ANC as a 'national unity front [through] which the national liberation of Africans will be achieved by Africans themselves' (1998, p.77). Also, African nationalism has to create a 'united nation out of heterogeneous tribes' and the freeing of Africa from foreign domination and foreign leadership. The emergence of this strand so soon after the convention illustrates an important point of this chapter – that different approaches to nationhood can exist simultaneously.

The Youth League saw South Africa as a country of 'four chief nationalities, three of which are minorities and three of which suffer national oppression'. It also saw the 'national organisations of the Africans, Indians, and Coloureds co-operating on common interests' (ibid.). And in looking at 'Vendors of Foreign Method', an oblique reference to communists, it insisted 'that we are oppressed not as a class, but as a people, as a nation' (ibid.). This conflating of an African identity with the concept of a nation emphasises the ethnic based approach to nationhood.

Greenstein points out that Anton Lembede, a key leader of the Youth League, when speaking on African national identity, invoked the memory of Shaka, Moshoeshoe, Hintsa, Sekhukhuni, Khama, Sobuza and Mzilikazi: 'Significantly, all these people worked and identified in their times with specific groups rather than with the general African collective ... At the same time, as they were appropriated by Africanists as heroes, they were also claimed by specific ethnic movements inside and outside of South Africa. The relations with the African heritage were thus much more complex than acknowledged by African nationalists (1995, p.16).'

Clyde ('C. R. D.') Halisi describes Lembede's approach as that of a black republican – thinkers who believe that 'African people themselves are the source of all legitimacy ... black republicans see democracy and socialism as inherent in the ways of the African folk. They are apt to assert, rather than theorise about such matters. The restoration of the rights of the African people is the negation of white rule and all that it means. African people are virtuous; degradation is a consequence of external corruption' (1988, p.132).

THE GROWTH OF NON-RACIALISM

Paralleling the above development in the ANC and its structures, such as the Youth League, was a growing radicalisation of South African Indian politics which saw the successful execution of the Passive Resistance Campaign of 1946, drawing from the experience of the mass protests that had congealed during the time of Mahatma Gandhi at the turn of the century. Indians, who had been subjected to specific forms of discrimination, were mobilised in this campaign by the leadership of Dr Y. Dadoo and Dr M. Naicker, leaders of the Transvaal and Natal Indian Congresses, respectively. By the end of the campaign, Essop Pahad (1988) argues, 'the foundation had been laid for greater co-operation ... (resulting) in the signing of the 1947 Dadoo-Xuma-Naicker Pact (p.90).' Doctor Xuma was then president of the ANC, and the pact has been referred to as 'The Three Doctors Pact'.

The incipient non-racial leanings of the ANC created problems for the more Africanist Youth League leadership – especially when they took over the reins of the ANC in 1949. They were, for example, scathing of the 'Three Doctors Pact'. Halisi cites the exchange between Peter Nkutsoeu Raboroko, who later became the PAC secretary of education, and Duma Nokwe, then secretary-general of the ANC: 'Nokwe emphasized the importance of multiracial democracy and the Africanists' own involvement in the construction of Indian-African unity in the form of the Three Doctors Pact. He asserted that multiracial democracy was revolutionary given the apartheid policy and criticized the vagueness of the Africanist position on the rights of all South Africans (1988, p.136).'

The adoption of the Freedom Charter in 1955, and especially the approach proclaiming that South Africa belongs to all who live in it, catalysed the eventual breakaway of the Pan-Africanist Congress. For Raboroko, 'the sacrifice of African nationalism on the altar of Charterism was the last straw ... (1988, p.137).' Halisi further argues that 'nationalism defined in racial and non-racial terms has to seek very different legitimising ideologies ... yet the ideological split between the Africanists and Congress was not clear cut and both groups claimed to desire a society in which racial distinction would be irrelevant ... the Africanists were not ideologically or politically autonomous enough to realign the overall orientation of African Nationalism and had great difficulty overcoming purely oppositionalist politics' (ibid. p.138). The Africanists, under the leadership of Robert Sobukwe and Potlako Leballo, broke with the ANC in 1958. The PAC believed the land belongs to Africans and that, according to Lembede, cross-racial co-operation may be desirable, but as explained by Reddy (1995) 'this must be between the African bloc and the non-European groups as units' (p.170).

The critical issue to deal with here is the way the ANC has managed potential tension between its non-racial position and its commitment to African leadership. The former position has been the core policy position of the ANC, especially since the 1950s. In 1957, Chief Albert Luthuli as ANC president, shortly after the adoption of the Freedom Charter and in the midst of debates with the Africanists, as cited by Ramutsindela (1997), argued that the ANC believes in a society in which white and non-white peoples of the Union will work and live together in harmony for the common good of the fatherland' (p.101).

In a 1968 interview, Oliver Tambo, then ANC president, explained that 'our programme of struggle is geared to what is known as the Freedom Charter, which is a statement of the objectives of our political struggle ... in terms of that programme, we fight for a South Africa in which there will be no racial discrimination, no inequalities based on colour, creed or race – a non-racial democracy which recognises the essential equality between man and man' (1987, p.70). The ANC's Morogoro conference held in Tanzania in 1969 was significant in that it admitted non-Africans to join the organisation as individuals. Non-Africans were admitted to the national executive at its Kabwe conference in 1985.

Previously, the various racial groups involved in resistance against colonialism and apartheid had been organised in separate formations very much 'their own' congresses. This practise had been perpetuated in the organisational structures operating in exile. The 1969 Consultative Conference of the ANC in Morogoro marked a departure from this approach, with Coloureds, Indians and whites accorded ANC membership, but still not allowed to assume leadership positions within the organisation. The argument for this, according to the Strategy and Tactics document of the ANC of the time, derived from the characterisation of the main content of the struggle as the liberation of Africans in particular, and blacks in general.

In particular:

This strategic aim must govern every aspect of the conduct of our struggle whether it be in the formulation of policy or the creation of structures. Amongst other things it demands in the first place the maximum mobilisation of the African people as a dispossessed and racially oppressed nation. This is the mainspring and it must not be weakened. It involves a stimulation and deepening of national confidence, national pride and national assertiveness. Properly channelled, and properly led, these qualities do not stand in conflict with the principle of internationalism. Indeed, they become the basis for more and more meaningful co-operation; a co-operation which is self-imposed, equal and one which is neither based on dependence nor gives the appearance of being so[6] (1969).

Any other approach, the ANC argued then, '... would amount to inequality (again at the expense of the majority), but it would lend flavour to the slander which our enemies are ever ready to spread of a multiracial alliance dominated by minority groups[7] (1969).' This was to change in 1985 at the Kabwe Consultative Conference when participation in leadership structures was opened to all races. The principle of 'African leadership' may not have changed but the organisational expression was taken to a different level. This principle quite correctly continues to be manifested in the practise of today's ANC, as can be seen in the weighing up, for example, of the composition of the election list.

Former President Nelson Mandela gave the commitment of the ANC to non-racialism when he said: 'Our people have reached out to one another across ... divisions ... to live out together the consequences of the profound but simple fact that, complex as history may have made our society, we are one people with one destiny[8].' Jordan (1997), explaining the ANC's 1994 slogan 'A better life for all', said: 'True to itself and its traditions, the ANC also addressed itself to the entire nation, rather than a section of it.' Mbeki, in his famous 'I am an African' speech delivered to mark the adoption of the South African Constitution in 1996, reiterated this theme: 'It is a firm assertion made by ourselves that South Africa belongs to all who live in it, black and white. It gives concrete expression to the sentiment we share as Africans, and will defend to the death, that the people shall govern (1998, p.34).'

6. ANC Historical Documents Archive. http://www.marxists.org/subject/africa/anc/1969/strategy-tactics.htm
7. http://www.sahistory.org.za/archive/strategy-and-tactics-statement-adopted-anc-morogoro-conference-april-may-1969-abridged
8. http://www.sahistory.org.za/article/address-accepting-honarary-doctorate-russian-academy-sciences

These 'positive future trends' of, *inter alia*, non-racialism, ensured that, even in the fiercest periods of clashes between forces of resistance and suppression, the conflict was not typified or presented as purely or totally racial, Jakes Gerwel told the National Conference on Racism in 2000[9]. It is the spirit of national reconciliation which he claimed was responsible for 'modern day South Africans avert(ing) a widely predicted civil war and racial conflagration and as the alternative produced one of the most acclaimed and democratic and diversity-accommodating constitutions in the world'.

THE 1997 ANC CONFERENCE

During 1997 there was an intense debate within the ANC about Africanism and non-racialism. Up to that point, the broad Africanist strand that existed in the ANC was committed to emphasising the centrality of the liberation which rose above ethnic identities. The resilience of the latter identities has, however, moved Carrim to write about the existence of 'a narrow Africanism' (1997a). This is opposed to the broad sense of Africanism where 'everybody who is opposed to racism and committed to uplifting the poor and to a South African national identity based on our geographical and cultural location as an African country is an Africanist'. Carrim articulates a position which most supporters of the Freedom Charter have argued: 'It has to be recognised that since Africans constitute the vast majority in this country, bore the brunt of the struggle against apartheid, are in general the most disadvantaged and overwhelmingly constitute the social base of the governing party, they will be the prime beneficiaries of this stage of our new democracy(1997a).'

Wally Serote argued that 'their (i.e. Africans) being indigenous to South Africa, their being in the majority and most importantly, their being the most oppressed in the country, dictates, and seeks, a special positioning for them within the liberation process and the resolution of the national question'. Carrim suggests that 'this approach of investing a greater African and class content to non-racialism must be distinguished from an exclusive Africanism which serves the interests primarily of an upwardly mobile narrow stratum of Africans rather than the mass of poor people' (1997b). The views of Serote and Carrim contrast with those of Peter Mokaba, who came to be associated with this narrow view. Writing in *The Star* while Deputy Minister in Mandela's Cabinet, Mokaba argued: 'The Africans ask

---

9. http://www.sahrc.org.za/home/21/files/Reports/national_conference_on%20racism%20report%202001.pdf

themselves ... if 60% of the 62% that voted the ANC into power is African, why is it that the percentages of other national groups in the leadership structures are more than their contribution to the democratic vote? (23 July, 1997).'

The debates took on a particular urgency as the ANC headed for its December 1997 National Conference. In a contribution to the pre-Conference debate, Jordan wrote that 'the ANC has always held that democracy, national liberation, and non-racialism, are inseparable. But we have equally forcefully said that for democracy to advance national liberation it must entail the empowerment of the oppressed and most exploited – Africans, Coloureds and Indians ... what honour could accrue to the ANC if it were to compete with the PAC on the issue of Africanism?' (1997, p.15). Responding to the type of charges made by Mokaba, Jordan argued that 'the electoral behaviour of Coloured and Indian working-class people is less likely to change until visible delivery on the part of the democratic government demonstrates that there could be sufficient resources for all the disadvantaged' (ibid.). Filatova criticised the discussion document, arguing that 'the ANC nation building text offers little to those who are neither African nor poor black' (1997, p.51).

In the lead up to the conference, Joel Netshitenzhe drafted a document, appended to this report, which provided the basis for a constructive consensus which seems to have held to this day. The final Strategy and Tactics documents adopted at the conference made the following points concerning Africanism:

- *The African people were themselves nudged and coerced to develop an ethnic consciousness that the system of colonial capitalism had undermined. Some among them were rewarded with bogus positions of status in apartheid institutions* (1997, p.9).
- *The affirmation of our Africanness as a nation has nothing to do with the domination of one culture or language by another – it is a recognition of a geographic reality and the awakening of a consciousness which colonialism suppressed* (ibid. p.6).
- *It defines the 'motive forces of transformation' as the 'African majority and blacks in general'. It also includes from 'the white community' individuals of 'rare foresight and integrity '... (who) made common cause with the national liberation movement* (ibid. p.9).

THE AFRICAN RENAISSANCE

Mbeki's close association with the idea of the African Renaissance has led to the mistaken conclusion by Filatova and others that he is an adherent of a narrow and exclusivist Africanist position. In fact, as the following extracts from his Prologue to *African Renaissance* show, his is a Pan-African ideology in the broadest sense. Mbeki writes: 'The new African world which the African Renaissance seeks to build is one of democracy, peace and stability, sustainable development and a better life for the people, non-racialism and non-sexism, equality among the nationals and a just and democratic system of international governance. None of this will come about on its own. In as much as we liberated ourselves from colonialism through struggle, so will it be that the African Renaissance will be victorious only as a result of a protracted struggle that we ourselves must wage (1999, p.XVIII).'

Critics have tended to seize on Mbeki's glowing references to African history to depict him as some quixotic dreamer, whereas he has actually concentrated more on the current challenges and future prospects of Africa. On one occasion Mbeki said, 'and as we speak of an African Renaissance, we project into both the past and the future ... we are trying to convey the message that African underdevelopment must be a matter of concern to everybody else in the world, that the victory of the African Renaissance addressed not only the improvement of the conditions of life of the peoples of Africa but also the extension of the frontiers of human dignity to all humanity (1988, p.241).'

This section can be concluded by taking cognisance of the three strands of Africanist thinking which emerged in South Africa in the course of the twentieth century:

- the broad outlook of the founding fathers of the ANC, which aims at Pan-African unity in a bid to overcome the effects of tribalism and ethnicity;
- the strategic question of African leadership over the non-racial anti-apartheid movement, and
- the narrow chauvinistic outlook which led to the PAC breakaway, and elements of which seemed to reappear during the ANC's 1997 debate on non-racialism.

MULTIPLE IDENTITIES

This section examines the postmodernist approach of seeing identity as a discursive device which is continuously redefined. The approach of encouraging and respecting identities against attempts at developing a dominant identity, as modernity tends to do, is explored here.

Given that the apartheid system sought to foster divisions along racial, tribal and ethnic lines, it would have been logical to expect such identities to have prevailed over national considerations. However, as Bhabha (1990) put it, 'it is from this instability of cultural signification that the national culture comes to be articulated as a dialectic of various temporalities – modern, colonial, postcolonial, "native"...' (p.303). And, as Chatterjee (1993) had pointed out, a key terrain which the elite strives to extend its dominance over is the 'arena of subaltern' politics.

Expanding on the subaltern school's approach, Greenstein introduces the notion of 'indigenous capacity' to alert us 'to the attributes of indigenous structures that shape the capacity of people to organise at the economic, political and identity levels, and employ their modes of organisation to sustain and open up avenues of independent existence and development outside the control of colonial forces' (1995, p.108).

ONE NATION / MANY IDENTITIES?

As mentioned above, the ANC Youth League depicted South Africa as a 'country of four chief nationalities, three of which (the Europeans, Indians and Coloureds) are minorities, and three of which (the Africans, Coloureds and Indians) suffer national oppression'. Alexander wrote that 'the classical liberal position on the national question in South Africa is the so-called four nations thesis' (1986, p.76). He argued that liberals saw the four major groups in South Africa co-existing in 'multiracial harmony' (ibid.) within a single state. According to him, the 'long-term strategic aim of the liberal establishment was, and remains, to co-opt significant layers of the black middle class' (ibid.).

Alexander proposes a one-nation theory which sees the 'struggle in this country as simultaneously one for national liberation and class emancipation' (ibid. p.77). He argues that the people of South Africa are being moulded into one unified nation by the twin forces of capitalist development and the class struggle resulting from it. The black workers have become the decisive force that will determine the direction of 'racial capitalism'.

As indicated in the introduction to this chapter, the search for national unity has been the holy grail of nationalist discourse. The importance of this has been explained by Slovo who argued that 'the modern nation state is not always the creation of the bourgeoisie', and that 'whereas the economic functions of the nation state created at the dawn of the capitalist era were served by the breaking down of ethnic, regional, language, and cultural diversions, in most of Africa ... colonial control for purposes of economic exploitation demanded ethnic fragmentation and inter-ethnic hostility'. Slovo continued: 'The historic process of spreading a national (as opposed to ethnic or tribal) consciousness and then national consolidation of existing state entities is, in the modern African era, generally a weapon of liberation and social advance (1988, p.144–145).' Jordan (2000) refers to this as the 'revolutionary perspective'.

Slovo further argued that 'despite the existence of cultural and racial diversity, South Africa is not a multinational country. It is a nation in the making; a process which is increasingly being advanced in struggle and one which can only be finally completed after the racist tyranny is defeated. The concept of one united nation embracing all other ethnic communities remains the virtually undisputed liberation objective' (Slovo, p.146).

The argument in this approach is that neither race nor ethnic affiliation determines membership of the nation. According to Jordan the nation's 'parameters are set by individual acts of voluntary adherence, which adherence requires the submergence of other loyalties to this larger unit; they are defined by a commitment to the country, its people and its future' (1988, p.118). It was recognised within the ANC/SACP alliance that there would always be a tension between the notion of national unity and sub-national identity. This has been articulated by, *inter alia*, Jordan who argued: 'The ANC recognises that, owing to the diverse origins of the South African population, there are inevitably and will continue to be cultural expressions of this diversity. The democratic state cannot, however, seek to legislate on such matters ... Neither can it abolish affinities based on such sentiment by administrative fiat ... We would insist, though, that sovereignty in a democratic state can no more be determined by accidents of biology any more than by those of philology. Indeed we would insist on "one country, one people, with one government – a government of the people of South Africa" that respects cultural diversity (ibid. p.117).'

During the 1950s the ANC stood at the vanguard of an alliance of racially-based organisations. Williams points out that 'the form of the Congress Alliance, of an alliance of four organisations each with a racially-defined constituency, allowed the ANC to reconcile its historical purpose as the voice of the African people with its commitment to a non-racial future for South Africa' (1988, p.75). This approach was emphasised by ex-president of the ANC, Oliver Tambo, who, as cited by Jordan, said: 'Let us in South Africa learn to stop being Bantus, Coloureds, Indians and whites. Let us be what we are, Africans in Africa. Let those who are committed racists who came to this continent determined to keep Africans in chains, to be perpetual white masters over blacks – let them persist in their role as foreigners on African soil (ibid. p.118).' This approach has been formally expressed within the ANC at key points in its history. The Freedom Charter, for example, proclaimed 'that South Africa belongs to all who live in it, black and white', and that '[a]ll national groups shall have equal rights'[10]. More recently, this approach was also evident in the ANC's Constitutional Guidelines, a set of pre-negotiations proposals drawn up by the ANC, where it declared: 'It shall be state policy to promote the growth of a single national identity … the state shall recognise the linguistic and cultural diversity of the people (Ebrahim, 1999, p.551).'

In its February 1991 Strategy and Tactics document[11], the ANC, while emphasising its opposition to ethnically-based mobilisation, placed particular emphasis on the role of the African majority: 'The African people (must) take the lead in combating any notions of racial or ethnic chauvinism and create the basis of the emergence of a common South African identity (1998, p.507).' At its 1997 Conference, the aforementioned Strategy and Tactics document explained the movement's position: 'Critical to nation building is the de-racialisation of South African society and the elimination of patriarchal relations. It means creating a society in which the station that individuals occupy in political, social, and other areas of endeavour is not defined on the basis of race, ethnicity, language, gender, religious, cultural, or other such considerations (1997, p.10).'

Black Consciousness, on the other hand, focused on imbuing black people with a higher degree of confidence, justifying this as an essential step towards democracy. As Biko expressed it: 'Liberation is of paramount importance in the concept of Black Consciousness (BC), for we cannot be conscious of ourselves and yet remain in bondage … being black is not a matter of pigmentation – being black is a reflection of a mental attitude. Merely by

---

10. http://www.anc.org.za/show.php?id=72
11. http://www.anc.org.za/show.php?id=107

describing yourself as black you have started on a road towards emancipation (cited in Reddy, 1995, p.184).' In many ways, the BC perspective was influenced by Garvey's emphasis on self-assertion, as well as Fanon's views on self-identity and revolt.

Alexander points out that the Black Consciousness perspective shared by some tendencies in the PAC sees the existence of 'two nations' in South Africa: an oppressing white and an oppressed black, sometimes referred to as a 'black nationality' (1996, p.81–82). 'Exponents of the Black Consciousness position have tended to conflate "race" and "class" to the point that in some versions all whites are projected as capitalists while all blacks are seen as workers … It seems to assume that all whites in South Africa, because they are not oppressed, cannot identify at a certain unspecifiable deep psychic level with the oppressed and with their struggle (ibid.).'

Superficial parallels can be drawn between this position and Mbeki's two-nation thesis. However, the two positions differ fundamentally in their starting points. Whereas Mbeki's is a continuation of the CST approach and located in the material differences between black and white people, the BC position begins from the psychological barriers between black and white people.

RESILIENCE OF ETHNIC / TRIBAL IDENTITIES

Phillip Dexter cites Debray in arguing that 'national identities are forged in opposition, and often most successfully in wars' (Tayob and Weiss, 1999, p.69). He then alerts us to one of the effects of the successful transitions South Africa is undergoing – 'it removes any significant "other" against which a South African identity can be forged … the pressure to revert to old, comfortable identities that are primarily based on perceived racial and ethnic identities are therefore very great, even if these identities are artificially created' (ibid.). Carrim has also commented on this, suggesting that 'the resilience in new forms' of ethnic and racial identities 'poses enormous challenges to the emergence of a broader South African national identity' (1997c).

In approaching the question of provincial demarcations, the ANC resolved not to draw the lines on an ethnic basis. However, as Mbeki pointed out, 'the reality is that the Eastern Cape has a Xhosa majority, in KwaZulu-Natal the majority are Zulu-speaking, in the Free State they are Sotho and in the North-West, Tswana (1994, p.4).' Mbeki stopped short of admitting that tribal/ethnic identity is a logical legacy of the separations forced by the apartheid system and re-embodied in South Africa's provincial system.

One particular form of identity which writers have picked upon is the seeming emphasis on Africanism in trying to trace the link between the Black Republic thesis and contemporary ANC thinking. Filatova cites the following as manifestations of Africanism:

- *Renaissance of African multiple cultures. The 'flowering of African cultures' which Slovo had propagated in 1992 has led to the growth of group self-consciousness and assertiveness (1997, p.58).*
- *Africanism … has gained momentum … (as in) the reinvention of black identity, styles and fashions, cultures, even ideology (Ubuntu), the discovery of Africanness … this Africanist tendency is expressed much more vigorously and in much stronger terms by the ANC leadership, communists among them, than either by the PAC or BC groupings (1997, p.52). (She sees South Africa's increased engagement in Africa as another illustration of this.)*
- *Political emotions and feelings of the 'non-African' minorities understandably play a much smaller role in the ANC's political considerations (ibid.).*

The views of Dexter, Carrim and Filatova have been cited to illustrate the point that there are concerns about the re-assertion of ethnic identities in post-apartheid South Africa. One response to the emergence or persistence of such identities is to declare South Africa a 'rainbow nation', thus establishing these identities as permanent features of the South African landscape.

THE RAINBOW NATION

The concept of the rainbow nation, echoing US civil rights leader Jesse Jackson's Rainbow Coalition, was popularised by Archbishop Desmond Tutu and also propagated by former President Mandela. It was meant to metaphorically encourage respect for the various cultures represented in South Africa. The problem with the notion is that, just as the rainbow consists of a fixed set of colours appearing in a fixed sequence, the rainbow nation concept could be seen as an attempt to 'freeze' the South African nation in its composition and hierarchy.

Filatova says the rainbow nation concept was meant to denote 'something intrinsically though not sharply divided and yet indivisible ... (it) was a successful albeit a romanticised representation of the Charterist interpretation of the South African nation' (1997, p.65). However, Dexter is less charitable, saying 'we are already showing signs of confusion in relation to the definition of a South African national identity where a murky, colonised, unclassed, ungendered, "rainbowism" rules' (1997, p.85).

Carrim sees the rainbow nation concept as reflecting the ANC-led government's commitment to nation building and national reconciliation. He points out that 'one nation, many cultures' (1998, p.51) was the theme of President Mandela's inauguration. He urges that such an approach should not be used to fossilise ethnic and racial identities. It should pave the way for deepening non-racialism, which does not mean to contradict African leadership, especially African working-class leadership. Carrim asserts: 'Failure to assert such leadership will serve to strengthen a narrow, exclusive Africanism, on the one hand, and an empty, artificial non-racialism on the other (ibid. p.55).'

The 1997 Strategy and Tactics document[12] gives an indication of the framework within which the ANC has been operating over the past two decades: 'The ANC recognises that individuals within such a nation will have multiple identities, on the basis of their make-up, cultural life and social upbringing. Such distinctive features will not disappear in the melting pot of broad South Africanism.' As long as the question of identity is restricted to a simply reductive understanding of cultures and a culturalist conception of race and ethnicity, as Gilroy (1992) put it, there will be a drift 'towards a belief in the absolute nature of ethnic categories' (p.50). This takes us down the slippery path of multiculturalism and a self-defined apartheid of eleven or more identities.

It seems that multiple identities are acceptable so long as they are benign. But what of the multiple identities of the emerging bourgeoisie which Woddis (1962) describes as standing Janus-like, exploiting 'its own workers and ensuring their submission to its own domination' (p. 274), while also coming into conflict with the 'big imperialist monopolies' (ibid.). Is the multiple identities approach an indulgence when, as the South African Human Rights Commission chairperson, Barney Pityana, in his opening address to the National Conference on Racism argued: 'The structures which

---

12. https://www.marxists.org/subject/africa/anc/1997/strategy-tactics.htm

history has erected, the mindsets and social practices, are not changing fast enough to meet the pace of time (2000, p.2).' For Pityana, it is important that 'we understand and appreciate the cultural differences and we must now challenge many of the social and cultural orthodoxies that have gone to make the taken-for-granted life-world of an Europeanised South Africa' (ibid.).

Accordingly, Gerwel (2002) emphasised that racism must not be seen as 'another form of expression of difference in our diverse society ... where poverty was so much a function of racial allocation of station, the achievement of the better life envisaged, meant a concrete addressing of the legacy of racism and the creation of circumstances where racism as felt practice would increasingly recede' (p.2).

A further question which needs to be answered is: From where do these multiple identities arise? Jordan argued that under apartheid 'the revival of African ethnicity had little to do with nostalgia for past greatness on the part of the Africans. It was even less the articulation of a "psychological urge", as the theorists of ethnicity claim, to cohere as members of a unique struggle for equality and freedom on the part of the African people ... Verwoerd argued that South Africa was not a common society. A historical accident had resulted in the artificial forcing together of members of a number of discrete nations. Thirteen of these were the "Bantu nations", the others were the Afrikaners, the Brits, the Coloureds, the Namas, and the Asians' (1997, p.10).

Capturing the tension between multiple identities, which people may consider fixed and a reformulation of identities, Duncan and De la Rey (2000), arguing that racial categories are discursively constructed and change over time, wrote about the racial category of 'Coloured' as follows: 'The Population Registration Act of 1950 legally constituted the category "Coloured" as a person who is not white or native. This category is under continual contestation under present-day South Africa. Individuals, who during the apartheid days were classified as Coloured, variously refer to themselves as "black", "so-called Coloured", and "Coloured" (p.15).'

The issue of fluidity of identities applies also to language and ethnicity among the African people in South Africa, a matter that is profoundly relevant to current discourse around the 'revival of tribalism'. In their treatment of the dynamics of the Mapungubwe state[13], Alex Schoeman and Sekibakiba Lekgoathi argue thus:

In the pre-colonial era, ethnicity was negotiable and reconfigurable and this flexibility continued, to a limited extent, even as the colonial and/or apartheid states were attempting to construct rigid ethnic boundaries through various forms of social engineering, such as the Native Affairs' Department project of classifying each and every African in South Africa into a 'tribe'. Before they were 'reified and named' by European colonial authorities 'through administrative and judicial procedures', African societies did not live in static, homogeneous, self-contained ethnic units but existed in extremely fluid, porous and heterogeneous entities connected to shifting boundaries that allowed for individuals and groups to move in and out and back and forth across these boundaries. Alliances of various forms were forged across these boundaries, not on the basis of linguistic or cultural affinity. In societies where the security and survival (both political and economic) of polities depended on having a large following and alliances with other groups, the rulers placed a high premium on attracting followers rather than worrying about how different their followers' language background and cultural practices were to the core ones. Thus ethnic affiliation played a very minimal – if any – role in determining group membership. It is very likely that this pattern manifest during the last 500 years also prevailed at Mapungubwe (p.41–42).

Schoeman and Lekgoathi also point out that '… Colonial conquest and rule did not capture static societies long set in their ways, but incorporated dynamic and changing societies including some quite relatively recently established political and social systems' (p. 47).

CRAFTING A NATION THROUGH THE STATE

Since the 1994 elections, the State has been playing an increasingly larger role in shaping the South African nation. Apart from the National Conference on Racism held in 2000 mentioned above, there has been an ongoing dialogue on various facets of nation building. At one level there has been a shift from emphasis on issues of consciousness as the basis for identity, to concerns pertaining to the economy, and political participation. The State has tried to address the former through affirmative action programmes to address worker and management representivity, as well as policies aimed at broadening black ownership of the economy and land restitution. Addressing the position of women as a means to tackle the patriarchal

---

13. MISTRA, *Mapungubwe Reconsidered*, 2013.

elements of South African society, as well as the abuse and discrimination faced by women on a daily basis, has come to be increasingly focused on a part of the process of nation formation and social cohesion. The experience of large numbers of migrants coming to South Africa, and the xenophobia or, as the NDP points out, 'afrophobia' it has engendered, introduced a new dimension to debates on national identity in South Africa.

One of the two most seminal developments in the past two years has been the Declaration and Programme of Action which emerged from the National Social Cohesion and Nation Building Summit in 2012. It was replete with symbolism that tried to connect it with the Freedom Charter. The conference was held in Kliptown, the venue for the conference which drew up the Freedom Charter in 1955. The summit was held in early July 2012, as close as diaries allowed to 25 and 26 June, the anniversary of the drawing up of the Freedom Charter.

The Declaration took as its starting point the well-known principle in the South African Constitution adopted in 1996 that 'South Africa belongs to all who live in it, both black and white, united in our diversity'. The second principle of the Declaration reveals how far down the road South Africans had travelled in defining their nation: 'South Africa is a unitary and sovereign state based on democracy, the rule of law, pursuit of equal human rights, non-racialism, non-sexism, and the equality of all persons.' It represents a decisive move from any race or ethnic conceptions of the nation to one that is articulated clearly in civic terms. The Declaration captured a wide range of obstacles to uniting South Africans: economic development, inequality, landlessness and homelessness, the burden of disease, poor education for the majority of pupils, crime and corruption, gender inequalities, racism and xenophobia. Implementing the 2030 Vision of the NDP was seen as an essential part of dealing with these building obstacles.

The second major development has been the drafting of the National Development Plan (NDP), also released in 2012. The opening lines of its 2030 Vision state: 'We have created a home where everybody feels free yet bounded to others; where everyone embraces their full potential. We are proud to be a community that cares'. Answering the question 'Who are we?' the vision statement emphasises: 'We are African. We are an African country. We are part of our multi-national region. We are an essential part of our continent (2012, pp.12–13).' Furthermore, 'Our multiculturalism is a defining element of our indigeneity … once, we uttered the dream of a rainbow. Now we see it, living it. It does not curve over the sky. It is refracted in each of us at home, in the community, in the city, and across the land, in abundance of colour (2012, pp.21–22).'

Chapter 15 of the NDP, entitled 'Transforming Society and Uniting the Country', is dedicated to capturing the ongoing process of nation formation. It also emphasises the role of the 1996 Constitution, describing it as 'a national compact that defines South Africa's common values and identifies our rights and responsibilities as people living together' (2012, p.458). Hence, it is not surprising that fostering the Constitutional values tops the list of what needs to be done. This includes the Bill of Responsibilities, which was developed by the Department of Basic Education and Lead SA[14] (South Africa) in 2011. The chapter then spells out the role of the family, education, media, sports and culture in fusing the nation. Equal opportunities, inclusion and redress are to be addressed through building capabilities of the citizens, righting the exclusionary practises of the past through transforming the economy and land reform, and promoting non-sexism and non-racialism. This state-led, civic approach to nation building is to be complemented by active citizenry and leadership. This must lead to a new social compact between government, business and labour so that all sectors of society can be involved in moving to a trajectory of higher growth and employment, increased investment, and savings.

CONCLUSION

The unity of all South Africans and the creation of a democratic society dominates approaches to the national question in South Africa. The roots of the democratic constitution can be traced to the first few decades of the previous century when the founding fathers of the ANC sought to create a society free of the demons of tribalism and racism; this can also be seen in the assertion that South Africa could be an independent, predominantly black republic. These approaches represented the modernist impulse which characterised the struggles of the oppressed European nations of the nineteenth century, and the people of Africa and Asia in the twentieth century.

The basis upon which South Africa was depicted as a special colony prevails today. This theory constructs 'two nations' – one which, despite the ushering in of democracy, is still privileged, and which used to be the colonising 'nation'; the other, the majority, was the colonised 'nation', and

---

14. A not-for-profit organisation (non-governmental)whose purpose it is to help build a socially cohesive nation.

continues to suffer from material deprivations. At the heart of the emerging South African nation exists an African core. Unity of this African core and the assertion of its leadership in the interests of all South Africans stands in contrast to the narrow chauvinism displayed by some approaches, and the negative tendencies of narrow identities and the patronage that attaches to them.

A final ingredient in the make-up of the South African nation is the existence of a multiplicity of identities. Should these be encouraged to exist, or should there be an overriding South African identity which subsumes these sub-identities? This question gains urgency as political, economic and social bases are opportunistically carved out on the basis of clan, ethnic or linguistic groupings.

The Social Cohesion Declaration and the NDP show how the resources of the State can be wielded in the interests of nation formation. They stand out as beacons of hope for granting Ms Luthuli's dream: 'My wish, before I die, is to see blacks and whites living harmoniously in a united South Africa.'

APPENDIX 1

NATION FORMATION AND NATION BUILDING: THESES ON THE NATIONAL QUESTION IN SOUTH AFRICA
JOEL NETSHITENZHE
JUNE 1997

Background

Colonial conquest in South Africa had two contradictory consequences. On the one hand, it brought together various disparate communities in one nation state. On the other hand, this very conquest was used by the colonisers to try and prevent the unity of these communities into one nation.

The discovery of diamonds and gold in the late nineteenth century heralded the advent of capitalism and, by the same token, a new epoch in the history of the country. Thousands of people who were previously separated in self-subsistence economies were either forced or attracted to the emerging industries to provide labour.

Transport networks were laid connecting the industrial hubs with the harbours. New towns emerged: further knitting together into a single economy communities which were previously separated. The hitherto peasant Afrikaner farmers began producing for the broader market, while Africans – dispossessed of their land – did not only become providers of labour, but also consumers of commercial products.

One natural result of this was the emergence of the colonisers' language(s) as a medium of communication through which economic activity was conducted. In the process, aspects of the colonisers' culture – material and otherwise – gained currency among all communities.

The importation of slaves and indentured labour by the Dutch East India Company from Indonesia, Malaysia and India also helped to shape the make-up of South Africa's population. Oppressed in the countries where they originated, these communities were subjected to the same colonial treatment in South Africa. Along with this was the emergence of the indigenous 'Coloured' community.

It is the irony of our history that the totality of this process, which crowned South Africa's evolution into one nation state, was the seed of subsequent decades of strife and bloody conflict. This is because the State was colonial in character, whether in the form of the Union in 1910 or the Republic in 1961. Power was handed over by the British conquerors to the settler colonial community to continue the subjugation of indigenous Africans, in particular, and the black majority in general.

The Essence of the 'National Question'

Whereas the 'national question' plays itself out in different ways specific to the concrete conditions in various parts of the world, it is fundamentally a continuous quest for equality by constituent communities which have historically coalesced into a single nation state, or the struggle for self-determination and even secession by communities within such states.

In the global context, the national question is fundamentally a quest for national sovereignty in relation to other nation states, especially the more powerful ones.

A number of basic principles should be taken into account in addressing this question in our country. These are summarised below in the form of ten theses.

Thesis I

The liberation movement in South Africa characterised our society as colonialism of a special type to describe the unique situation in which both the colonisers and the colonised shared one country.

The basic conclusion arising from this is that the national democratic revolution (NDR) is, in essence, an act of addressing the 'national question': to create a united, non-racial, non-sexist, and democratic society. The 'national character' of the NDR is therefore the resolution of the antagonistic contradictions between the oppressed majority and their oppressors, to resolve the national grievance arising from colonial relations.

Thesis II

National oppression and its legacy are linked almost inextricably to class exploitation. So closely linked are they that among the debates on the characterisation of South Africa under apartheid was the question whether national oppression was a necessary condition for South African capitalism, or whether South African capitalism was a necessary condition for national oppression.

Be that as it may, what this emphasises is that national oppression can only be successfully addressed in the context of socio-economic transformation.

This entails much more than competition among the 'multiracial' middle strata for material benefits accruing out of the achievement of democracy, a phenomenon to which concepts like 'black empowerment' popularly tend to be reduced. Rather it means, above everything else, improving the quality of life of the poor, the overwhelming majority of whom are defined by South African capitalism as blacks in general, and Africans in particular. In other words, consistent implementation of the RDP is an essential part of addressing the national question.

Thesis III

A nation is not equivalent to a classless society. In any case, this would be a contradiction in terms because the latter is by definition an international phenomenon, requiring the 'withering away' of nations as such.

A nation is a multi-class entity. Under a system of capitalism it will have its bourgeoisie, middle strata, rural communities – rich and poor. The objective of the NDR is not the creation of a socialist or communist society, though its progression, for those who adhere to these aims, does not exclude these long-term consequences.

Among the central tasks of the NDR is to improve the quality of life, of especially the poor, and ensure that in the medium- to long-term the station that individuals occupy in society is not defined by race. The opposite is essentially the case in present-day South Africa, where the poor are by definition essentially black, and where the majority of the rich are by definition white.

An important subscript to this is that the NDR also entails, consciously or subconsciously, the building of a black bourgeoisie. The tendering conditions that government has introduced, and the nudge on the private sector to promote all kinds of 'empowerment', illustrate this. The reality is that the bigger and more successful this black bourgeoisie becomes, the less will it exhibit race consciousness, for instance in its attitude to workers.

In the same vein, the unfolding NDR has also meant the rapid development of black middle strata, a process that is bound to accelerate even more as opportunities open up in various areas of life.

The democratic movement must seek to influence these classes and strata – both black and white – to take active part in the realisation of the Reconstruction and Development Programme – for them to act in a way that promotes South Africa's true interests.

Thesis IV

Apartheid was most successful in crippling working class unity; and that legacy is still felt acutely today.

The ANC enjoys the support of the majority of Coloured and Indian middle strata. What we usually refer to as the 'Coloured' and 'Indian' question is in large measure an expression of fears of the working class (including the unemployed) among these communities that the rise of the African worker and the African poor directly impacts on the comparative privilege that apartheid afforded them. This applies similarly to white workers, which is partly the reason why many of them constitute the mass base of the ultra-right. There are of course other important elements that come into play such as language, religion, racism and the spatial separation of communities.

But this unique situation underlines the centrality of building working-class unity as a major element in forging the South African nation.

Thesis V

The 'national question' is also, and importantly, a superstructural phenomenon at the level of consciousness, 'feelings' and perceptions. Thus, it has a potent and dynamic momentum of its own, underpinned by such factors as language, culture and religion. To this extent, the socio-psychological element of the national question can be used effectively to promote the process of nation formation, or even to undermine it.

One of our greatest successes in the transition has been to promote the 'feeling' of pride in being South African, including through sport and other issues that may seem innocuous. Thus, capturing the national imagination through the Campaign for a New Patriotism is critical to nation building.

Yet, the socio-psychological phenomenon on its own is not sustainable without socio-economic transformation; nor can it be accepted as universally credible in a situation in which those privileged by apartheid do not accept that they have to lose some of these privileges. The rumblings on such issues as education, welfare grants, labour matters, and so on are a reflection of this problem.

Thesis VI

Individuals are social beings with different social experiences, class backgrounds, political histories, religious affiliations, as well as sport and music preferences. With regard to the national question, race, ethnic origins, language, and sometimes religion have an important role to play in defining a person's identity. Above all, the fact of belonging to this country, and this state, is itself a critical attribute.

Therefore, individuals will evince multiple identities: for instance, being a South African with a specific mother tongue, class position, political and religious affiliation, and so on. These identities do not die in the melting pot of broad South Africanism. Rather, they can all co-exist in healthy combination, the fundamental question being: which identity assumes prominence and under what conditions?

To deny the reality of these identities by the democratic movement is to create a vacuum, which can easily be exploited by counter-revolution.

However, the main thrust of the NDR is not to promote fractious identities but to encourage the emergence of a common South African identity. At the same time, it should be noted that some of the identities associated with 'culture' or 'ethnicity' or 'religion' can, in fact, be contradictory to the building of a new nation based on principles of equity: for instance, to use these attributes as an excuse to perpetuate gender oppression, or to campaign for racial or ethnic divisions among citizens.

Thesis VII

Deriving from its characterisation of apartheid colonialism, the ANC was correct in asserting, in the Strategy and Tactics documents from the Morogoro and Kabwe Consultative Conferences, that the main content of the NDR is the liberation of black people in general, and Africans in particular. They are in the majority, and they constitute an overwhelmingly larger majority of the poor.

Related to this is the identity of the South African nation in gestation: whether it should truly be an African nation on the African continent, or a clone of, for instance, the US and UK in outlook; in the style and content of its media; in its cultural expression; in its cuisine; in the language accents of its children ... What is required in this regard is a continuing battle to assert African hegemony in the context of a multicultural and non-racial society. It is subject to debate whether the popular imagery of a 'rainbow nation' is useful in this respect.

There is, however, an important role that it does play as popular imagery. But if used to express the character of South African society as one made up of black Africans who pay allegiance to Africa, whites who pay allegiance to Europe, Indians who pay allegiance to India, and Coloureds somewhere in the undefined middle of the rainbow, then it can be problematic. For it would fail to recognise the healthy osmosis among the various cultures and other attributes in the process towards the emergence of a new African nation.

Thesis VIII

Morogoro was correct further to assert that this main content of the NDR should find expression in the leadership structures of the ANC and indeed of the country as a whole – what is usually referred to as 'African leadership'.

However, this principle does not mean mechanical proportional representation in leadership structures: that we should do 'ethnic, racial, language, gender and class arithmetic' in composing leadership structures.

The principle of African leadership and balanced representation in racial, gender, ethnic and class terms is a broad one which should find broad expression in actual practise. Yet, attention should always be paid to these broad parameters because a critical mass can be reached where perception of dominance can take root.

The principle of African leadership does not mean derogating from merit: in any case, one cannot proceed from the premise that it is people other than Africans who are endowed with merit. However, apartheid deliberately denied opportunities to blacks in general and Africans in particular. Therefore, it is critical that deliberate steps are taken to empower them to play their requisite role. Affirmative action is meant to address this, and naturally, it is those who have been most disadvantaged who will be the foremost beneficiaries of such a programme.

Thesis IX

The national question is never fully solved, precisely because it is not merely a material question, nor one related only to various forms of power, precisely because attached to it are emotional and psychological factors, and precisely because people will continue to have multiple identities.

Rather the challenge is to maintain a healthy equilibrium between centrifugal ('disintegrative') and centripetal ('integrative') tendencies.

Indeed, as we seek to integrate South African society across racial, language, ethnic and other barriers, we are also engaged in the process of developing those individual elements that distinguish these various communities from one another.

It will not be possible to achieve the kind of balance that will satisfy everyone for all time, even if the broad principle is attained in practise. This is aggravated by the fact that, as individuals compete for positions in politics, the academic terrain, the economy, and elsewhere, the more unscrupulous ones among them will seek to use criteria that exclude those who have all along been disadvantaged, or to use the racial, ethnic and/or language 'card' to advance their personal ambition.

Even within the ANC tensions will flare up from time to time, especially in periods such as preparations for National Conference and other allocations of positions of power and influence.

Thesis X:

The process of nation formation depends on objective conditions such as the fact of an integrated national economy, the historical evolution of a nation state, national identity, and so on. This objective environment is itself a product of human activity, in our situation represented broadly in the act of colonisation and the struggle against it.

This struggle was itself an important and conscious act of nation building. To this extent, the ANC (and other political movements), the new government and organs of civil society have a critical role to play in facilitating the emergence of a new nation: in nation building.

This includes striving for consistent and thoroughgoing democracy, effecting socio-economic transformation and encouraging a New Patriotism. It must also include the elimination of the geographical separation along racial and ethnic lines in the programmes to provide housing and other services.

CHAPTER FOUR

SECTION I:

LINKING NATION FORMATION AND SOCIAL COHESION

Introduction

In this chapter (which consists of two parts) social cohesion and its relationship to nation formation are examined. There is a theoretical and conceptual framework for social cohesion, linking the framework to nation formation and proposing a set of indicators for measuring it, in the first part. The second part takes up the issue of the commemoration of public holidays as a case study, and proposes creative ways in which the vexed issue can be dealt with as part of the process of promoting nation formation and social cohesion. The chapter draws largely from submissions that the Mapungubwe Institute (MISTRA) has made to various government entities to contribute to their reflections on these issues.

Since 1994, key legislation has been passed to promote national unity, equality, and to entrench and protect human rights in South Africa. The Interim Constitution (Act 200 of 1993) and the Constitution of the Republic of South Africa (Act 108 of 1996) enabled the establishment of: the Human Rights Commission (1994); the Truth and Reconciliation Commission (through the Promotion of National Unity and Reconciliation Act (1995)); the Commission for Gender Equality (1996); the Youth Commission (1996); the Promotion of Equality and Prevention of Discrimination Act (2001); the Commission for the Promotion and Protection of the Rights of Cultural, Religious and Linguistic Communities (2002), and the Pan South African Language Board (1995). In conjunction with economic policies aimed at black empowerment and equity, the cluster of laws and institutions set out to fundamentally transform South African society, promote national unity, reconciliation and social cohesion.

In 2007, an ad hoc parliamentary committee, chaired by Professor Kader Asmal, was mandated to investigate the effectiveness of these Chapter Nine[15] constitutional institutions and other related bodies. The report was completed in 2007 and found inconsistent financial management systems, governance tensions, inaccessibility and lack of co-ordination in the overall system. Recommended was a rationalisation of all the human rights bodies into a single South African Commission on Human Rights and Equality incorporating the Human Rights, Youth, Gender, Cultural, Religious and Linguistic Communities Commissions.

The existence of these laws and the work of these bodies greatly assisted in monitoring and combating discriminatory practises and human rights violations. However, the deeper structural features of minority rule and race-based inequality have as yet not been completely dismantled. Hence, the transformatory electoral mandate of the 2009 election, captured in the ANC's election manifesto, translated into outcomes, identified 'active and responsible citizenship', which included the promotion of social cohesion, as Outcome 12. This outcome was assigned to the Ministry of Arts and Culture. In implementing this, the ministry appointed the Mapungubwe Institute (MISTRA) to assist in devising a strategy for nation building and social cohesion. This strategy was tabled and discussed at a national Nation Building and Social Cohesion summit held at Kliptown in July 2012 where a declaration which contained the main principles and recommendations of the strategy was adopted. The first section of this chapter is based on MISTRA's submission on the strategy.

The need for linking nation formation to social cohesion arises, as Chidester, *et al.* (2003) established, from the fact that the persistence of stark divisions and inequalities produced by colonialism and apartheid persists in post-apartheid South Africa – in its economic and its social life; while the postcolonial state, under the condition of globalisation, 'has lost some of its locus for social cohesion'. In the light of this, the National Development Plan (NDP) states that access to economic resources and quality education remains largely based on 'race, gender, geographic location, class, and linguistic' factors (2011, p.412).

If left unchecked, this will not only persist indefinitely but could also

---

15. The institution is so named because of Chapter Nine of the Constitution, which gave birth to these bodies.

worsen to ultimately threaten the long-term sustainability of democracy in South Africa. To counter this, public and private institutions, in partnerships with communities and citizens of South Africa's diverse society, have sought to work together in attempts to build an inclusive, just and cohesive society in which not just a privileged few but all members of society live in peace and prosper together. Despite these efforts, inequalities and exclusions have not been eradicated.

As a point of departure, the linking of nation formation and social cohesion as processes should be grounded in local meanings, embedded as they happen to be in community, social ideas and cultures, and the dynamic interaction among the various South African communities. All human societies, at both local community level and larger intercommunity and national-life level, require sets of shared values, norms, visions and goals to secure co-operation and foster bonds of belonging.

In the context of South Africa, it can be argued that the concept of ubuntu articulates a social humanism of interpersonal care, sharing and a commitment to the greater social good. It posits the individual human being as a social construct in a public culture of human reciprocity and solidarity. In this view, an individual is not an entity severed from other human beings. Rather, the individual is human by virtue of other humans. This unreserved humanist and inclusive social ethos, as Ramose (2004) suggests, places every individual in a social relationship with other individuals. This interconnectedness, based on valuing and respecting all human beings, is the foundation of social solidarity. It constitutes a social compact of rights and responsibilities animating and regulating social life. Any strategy on social cohesion and nation formation should be grounded in this. Hence, the preamble to the Constitution of South Africa declares: 'We the people of South Africa … believe that South Africa belongs to everyone who lives in it, united in our diversity.'

SOCIAL COHESION AND ITS MANIFESTATIONS

'Social cohesion,' according to Jenson, 'is a concept with a history. It is not simply an academic concept or a catch-all word meaning many things. Rather, it is what is helpfully termed a "quasi-concept" – a hybrid operating within policy communities (2010, p.3).' Jenson cites Bernard, who proposed this classification, and described a hybrid concept as a construction 'with two faces' that can be applied scientifically while retaining 'a vagueness that makes them adaptable to various situations, flexible enough to follow the meandering and necessities of political action from day to day' (1999, p.2).

According to King (2009), the concept of social cohesion was popularised in the 1990s. This was at a time when the effects of globalisation unsettled societies across the world, thus threatening the legitimacy of the State and social cohesion of societies, and with it, the welfare and dignity of the citizens. In addition, Offe (2006) asserts that in many parts of the world citizens have become disaffected with state organisations and public institutions, evidenced in the declining participation in national and local elections. However, a concern with the stability and integration of communities and societies dates back to the advent of industrialisation and urbanisation and the disruptive effects of this on closely bonded and well-integrated local community life.

However, in recent times Jenson recounts that the Organisation for Economic Co-operation and Development (OECD) was one of the first international bodies to take social cohesion on board, 'diffusing' it 'among its members' in the early 1980s. Soon after, Jenson says, the European Union (EU) 'declared that the economic and social cohesion of Europe was a main goal'. In response to this, the Council of Europe, responding to the growing poverty and social exclusion in many parts of Europe, established a Directorate of Social Cohesion. In 2001, the EU developed a position document which stressed that social cohesion is not conceived in any 'traditional homogenising' in terms of a single dominant national culture, but in terms of an 'open and multicultural society'. The object of this was to provide all citizens 'access to opportunities to secure their basic needs; to progress; to protection of their rights; and to dignity and confidence' (Jenson, 2010, pp.4–5). This sent the concept into wider circulation.

Modern nation building, on the other hand, dates back to the struggles for national independence in the nineteenth century, which saw a spirit of nationalism, driven by struggles for independence, across the globe. So just as the disintegration of local communities dates back to violent contact with advancing colonists, the South African struggle for national liberation and national unity is not only something, as Chapter Three made clear, that dates back to the early twentieth century.

Since becoming a democracy, however, new conditions and challenges face South Africa. As the indicators for measuring social cohesion proposed below make clear, the race-based social and economic divisions of the past, and practises of exclusion, have not been eliminated from society. The threat this poses to the long-term stability and development of the society has accentuated the need for policy intervention programmes aimed at constructing a more inclusive and cohesive society. While the factors which drive social tension, conflicts and fragmentation can be readily identified and addressed, the extent to which this would result in higher levels of social cohesion can be called into question. For this reason, social cohesion draws attention to the way in which economic, social and cultural factors and practises have to be drawn into a multidimensional strategy, underpinned by values which inform social conduct and promote social co-operation and interaction in, and between, communities, and in relations with state institutions at local, provincial and national levels.

SOME DEFINITIONS

Given their conceptual proximity, it may be useful at this stage to differentiate between social cohesion and nation building. Social cohesion is defined as the degree of social integration and inclusion in changing communities in a diverse society with a history of division and inequality. In terms of this definition, a community or society is cohesive to the extent that the inequalities, exclusions and disparities based on ethnicity, gender, class, nationality, age, disability, or any other distinctions which engender divisions, distrust and conflict, are reduced or eliminated in a planned and sustained manner. This should be underpinned by community members and citizens as active participants working together for the attainment of shared goals, designed and agreed upon to improve the living conditions for all.

Nation building is associated with the reconstruction of a national identity based on geographic, cultural and political features. This is done with a view, in part, of legitimising state-societal relations. Nation building relies for its raison d'être, among others, on available symbolic traditions, customs and beliefs to draw up a folder of national characteristics.

A nation state can be an amalgam of assorted social groups owing allegiance to the State and its institutions. The erosion of national identity emerges when disparate identities such as race, class, ethnic group and gender assume prominence at the risk of undermining national consciousness and identity. As discussed in previous chapters, nation building can be defined as the amalgam of actions undertaken by various actors in society, including the State, to promote nation formation (the emergence of a united nation). Apart from the economic and political realms, nation formation should generally take place in cultural spaces.

What is meant by national identity? Postulates of national identity, although offering different explanations, for our purpose, denote constructed and changing entities of description which are influenced and impacted by political, technological, economic and social factors. National identity thus allows the formation of roots, community and shared descriptions. The rituals and symbols of national identity facilitate consciousness that unites society around a national character, common language and a shared purpose.

With regard to social cohesion, the Department of Arts and Culture defines this 'as those factors that have an impact on the ability of a society to be united for the attainment of a common goal. It is the extent to which members of a society respond collectively in pursuit of these shared goals and how they deal with the political, socio-economic, and environmental challenges that are facing them' (Presentation on Social Cohesion, Portfolio Committee, 26 May 2010).

In mapping social cohesion in 1999, Jensen (2010) identified five dimensions structured in binary patterns of positive and negative attributes, as follows:

belonging —— isolation

inclusion —— exclusion

participation —— non-involvement

recognition —— rejection

legitimacy —— illegitimacy

This model has been adopted and applied to South Africa by Cloete and Kotze (2009) and by Struwig, *et al.* (2013). It has been extended for this project as set out and defined below:

- **Belonging:** To be part of, and to experience, a sense of affiliation to the community and the larger society. It involves processes of identification and acceptance within a community and larger society. In a diverse society such as South Africa, it requires identification with, and acceptance of, groups. Its opposite is isolation.
- **Inclusion:** To be included on an equal basis in all social activities and rights and to have equal access to all life opportunities. Its opposite is exclusion.

- **Participation:** Unhindered participation means active involvement in community and social activities, programmes and events. This is opposed by non-involvement.
- **Recognition:** To recognise, acknowledge and value differences without discrimination. It is negated by rejection.
- **Legitimacy:** Integrity and social legitimacy of public bodies and leaders representing community members and citizens. This is undermined by illegitimacy.
- **Shared values:** In societies with diverse cultures, it is to be expected there will be diverse, and even divergent, values. It is thus important for citizens to subscribe to a basic set of shared values such as democracy, freedom, equality, justice and mutual respect. This is contrasted by the absence of shared values.
- **Co-operation:** A willingness to co-operate and work on community and social projects with diverse citizens, as opposed to non-co-operation.
- **Belief:** Confidence in the future of the community with the conviction that the future of the community depends on the action of the community members. The notion of self-worth is integral. Scepticism and a lack of confidence is its opposite.

According to Emery and Flora (2006) and Jim Cavaye (2006), community and social development are based on eight resources referred to as forms of capital. These are:

Environmental Capital: The natural environment and geographical location of a community and/or a society including its land, climate and natural resources. South Africa's geographic environment is diverse, supports a diversity of natural life and is rich in natural resources. Historically, the natural resources and most productive part of the land were controlled by a minority and still remain so. In the present context, the development of natural resources has to be conducted within a framework of environmental protection.

Cultural capital: The customs, traditions, language and religion of a community. It includes the community's outlook on, and understanding of, the world and encapsulates the way of life of a community, its heritage and its creative, inventive and aesthetic modalities. South Africa is a culturally diverse society consisting of African, Asian and European cultures. Under colonialism and apartheid, African and Asian cultures were marginalised, while European cultures were privileged. A transformed and inclusive community will redress the cultural imbalances of the past on the basis of equality. It will further seek to bridge the divides erected between cultures under segregation.

Human capital: The knowledge and skills of community and society needed for economic, technological and scientific development. Quality education and training in South Africa was designed to serve a minority. As a consequence, the country suffers from a skills deficit as it works to repair the primary school system and to achieve universal primary education access that is in line with the United Nation's Millennium Development Goal 1 and is the government's Output 1.

Social capital: The bonds that tie individuals and communities together and the bridges that connect groups, organisations, associations and communities.

Political capital: The access by members of the community to public and representative bodies where policies are developed and decisions made on programmes and resource allocations. While there is a high level of participation in national, provincial and local elections, there is a breakdown at community level between elected members and officials on the one hand, and community members on the other. This is evident in the widespread service delivery protests in many parts of the country, despite the existence of mandatory integrated development plans and social cohesion as a key performance area for local governments.

Financial capital: The financial resources at the disposal of the community and society for investment in development directed towards capacity building, local, and national economic initiative businesses.
Construction capital: The constructed environment (assets) of houses, buildings and infrastructure, or roads, railways, ports and telecommunication networks as well as energy-generation and supply grids.

To recapitulate, a society such as South Africa, as a cohesive and unified entity, should be characterised by:

- a sense of belonging for all its diverse citizens and members;
- a shared vision among diverse citizens on the future of their community and society;
- a broadly shared set of public values and norms for social conduct;
- equal opportunities for development and advancement for all people, regardless of culture, gender, status, age, ability and region;
- positive valuation of diverse cultures, languages and religions;
- respect and tolerance for political and ideological differences;
- regular interaction, exchange and co-operation among its diverse members;
- respect for constitutionally-based laws, international law and local regulations complying with such laws;
- a high level of awareness of the rights and obligations of citizens;
- a proud consciousness of being South African;
- active participation of citizens in public institutions, decision-making processes, projects, events and celebrations at all levels of society;
- democratic and peaceful resolution of disputes and disagreements;
- integration of immigrants into society, and
- transparent and accountable handling of public affairs by public representatives and government officials.

THE INTERRELATIONSHIP OF SOCIAL COHESION AND NATION BUILDING

With these characteristics set out, it is therefore necessary to locate social cohesion and nation building at the specific *levels* of their practical operationalisation in public life. At the same time, it is important to draw attention to their interconnections and mutually reinforcing and potentially disrupting effects. Accordingly:

- **Social cohesion** is generally **community-based** and located at a **micro-social and sub-national level**.
- **Nation building**, on the other hand, is **nationally orientated** and thus located at the **macro-social level**.
- **Intercommunity cohesion located at the district and provincial or meso- level of intercommunity life** is necessary as the gap between the sub-national and the national stated above in a country the size of South Africa is great, requiring an intermediate level of social cohesion.

An integrated approach to nation formation and social cohesion, therefore, must engage and link up with all three levels of public life. In this regard, social cohesion and national unity is a layered and integrated approach. The macro-level of nation building depends for its success on the performance of micro- and meso-co-ordination and performance. Likewise, the effectiveness of the meso- and micro-levels depends on the performance at macro-level.

Put plainly, national, provincial and local policies and their effective implementation are interdependent and interconnected. Any gap or misalignment between these levels in critical jurisdictions will result in the fragmentation of governance, and with it, the fragmentation of society.

While this is not a diagnostic of breakdowns in relation to co-operative governance, the crises in provincial and local government that became manifest in the country soon after the advent of democracy pointed towards structural and operational fragmentation at all levels of governance. The severe social and other consequences of these crises are openly acknowledged and there are attempts by government to attend to them – hence, among other initiatives, the strategy developed by government for social cohesion and nation building.

These are the historical and present contexts which nation formation and social cohesion initiatives have to acknowledge to achieve the progressive realisation of a South African society as an inclusive, cohesive, sustainable, dynamic and durable society, fully integrated into Africa and the world. To actualise this calls for concerted and co-ordinated work on several interfacing domestic, regional and global developments. This work must, per definition, begin at home.

To monitor and measure the impact of social cohesion and nation building policies and programmes, indicators are needed. To this end, Atkinson and Marlier (2010) recommend that the design indicators adhere to five basic principles. These indicators have been adapted for South African purposes and are recast as eight features, rather than principles, to be built into the indicators. They must therefore:

- clearly determine the nature and extent of the specific problem of inequality and social exclusion;
- be both quantitatively and statistically validated;
- be generally agreed upon and accepted by policy makers, programme managers and community participants;

- be context-specific and adaptable;
- be aligned to the patterns, tempo and direction of change;
- be revised and adjusted in response to new and unforeseen developments;
- be attainable and adequately resourced and supported, and
- be benchmarked and interpreted for comparative purposes locally, nationally and internationally.

Developing indicators requires drawing on quantitative, that is objective, national, provincial and local development indices combined with experiential personal data, analysis and interpretation. The design, while attentive to global benchmarks, must be rigorously grounded in the particularities of South Africa. This will ensure that development indicators are socially contextualised. Directly related to this is the necessity to ensure that *experiences* of social inclusion and well-being specific to South Africa are measured.

The following section outlines the steps required to ensure maximum support for a national programme on social cohesion and broad support for the principles and indicators of the programme. It is concerned with actualising the strategy. The following steps are widely recommended:

- mainstreaming social inclusion and nation formation in development plans and initiatives nationally, regionally and locally;
- mobilising all the key participants, stakeholders and institutions;
- building national support for the strategy and its objectives;
- involving communities at all stages of planning and implementation;
- building the requisite capacity and skills;
- ensuring transparency and accountability, and
- combating nepotism, patronage, and corruption.

INDICATORS OF SOCIAL COHESION

The indicators presented below are designed to establish their cumulative impact on the specific and general forms of social inclusion/exclusion and the effect of this on social cohesion and national unity. At the same time, the direct and indirect relations of the arts, culture and heritage to these are highlighted, the purpose being to interconnect different spheres and aspects of society in an effort to arrive at an integrated strategy.

However, as Struwig, *et al.* caution, in measuring social cohesion the indicators should not be applied to 'disaggregate' the approach to social cohesion by focusing on any one of the indicators in isolation or on arbitrary clusters. Since: 'if social cohesion can be reduced to a cluster of social conditions, can it truly be assessed by considering the sum of relevant indicators such as patterns of job creation and education? Many claim that this is simplistic and that social cohesion suggests a much larger, overarching quality or condition in society which drives these indicators or emerges from their combination (2013, p.401).' The view taken in this report is that social cohesion operates and emerges from a complex and multidimensional process in which the various indicators impact on each other and on society and its members, producing either inclusive and cohering effects, or excluding and fragmenting effects. This explains the emphasis on the multidimensional nature of social cohesion in the section above dealing with the dimensions of social cohesion.

The statistical data referred to below draws on the *South African Development Indicators*, 2010–2011 and 2012; and they are examined cursorily, merely to illustrate their implications for social cohesion.

SLOW ECONOMIC GROWTH AND TRANSFORMATION

From 1993 to 2012, the highest gross domestic product (GDP) growth was 5.6% in 2006. It fell to 5.5% in 2007. The lowest was -1.5% in 2009 in response to the global recession. It increased to 2.5% in 2012. Growth for 2013 is estimated at no more than 2.0%. This means that the much needed expansion of the economy to drive down unemployment has not materialised. The goal for real growth remains at 6%.

Black economic empowerment (BEE) aimed at economically empowering historically disadvantaged South Africans peaked in 2003 and 2004 at approximately R660 billion. This was in the wake of the publication of the Broad-Based Black Economic Empowerment (BBBEE) Act which had just been passed at the time. In 2009 it slowed down and dropped to approximately R160 billion. Fast-tracking sustainable BEE is considered a high priority for inclusion.

The percentage of top black managers in the private sector rose from 12.7% in 2000 to 32.2% in 2012. The appointment of senior black managers rose from 18.5% to 39.4% over the same period. The appointment of top black female managers rose from 12.4% in 2000 to 19.5% in 2012, while that of senior female managers rose from 21% to 27% over the same period. While there is a positive trend in the employment of black managers, it is less so in the case of black females. This calls for intensification of transformation and an increase in demographic and gender representivity in senior management.

The slow pace of economic growth and transformation impacts directly on the capacity of the State to expand economic participation and inclusion for all South Africans. It therefore relates directly to continued economic exclusion, unemployment, and poverty and inequality for those historically excluded from productive and gainful livelihoods. It is further linked to many of the other social problems, and the material and cultural deprivations inflicted on historically excluded communities.

UNEMPLOYMENT AND SOCIAL EXCLUSION

Approximately 9.5 million people were employed in 1995. Although employment expanded from 1994, relative to population growth and numbers entering the labour market, the unemployment rate increased. The employment figure increased from 11.2 million in 2001 to 13.8 million in 2008. It declined to 12.7 million in 2010 due to the global economic crisis, resulting in massive job losses. Unemployment, which peaked at 31.2% in March 2003, dropped to 25% in 2007, to rise again to 24% in 2009. For 2012 the official unemployment rate was at 25%, while the expanded definition of the *South African Survey* (2010–2011) pegged it at 36.5%.

High levels of unemployment are both a historical phenomenon in South Africa related to the structure of the economy, and a consequence of the aggravated current global conditions.

POVERTY, INEQUALITY AND SOCIAL EXCLUSION

Poverty is the consequence of social and economic exclusion. It serves to exclude the poor from participation in the mainstream economic, social and cultural life of a society. It assaults the dignity of the individual and curtails life-chances for personal advancement. With regard to income poverty, the percentage of those living below the poverty datum line of R322 per person declined from 53% of households in 1995 to 48% in 2005.

The richest 10% of the population received 40% of the national income, while the poorest 40% received only 5% of the national income. This points to huge inequalities with 70% of the income going to the richest 20% of the population, while the poorest 20% receive about 2.3% of the national 'cake'. While average real incomes have increased, inequality remains stark along racial lines.

Poverty and inequality remain major challenges for South Africa. The Gini coefficient indicates that inequality remains high. South Africa ranks among the most economically unequal societies in the world.

SOCIAL SUPPORT

South Africa has an extensive social assistance support network that involves a number of interventions:

The social assistance programme covers over 15 million South Africans, up from 2.4 million in 1995, with the major share being 9.57 million recipients of the Child Support Grant (CSG), which is provided to children in need up to their eighteenth birthday. The Child Foster Care Grant (CFCG) is extended to families who take care of orphaned children. There is also the Old Age Grant (OAG), the War Veterans Grant (WVG), the Disability Grant (DG), the Child Dependency Grant (CDG) and the Grant-in-Aid.

In 2010–2011 government spent R87 billion on social grants in response to the rising unemployment caused by the global recession. In 2011/2012 this increased to R96 billion at a constant average of 3.4% of GDP and was coupled to the government's War on Poverty Campaign and a comprehensive Anti-Poverty Strategy targeting the most deprived local communities to empower households to lift themselves out of poverty by linking the social grants to economic development.

These trends play themselves out in relation to access to formal housing, potable water, electricity, land distribution, health and nutrition, as well as education. In most of these instances (except for land redistribution, which has been mediocre) progress has been registered in uplifting communities that were excluded and marginalised under the apartheid system. The majority of the population now have access. Yet, quality of these services has, in significant instances, been poor. Community protests around services reflect, in part, this reality.

Social cohesion should also be measured in terms of community safety, gender equality, manifestation of discrimination, youth development, corruption and active citizenry. We elaborate briefly on some of these indicators below.

CRIME, SAFETY AND SECURITY

According to the number of serious crimes per 100 000 of the population, this declined from around 5,516 in 2000/2001 to 3,679 in 2010/2011 to 3,608.8 in 2011/2012. In light of the fact that crime of all categories remains persistently high in South Africa, the reduction over the last two years is marginal. Also, it falls below the goal of reducing it by between 4% and 7% over the period 2009–2014.

Unsafe communities create fear and distrust among citizens. Insecurity hinders free and open social interaction as people retreat and hide behind high walls and security gates. Personal experience of crime has a traumatic effect on individuals and families. Crime is thus a threat to social cohesion and nation formation.

GENDER EQUITY AND SOCIAL EXCLUSION

Compared globally, South Africa has the highest percentage of women in legislative bodies at all levels of government. However, the position of women in society remains beset by inequality, exclusion and discrimination. Women are still more vulnerable to unemployment, exclusion from access to resources, decision making and the unhindered exercise of their constitutional rights and opportunities within the family, at work and in the public domain. In this regard, the Commission for Gender Equality (2001) identifies what is referred to as 'ten top stumbling blocks in the way of the empowerment of women in South Africa'. These are:

- patriarchy as a source of oppression in the family and society;
- poverty, which is higher in female-headed households than in male-headed ones;
- women excluded from domestic power sharing and decision making;
- violence against women;
- access to land and economic resources;
- HIV/AIDS, tuberculosis, and other chronic diseases;
- underfunding of public agencies to promote gender equality;
- inadequate service delivery of housing, water, sanitation, and electricity;
- exclusion of women from traditional authority, and
- low involvement of men in gender equality matters.

These curtailments reside in the social and economic structures of a society; and they confine many women to reproductive and domestic roles in the family and to temporary productive roles. They result in sharp differentiations in the social and livelihood assets of women and men, as well as in their asymmetrical power relations. Sustained by discriminatory, restrictive and even sexist ideologies and practises, the construction of a fully non-sexist and non-racial democracy requires programmes and interventions aimed at empowering women.

DISCRIMINATION: SOCIAL EXCLUSION INFORMED BY IDENTITY

There are three important forms of identity-based exclusion which need to be considered.

Racism: This refers to the institutionalisation of racist policies and practises based on the ideologies and beliefs of racial superiority. It was practised throughout the colonial era in South Africa and systematically institutionalised under apartheid.

While racism was outlawed in 1994 with the abolition of apartheid, social attitudes, access to resources and life opportunities in South Africa still remain largely race-based. In addition, minority and extremist right-wing groups, organisations, and members of such communities, continue to harbour and cultivate racist ideas and promote behaviour which results in acts of racist abuse in public and work places, on sports fields, as well as in, and between, communities. It is widespread in social and other informal media. The remnants of racism remain visible in the spatial divisions of human settlements. The eradication of racism is therefore critical for achieving human equality as the basis of social inclusion and solidarity.

Ethnicity: In addition to racial divisions, the diverse linguistic and cultural groups in South Africa were encouraged to embrace narrow identities, especially through the Bantustan system. On the basis of these divisions, educational and cultural practises were promoted which fostered tribal prejudices, identities and rivalries.

Used as power bases and sites of patronage, ethnicity, like racism, undermines equality and merit and undermines social cohesion. Such practises should therefore be discouraged and not rewarded in public life.

Attacks against migrants: The term 'migration' is used to denote movements by people from one legally defined geographical space to another. South Africa experiences two forms of migration: internal or in-country migration, and external migration; the latter, both legal and illegal, from outside South African borders.

Both forms of migration, generally into urban areas, contribute to the spread or formation of informal settlements and result in competition for limited resources and work opportunities and, under conditions of widespread poverty, frequently result in violent confrontations. This was the case in 2008 when, as the Human Rights Commission reported, 'community members from African countries were targeted, leaving 62 people dead, hundreds wounded and contributed to the displacement of at least a 100 000 people or more' (2010, pp.11–12). The attacks were marked by intense ethnic stereotyping, intolerance and violence reminiscent of the racist brutalities of South Africa's past. Accordingly, Landau (2011) does not see the attacks as random crimes and spontaneous violence, but flowing from a long history of spatial controls and exclusionary practises, brutalising South Africans in their attitudes to foreigners who they see as enemies from within.

Although this was not the first incident of violence against foreign nationals, the scale and the brutality of the attacks were unprecedented. In this regard, the attacks and the continued tension between locals and immigrants pose a challenge to social cohesion.

To prevent this from recurring, the South African Human Rights Commission (SAHRC) Report makes wide-ranging recommendations, including the requirement that public agencies and civil society must 'ensure that all social conflict disaster plans and integration plans include clear and transparent policy on reparations' which would 'include all persons regardless of immigration status to reparations', constitutional protection, justice and safe reintegration or humane repatriation.

YOUTH DEVELOPMENT

The National Youth Policy (2009–2014), developed to identify gaps and accelerate the development of youth, states:

Youth development should be viewed as an integral part of addressing the challenges of South Africa's development. It should also be seen as a central process of building a non-sexist, non-racist democratic society, and must be approached with the same vigour as all other processes of transformation. The development of young people must also be aligned to the government's approach to addressing poverty and underdevelopment, as well as a mechanism for promotion of social adjustment, social cohesion, and economic emancipation attained through comprehensive, integrated, cross-sectoral and sustainable policies and programmes that seek to bring about tangible improvements in the quality of their lives.

The policy acknowledges the diversity of youth in South Africa and identifies the following as priorities:

- young women
- youth with disabilities
- unemployed youth
- school-age and out-of-school youth
- youth in rural areas
- youth at risk.

The latter category is further specified to include youth living with HIV/AIDS, youth-headed households, youth in conflict with the law and youth abusing dependency-creating substances. It also spells out the rights and responsibilities within a democracy and proposes a range of policy interventions in relation to education, economic participation, health and well-being, social cohesion and civic participation, and national youth service.

The National Youth Policy is very closely aligned to national priorities and includes the youth's right to cultural expression.

The unemployment rate among the youth is estimated at close to 50% and they constitute about 70% of all the unemployed. The youth employment ratio of 15–24 year-olds looking for work is about 13.2% in South Africa, compared to 40% in countries at the same level of development in Latin America and Asia. Eighty-six per cent of the unemployed youth have not gone beyond Grade 12 and two-thirds have never worked. A youth-focused strategy of inclusion, skills training and employment is thus of critical importance.

Perceptions of Corruption and Basic Service Delivery

Perceptions that corruption has increased persist. This has pushed South Africa from 43rd in the Corruption Perception Index in 2007, to 55th in 2009; and between 2011 and 2012, South Africa moved from 64th to 69th, indicating a rise in negative perceptions. Recent anti-corruption measures that have been taken to counter this include the establishing of an inter-ministerial committee on corruption, an anti-corruption unit in the Department of Public Service and Administration, and a tender compliance unit in the National Treasury.

Incidents of corruption fuel negative perceptions and serve to undermine public confidence and trust in public representatives, officials and institutions. They can lead to withdrawal from participation in public life, and/or to a generalised spread of corrupt practises to become a social norm; both of which invariably result in social disorder, conflict and fragmentation.

Active Citizenship and Identity

The strength of civil society in South Africa, measured by affiliation to voluntary religious, sport and recreation, music, labour, political, environmental, professional and charitable organisations, indicates a high level of civic participation and a considerable desire to hold government and public bodies accountable. This further suggests that the potential for participatory government at local level is relatively good for a middle-income country.

This is underscored by the high levels of participation in national, provincial and local government elections. However, while levels of registration of eligible voters have been above 75%, the turnout of registered voters has been declining from 89% in 1999 to 77% in 2004, with a slight increase to 77% in 2009. These figures, however, correspond to global trends.

Confidence in a positive future for all in South Africa was at 72% in 2000; it rose to 85% in 2005; plummeted to 58% in 2012. This decline is attributed to the economic crisis. Overall optimism about an inclusive future for all periods was above 50% for all races.

Public approval of the state of race relations was at 72% in 2000. It dropped to 40% in 2001 to rise to 60% in 2004. In 2010 it was 50%, and had plummeted to 39% in 2012. This should be of concern since the statistics relate directly to the objective of building an inclusive non-racial society and nation.

Related to the above is the identity of citizens based on self description. Citizens who see themselves as African rose from 18.4% in 2004 to 25.8% in 2007; 32.6% in 2008; and 30.2% in 2009. This points mainly to a growing identification with Africa. Citizens who see themselves primarily as South African averages at just above 50% in this period. Those who describe themselves by race average around 8%. Language self-descriptors were on average 5.3%, pointing to a decline in ethnic identification.

Taken together, these indicators provide an overview of all the threats related to building a cohesive and united society. The relative degree of the threat posed by each can thus be rated to assist with deciding on what to focus and what to prioritise.

At least at the level of public policy, there is a high correlation between national development policies on the one hand, and social cohesion and nation building on the other. As shown by the data presented above, the challenge, clearly, is about implementation – not only in relation to public services but also on such issues as job creation, discrimination in communities and at work, corruption and other indicators which depend on actions of all of society.

SECTION II:

CASE STUDY ON SOCIAL COHESION AND COMMEMORATION OF NATIONAL HOLIDAYS

South Africa has 12 public holidays as determined by the Public Holidays Act of 1994. National holidays form part of the collection of National Symbols, such as the national flag and the coat of arms, and are designed to facilitate the process of building a cohesive and inclusive society. Partaking in national holiday activities is meant to enhance a national consciousness about values enshrined in the Constitution.

The following days are standard holidays formally observed in most parts of Africa and the world: New Year's Day, Good Friday, Family Day, Christmas Day and Day of Goodwill. These will be termed normative public holidays, or Group One days.

For purposes of this study, the focus is on Group Two days, introduced or redefined after the attainment of democracy in 1994: Human Rights Day, Freedom Day, Workers' Day, Youth Day, National Women's Day, Heritage Day and the Day of Reconciliation. At issue is the place and meaning of these public holidays for a society coming to terms with its past and looking ahead to the future. Beyond this is the question of how the days should be observed, both in line with their formal meanings and in a manner that involves the majority of society.

Group Two holidays are meant to draw attention to both tragic and joyous moments in the evolution of the South African nation and nation state, defining who we are, what we should not have been and what we should be. They are meant to foster nation formation and social cohesion beyond divisions based on race, religion, ethnicity and class; and to assist in cementing a foundation for progressive policy change, social capital, as well as institutional and interpersonal trust.

Most of these ideals are commonly shared among the overwhelming majority of South Africans – derived from self-interest and, to an extent, an appreciation of the common interest. However, this does not necessarily translate into an acceptance of the symbolism that is currently attached to all the Group Two public holidays.

This section is primarily based on MISTRA's interactions with the Gauteng Province's Department of Sport, Arts, Culture and Recreation. It interrogates the motivation behind national holidays as possible platforms for promoting nation formation and social cohesion, and reflects on creative ways in which these holidays can be commemorated to ensure wider participation and appreciation of their importance.

South Africa is a country shaped by a legacy of discrimination and oppression. The history of the country is represented by domination by a few over many other social groups. This created a dynamic of exclusion and inclusion which persists, in various forms, to this day.

The issue of the extent of popular legitimacy of the national (specifically Group Two) holidays and how they should be observed arises because our society is defined by a variety of fault lines. As such, there is bound to be contestation around the meaning of events and milestones in our history. Precisely because such history, in the main, pitted sections of society against each other – defined mainly around race and class – most Group Two days invoke mixed emotions and are often contested.

Because the legacy of the past has not been totally eradicated, the meaning of tragedy and joy as represented by these holidays is inverted in the psychology of the erstwhile contestants. To some extent, this also applies to the issue of class and gender.

And so the question arises whether we should have national holidays that draw on these contested experiences at all! On the other hand, we can retain the holidays and accept that contestation will continue to simmer both above and below the surface. We can then let sleeping dogs lie and hope that, over time, as the nation evolves and achieves greater levels of unity and cohesion, these holidays will be widely accepted across society.

Both of these arguments are erroneous. The first argument posits national unity as being shorn of fundamental human values and can have the effect of equating justice and injustice. The Constitution of the Republic of South Africa answers this question without equivocation in the values that it espouses including in the ringing injunction in its preamble:

We, the people of South Africa,
Recognise the injustices of our past;
Honour those who suffered for justice and freedom in our land;
Respect those who have worked to build and develop our country; and
Believe that South Africa belongs to all who live in it, united in our
diversity.
We therefore, through our freely elected representatives, adopt this
Constitution as the supreme law of the Republic so as to –
Heal the divisions of the past and establish a society based on democratic
values, social justice and fundamental human rights;
Lay the foundations for a democratic and open society in which
government is based on the will of the people and every citizen is equally
protected by law;
Improve the quality of life of all citizens and free the potential of each
person; and
Build a united and democratic South Africa able to take its rightful place
as a sovereign state in the family of nations.

The struggle against apartheid was premised on building a new South African national identity. Understanding the history of colonialism and apartheid informs the strategic choices subsequently made in the democratic period and the universal national aspiration to become a united, prosperous, and stable society.

The second argument encourages the notion that nation formation and social cohesion can be attained without agency as a natural evolution of human consciousness. It can be asserted, quite correctly, that attainment of these objectives depends on a variety of other factors. Not least among these are issues of economic well-being, extent of social equity, platforms of integrated social interaction, spatial dynamics, mutual appreciation, knowledge of languages and culture, and so on.

However necessary these factors may be, they are not a sufficient condition for nation formation and social cohesion. Symbolically invoking moments of joy and sadness in society's collective memory is a critical part of the agency to encourage unity and cohesion. Importantly, in the dynamic of cause and effect, symbolic gestures such as national holidays can facilitate common practical efforts to address that which is bad and wrong in society, and encourage that which is good and right.

In this sense, national holidays speak to the goal of engendering a cohesive society – a people united in diversity. National holidays highlight the progress made to mark values of humanness espoused in the Constitution and its Bill of Rights.

The holidays are meant to promote the aims of development and transformation which include: addressing interpersonal and institutional trust, promoting material and spiritual well-being, contributing to the country's understanding of itself and self-belief, forging a sense of community through common symbolic actions and assisting to address challenges of social conduct.

National holidays are a public good indicating mutual responsibility of realising the goal of building a better life for all. They are value-laden – and the objectives for which they were selected in the first place demand that they should be consciously promoted. They require combined championship and advocacy from all those who share in the welfare of South Africa. It should therefore be accepted that appreciation of their meaning and symbolic value requires deliberate action, and that universal attainment of such appreciation would be evolutionary and adaptive, rather than realised by imposition or fiat.

The question can be raised whether there should be concern at all about this issue: if the majority of South Africans – particularly those who engaged in the struggle to eradicate the system of apartheid and are drivers and beneficiaries of the programmes of social change – are fully in sync with the thinking of the State on the character of the holidays. The challenge, however, is about the legitimacy of the holidays, as well as the popularity of the forms of their observance. Two critical issues should be kept in mind in this regard:

First, the cynicism among some regarding these holidays – few as these may be – can steadily and increasingly infuse the rest of society. In part, this is because many of those who harbour such sentiments have a public voice far louder than their numbers may suggest; they control many platforms of discourse; they own most of the wealth and income; they are employers; and many of them are central in information- and value-mediation as teachers, religious leaders, journalists, and talk-show hosts, intellectuals, researchers, and so on.

Second, a positive sentiment without concrete steps to actualise it stands the danger of withering in the fullness of time. The forms of celebration, in most instances, involve a few people at designated events, even if there can be subsidiary activities or geographic rotation of the public functions. The standard form of these events results in a situation in which interest among those not involved wanes, including among those who embrace the sentiment about what the holidays represent. This can be precipitous because holidays lend themselves to 'holiday conduct'.

National holidays are established to bring together the country's diverse communities in support of shared national objectives, including nation building, social cohesion, and national identity. National holidays represent an attempt to construct national symbols which integrate the diverse histories and heritages of South Africa. National holidays are significant in their linking of particular events in our nation's history. National holidays are intended to profile a complex history of oppression, resistance, engagement, heroism and combined triumph.

Established to promote nation formation and social cohesion, national holidays aim to promote new political and social values and to nurture a broader understanding across race, gender, religious and class differences about who we are and the ideals to which we aspire. This relates to the objective of building a nation state that accommodates the plurality of social interests while carving a prosperous and equitable society.

Simply put, the aim of national holidays is to promote national identity and shared values beyond social group membership. Given the fractured nature of our past, the goal of post-apartheid South Africa has always been to privilege an overarching identity above social group consciousness, inspired by the injunctions in the Constitution and Bill of Rights.

Even though South Africa is a heterogeneous society with varied cultural formations and social affiliations, nation formation remains the goal for society as a whole. Promotion of national pride is both an intended outcome, and a means to instil in every citizen and resident optimism about reaching the national goals. National holidays symbolise the accumulated narrative of our fractured and divided past, and the promise of the future.

SYMBOLISM OF NATIONAL HOLIDAYS

Public holidays advance national objectives by promoting the symbolism of heroic acts (celebrating the agency of the liberation struggle); that which should not have been (remembering repressive acts which should not recur); and what we should always be (popular united action and appreciation of sectors of society, including women, workers, and youth).

Human Rights Day was established to promote a human rights culture based on identifiable values of justice and tolerance. The symbol of Sharpeville recognises both repression and defiance.

Freedom Day celebrates the attainment of the franchise for all, underlying the popular act that marked the beginning of a new era of democratic governance. The day places the mass of South Africans rightfully at the centre of the process of change.

Workers' Day symbolises the solidarity of all workers across racial, gender and national divides. Its formal observance in South Africa recognises workers' rights as part of the pantheon of human rights, and reflects an appreciation of workers' role in wealth creation and their historical efforts for an equitable system of social relations.

Youth Day commemorates the activism of young people against an infringement of their rights, starting with the demonstration and repression in Soweto in 1976. It marks a recognition of bravery and creativity of young people that can lift a nation to new heights.

Women's Day celebrates the heroism and initiative of women reflected in the planning and management of the anti-pass demonstration to the Union Buildings in 1956. Contained in the symbolism of this experience is a critical message not only about non-sexism and gender equality, but also non-racialism.

Heritage Day is intended to pay homage to all cultures in the land. It pivots around King Shaka (his birthday), a symbol of the precolonial endeavours of nation formation.

Day of Reconciliation marks one of the best symbolic representations of the ugliness of war. The heroism that the Battle of Ncome River symbolises among the contending forces lives in folklore, and it formed the pillar of new initiatives in later years such as the formation of Umkhonto we Sizwe, whose armed activities were launched on this day.

Several challenges are associated with the form and content of the observance of national holidays. Are all of them effective in promoting with integrity public awareness of South African history and aspirations? Are they triumphalist and thus by definition exclusionary? Are they used positively or adversely for rallying society around a common vision? While they seek to define a new national narrative, are there creative ways in which this objective can be popularised across all sectors of society?

Beyond the issues of contested historical narratives and national identity, what other factors impact on these challenges?

Narrow politicisation of national holidays: A perception prevailing among certain quarters of society is that national holidays have been appropriated to serve solely the interests of the ruling party to the exclusion of other party political affiliations. While this has changed somewhat with the involvement of all parliamentary parties in some of the official events, it is seen as shallow symbolism. What are billed as events geared towards bringing society together are seen as assuming a partisan form and content – reflected, in part, in the communication of the various political parties on these occasions.

Commercialisation of national holidays: Some in the business sector have seized on the holidays to advance a self-serving commercialism. The moral force of these public holidays is thus compromised. This also applies to the Group One holidays, reflecting a broader challenge of social organisation, outlook, culture and mores. Both sets of holidays are thus taken as paid rest days in which to engage in whatever pleasure may tickle citizens' fancy, including retail binges.

Unresolved social issues: Limited progress has been made in erasing the fault lines within South African society. Thus, there would be a sense among the disadvantaged that society has been corralled into a false reconciliation, given the backlogs in the provision of services, and inequality in access to wealth and opportunities. On the other hand, some of the ills of society such as crime and corruption (and potholes) and corrective actions by the new state are seized upon by the privileged as reflective of 'falling standards' and 'reverse discrimination'. National holidays are thus seen variously as representing progress or the lack of it, success, or failure.

Perceived marginalisation of other stories: Group Two holidays represent the emergence of a new society – that some are still uncomfortable with – and they replaced or redefined the pre-1994 set of holidays. Thus, by definition, they are seen as marginalising other stories. In this regard, there are arguments advanced by some that these Group Two holidays present purely political moments in history and that they have reference to only one group or other in our society. In other words, while formal elements of the status quo ante and its practises are being abolished, the ideas linger on.

Cynicism regarding national holidays: Segments of the South African population believe that their voices matter little to those in political office, even though to some the reverse might be more apposite. Could it be that those constituencies that identify with national holidays and related events do so because they perceive of the system as representing their interests and vice versa? To an extent, this issue recounts the relationship between national identity, citizenship, power relations and new value systems.

POSSIBLE NEW APPROACH TO NATIONAL HOLIDAYS

A renewed effort is required to promote national holidays in a manner that would, over time, ensure their near-universal acceptance. This requires creativity in conceptualisation and in the detail of form. It requires an appreciation of the dynamic between the formal and the informal – and the defining impact that the latter can have on the former, and on public consciousness generally. It also requires prioritisation in defining the role of the State, and state functions for each of the holidays.

In this regard, the pervasive popularity and near-universal common manner in which some of the Group One holidays and other days that are not holidays are observed, is quite instructive. This variously applies to instances such as Christmas Day and Mother's Day – and the manner in which families, communities and the media have found ways of transmitting the same open and subliminal messages around these days. Experience in other countries (such as Zambia, Mozambique, US, Denmark, UK and China) does, to some extent, show that creative ways can be found to establish common ways of observing public holidays in smaller social units, without necessarily assembling in large numbers or invoking formal state functions.

An improvement in the popular appreciation of the holidays and the manner in which they are observed should include:

• Renewed and creative civic education on the importance of the holidays involving the State through its relevant line function departments and organisations in civil society and industry. This can include a formal joint declaration that these days are a public good and property to be owned by everyone.

• Some of the holidays should be prioritised as formal state events with standard forms of celebration. Others should take a lighter note, yet without subtracting from their symbolic importance. This requires subtlety of message and form, appreciating that changing consciousness is a protracted process.

• The forms of celebration should emphasise involvement of the youth – in a variety of ways – such that their particular experiences in such activity remain embedded in their consciousness into adulthood.

At the generic level, there are positive practises that have been introduced in recent years that should be retained: these include thematic campaigns for the month on which the holiday falls; specific events led by the relevant government institutions, and mobilisation of the media to participate in and promote these activities.

What requires serious consideration is the selection of forms of activities, taking into account how these can help inform a new consciousness and become embedded in the 'culture' of families, communities and sectors of society.

In line with the above, specific proposals are contained in Annexure I. The basic proposal is that Freedom Day should be commemorated as the *pre-eminent* public holiday: South Africa's national day. The others should be observed as commemorative days in two categories: semi-formal and informal.

What is critical in taking the discussion forward is that the ideas on these changes should come from, and be seen to be coming from, a consultative process rather than as a formal decision of government. The ongoing consultations on social cohesion could be the forum where these and other ideas are canvassed, and emerging from that, a consultative process could be initiated, culminating in concrete proposals adopted at a smaller but representative forum. A group of eminent persons could be assembled to lead the process, and to act as the public face of the initiative.

HOLIDAY	STATUS	ACTIVITY	RESPONSIBLE
Human Rights Day March 21	Semi-formal observed	Select a theme from the Bill of Rights. Conduct debating contests in secondary schools from the beginning of the year on the theme, culminating in a national contest involving one school per province on Human Rights Day. The Judiciary and legal fraternity, including retired judges and other legal practitioners, can take charge of the adjudication process, with the Constitutional Court judges, and whomever else they select, taking charge of the final contest.	**Constitutional Court,** assisted by the Department of Justice
Freedom Day 27 April	Formal, and observed as the pre-eminent national day	Celebrating the nation state and its popular legitimacy. Promote state symbols and state authority: military and civilian march past with the President taking salute. Continue with the National Orders function in the evening. On the last school day before the holiday, distribute small flags and a pennant with Coat of Arms in all public and private primary schools (depending on cost, to all pupils or to the 20 best-performing students per grade).	**State:** The Presidency, SANDF and the Department of Basic Education
Workers' Day 1 May	Informal and semi-formal	Rally and/or march organised by the union federations. One of the aims, in addition to popularising workers' rights, should be to encourage class solidarity across race and ideology. As such, the condition for state participation (President or Deputy President) should be that the event is jointly organised by all the federations.	**Trade Unions** and the Department of Labour

HOLIDAY	STATUS	ACTIVITY	RESPONSIBLE
Youth Day 16 June	Semi-formal	Combined finals, in one venue on the same day, of Rugby Craven Week and Football ('Kalamazoo') Mokone Week on Youth Day. This will be preceded by provincial competitions, and then groups of provinces (coastal and inland) leading to the selection of the finalists. On the day, the participants (and others) can visit the Hector Pieterson Museum.	**SARU, SAFA** and the Departments of Education and Sports & Recreation
Women's Day 9 August	Semi-formal	Women's Day concerts in each metro and district (or each province) with women musicians and poets as main performers. Museums, art galleries, libraries, and media should all be encouraged to have a theme on the role of women in society – beyond stereotyped gender roles. Each pre- and primary school should devise creative ways of preparing a present for each boy-child (prepared by the girls – as a reversal of stereotyped roles) and combine this with a theme against bullying. National competition among primary school children for the best poem on the role of women in society. 'Men's lunch day' within families: where men prepare lunch; and radio programmes in the afternoon for families to share light moments about the experience.	**Gender Commission**, the Ministry of Women, Children and People with Disabilities, and municipalities.
Heritage Day 24 September	Informal and semi-formal	Provincial high school music festivals: choir competitions leading to the national final on Heritage Day. Provincial activities along the lines of current cultural events. Grand event in the evening: a national cultural variety show at the State Theatre attended by the President. Informal activities that include the so-called 'National Braai Day'	**Department of Arts & Culture, provincial governments**

HOLIDAY	STATUS	ACTIVITY	RESPONSIBLE
Day of Reconciliation 16 December	Informal	Promote interaction among neighbours and communities through activities that they themselves identify, such as street carnivals, braais, and street games. Start with early morning ceremony at Freedom Park.	**Municipalities**

CONCLUSION

Nation formation is an evolutionary process that may take many decades, if not centuries. It requires agency in the form of promotional activities by various sectors of society – what can be characterised as a consensual act of nation building. An element of such agency should be deliberate efforts to promote social cohesion, combining matters related to promotion and enforcement of non-discriminatory practises, symbolic acts that help unite society, and improvement in the material conditions of the people, especially the poor.

Because of the profound disparities inherited from society's colonial and apartheid past, the various elements required to attain social cohesion will take long to materialise. However, it should be appreciated that a minimum level of social cohesion and sense of nationhood is required to attain the ideal society envisioned in the Constitution. In other words, to attain a united and socially cohesive nation requires at least an appreciation of a common destiny across all sectors of society and continuing improvements in the all-round lived experience of the majority in society. Some of the instruments that can be used in this regard are national symbols, of which national holidays are part.

CHAPTER FIVE

WESTERN CAPE, HOUT BAY

Introduction

Hout Bay is situated in a valley behind Table Mountain on the Atlantic seaboard of the Cape Peninsula some twenty kilometres south of the city centre of Cape Town. The story goes that Jan Van Riebeeck visited the area in 1653 and observed in his journal 'the forests are the finest in the world and contain timber as long, thick and straight as one would wish'. He promptly gave the place the Dutch name *Hout Bayken*. The abundant timber in this valley became the main source of supply for the building of the Castle and for ship repairs. Then manganese mining took off briefly before it was overtaken by a thriving fishing industry – with a canning factory opened in 1904 at the harbour.

The main types of fish caught are tuna, crayfish and snoek. South Africa exports about 80% of its fish. With the decline in commercial fishing, tourism today constitutes the main source of income for the local economy. Besides fishing, outdoor activities include hiking, sailing, surfing, kayaking and cycling. The area is part of Ward 74, which in turn forms part of Subcouncil 16 (Good Hope) of the City of Cape Town. The following areas are key to our research activities.

HANGBERG

Hangberg is a predominantly Coloured residential area just above the harbour. An estimated 40 000 people live in this area. Historically a fishing village, it used to provide employment in the fishing industry. With the decline of this industry most residents are now unemployed. A combination of desperation to make a living and the frustrations posed by the regulation of the fishing industry through the quota allocation system has led many fishermen to turn to poaching to supply the growing international market. According to community members, the poachers are highly organised and competitive.

Competition often leads to fights between different poaching gangs and between gangs and the police. Children growing up look up to the poachers as role models.

Another social problem in the area is drugs and especially 'Tik',[16] which is consumed even by children.

The school dropout rate appears high because of the absence of a high school in the area; parents often keeping kids at home to help in scraping a living together. There is a process of peace building following the events of 21 September 2010 over land and housing in the area.[17]

IMIZAMO YETHU

The community of Imizamo Yethu, of about 40 000 residents, is made up of 3,900 families settled on 18 hectares of an original 34 hectares bought by the government from the Department of Forestry to settle the original 455 families. To date, more than 18 000 houses have been built in the area, of which 15% of them are made of brick. The community consists of approximately 70% black African, 10% Coloured and 20% non-South African Africans: mainly Namibians, Malawians, Zimbabweans, Ethiopians, Somalians and Congolese. There is a satellite library that teaches isiXhosa (the predominant African language of Capetonians, many of whom originate from the Eastern Cape) to fellow Africans living in the area.

THE VALLEY

The Valley is the predominantly white residential area of Hout Bay where mostly high-income South Africans and a few foreign property owners live. The domestic workers of The Valley live in Imizamo Yethu and Hangberg. The Ratepayers Association in this area is perceived to be interested in restricting the expansion of Imizamo Yethu and Hangberg, sometimes to the extent of supporting forced removals of communities in some sections of

---

16. Tik is an odourless, crystal-like substance. It is a stimulant that speeds up the functioning of the vital organs, e.g. the heart. It is highly addictive and harms the functioning of the central nervous system. (http://www.drugcentre.org.za/druginfo_tik.html
17. On this day, 62 Hout Bay residents were arrested and 18 were injured in a clash between metro police and civilians. Violence broke out when community members clashed with metro police as the City of Cape Town dismantled illegal structures in the area on Tuesday morning (*Mail and Guardian* [online] 21 September, 2010).

these townships. The perception is based on an argument to keep Hout Bay a nature reserve, and preserve the current spatial patterns and land allocation.

The purpose of this research project was to:

- research the different interpretations and meanings that diverse social actors in South Africa attach to the concept of nation formation and social cohesion and calls for implementing these;
- examine and study the different ways in which the different social actors act and respond to these theoretical and social constructs and thus enter into contestations of such ideas and investigate the important role of the State in mediating those contestations, and
- examine how the different social actors respond and give meaning to state policies and intervention practises.

Based on the project documentation and brief provided for the research project, a broad conceptual approach to the field research was developed which informs the questions asked and the discussions pursued with the individuals and organisations that had been identified. This section briefly sets out the conceptual approach.

UNDERSTANDING NATION FORMATION AND SOCIAL COHESION

By way of introduction, and without directly asking the question 'what do you understand by nation formation and social cohesion?', there was an attempt to gain an awareness of the respondents' perception of the nation building project in South Africa and how far the country has come generally in actualising this. The discussion then focused on how the nation building and social cohesion project plays itself out in the specific community and on whether there is a shared sense of community identity and a desire on the part of the community to work towards and achieve social cohesion. In general, this allowed the respondents to provide an impromptu assessment as to whether or not social cohesion exists, and whether it is possible to achieve it.

FACTORS THAT PROMOTE OR IMPEDE NATION FORMATION AND SOCIAL COHESION

During the interview/conversation, there was focus on specific dynamics that have an impact on, and could either promote or impede, nation formation and social cohesion. These include the following:

Spatial distribution: To what extent does the geography and physical layout of the area impact on nation formation and social cohesion? How has the planning for, and allocation of, housing, schools and recreational facilities changed since 1994 and how has this impacted on nation formation and social cohesion?

Social interaction: Since 1994 has there been more social interaction between different groups in the community? What has made this possible or difficult and is there a discernible outcome, either negative or positive? Are changes in social relations and interaction gradual, and are there specific interventions that have contributed to changes over the years?

Political dynamics: To what extent does allegiance to political parties or a political tradition (historically and currently) impact on achieving social cohesion? Do the political dynamics in the community (formal and informal) contribute to the promotion, or the breakdown, of social cohesion?

Socio-economic disparities: Do issues of unemployment, poverty, access to social and welfare services and social class impact on social cohesion? What degree of social capital exists in the community and how does this contribute to social cohesion?

Migration: Does the presence of newcomers and foreigners impact on the level of social cohesion in the community? Are there indications of tension between 'insiders' and 'outsiders'?

Role of institutions and organisations: How do the interventions and actions of institutions and organisations impact on the willingness and ability of the community to achieve social cohesion? Here we focus on the role of government and state institutions (local, provincial and national levels), NGOs and CBOs, formal and informal organisations, and associations such as faith communities, stokvels, funeral societies, sports clubs and business in both the formal and the informal sectors.

We interviewed individual activists who belong to organisations and could therefore reflect both their individual and organisational experiences, views and perspectives:

Denis Goldberg is an ANC veteran, Rivonia trialist and former long-term political prisoner. He lives in The Heights in Hout Bay. To get to his house you have to drive through Hangberg, a predominantly Coloured township. From the balcony of his house you can see Hangberg fishing village spread out below. Although he is 'retired' he is still active in the ANC and gets invited to talk at schools and other social gatherings. He is involved as a patron in the Kronendal Music Project – a project run by a young white UCT music graduate to teach jazz to the children of the divided community of Hout Bay – Hangberg, Imizamo Yethu and the Valley. The jazz band has been invited to Germany. He was met on a Monday midmorning at his home (Fieldwork Notes, 2012).

Kenny Tokwe is originally from Sada Township[18] in Whittlesea, Eastern Cape. He came to Cape Town in the early 1980s after a spate of detentions following his involvement in student and political activities. Once he arrived in Hout Bay he got involved in the struggles of the shack communities in five squatter camps there for the right to live in the area. In his own words he helped 'organise the community to fight for Hout Bay to belong to all who live in it'. Through contact with an Irish philanthropist, Niall Mellow, Kenny travelled to Ireland, which opened the door to a housing project in the Hout Bay area[19]. Kenny now works as a community development worker (CDW) there. He was interviewed at the offices of the ANC in Imizamo Yethu (Fieldwork Notes, 2012).

Donovan van der Heyden is a voluntary community development worker working on youth development, land and housing reform and also represents the traditional fishers. He is passionate about community work –

18. Sada Township was a settlement set up by the apartheid government in the 1970s to house thousands of black families displaced under the Group Areas Act from the Western Cape. For further information on the area see: http://www.sahistory.org.za/places/sada
19. Two hundred Irish volunteers travelled to South Africa in 2003 under the auspices of the Niall Mellon Township Project to build homes for residents backed by interest-free loans. Volunteers returned in the subsequent years. (http://www.capetownmagazine.com/news/imizamo-yethu-builders-back-to-see-progress/10_22_977)

local economic development, struggles of traditional fishermen for survival and access to land and housing. He has deep roots in community activism (Fieldwork Notes, 2011).

Florince Clark is an outreach worker at Hout Bay Community Awareness Rehabilitation Education Support Service (C.A.R.E.S.). Her work involves encouraging recovering drug and alcohol addicts to change their drug taking habits. She says that as far as she is concerned, the rich have become richer and the poor have become poorer. 'Here people get more children even if they can't afford it. It's still the same: the whites stay in The Village, the blacks in Imizamo Yethu and the Coloureds in Hangberg (Fieldwork Notes, 2011).'

Roseline Booi is also an outreach worker at Hout Bay C.A.R.E.S. and works with Florince. 'If you see a white guy walking around in this area you know he's coming to buy drugs. And if you see a Coloured or black person walking in the village, the white people think he's coming to steal,' says Roseline. Both Florince and Roseline's stories, we shall see, are examples for this community of how it can heal itself of discrimination, oppression, lack of dignity and violence (Fieldwork Notes, 2011).

Phumla Madikizela is a social worker employed by Hout Bay C.A.R.E.S. She lives in a tiny shack in Imizamo Yethu with her husband and three young children. Although C.A.R.E.S. has offices in Hangberg, it is in Imizamo Yethu that Phumla provides her services (Fieldwork Notes, 2012).

Natasha Meter and **Shamiega Wyngard** both live behind Philadelphia Flats and belong to the Hout Bay Civic Association. They tell a story of how on 21 September 2010 the Council wanted to put people out of their 'Wendy houses' saying they could not build on the nature reserve. 'We were not allowed to build above this "slot". They came with a mediator. A few weeks ago people were issued with eviction notices. The walls of the flats, the floors are cracked. And if your toilet is blocked you must wait for weeks for them to fix it. *Ons kry nie services nie*, and your windows, you must find a private person to fix it (Fieldwork Notes, 2011).'

Florince and Roseline introduced Natasha and Shamiega to the researchers on a weekday afternoon on the balcony of their house at the top of Hangberg, just behind Philadelphia Flats.

Jasmiena Davids was born and raised in Hout Bay. Married according to Muslim law, she has seven children. She used to stay on The Sentinel,[20] and with the Group Areas Act they were moved from there to the harbour. The area has seen lots of changes according to her, '... before, never had children taken drugs like Tik but only big guys smoked dagga. Today there are also guys who poach perlemoen, crayfish. In the past, poaching never used to be this big. When the factories closed fishermen were left without jobs and today poaching is one of the few options for these men.'

Jasmiena was met at her house, which doubles up as a preschool run by her daughter. She and her daughter were looking after 10 children at the time (Fieldwork Notes, 2011).

David Africa has worked in the Western Cape as a political activist since the 1980s. He has lived in Hout Bay since 2007 and is connected and in touch with people from different organisations there, especially in Hangberg and Imizamo Yethu. David is curious about issues of race, class, social integration, and separation, especially as they impact on Hout Bay and on some of the challenges that development has brought to Hout Bay, namely the influx of migrants and refugees. He has a particular interest in how one can develop a progressive political project in Hout Bay that deals with the issue of social cohesion and nation building (Fieldwork Notes, 2011).

Ravone is a fisherman. He says he and his fellow fishermen used to have a lot of freedom for fishing. But with the concerns about overfishing and declining resources the quota system was introduced. He feels that the people who have benefited from the fishing quota system are big businesses. According to Ravone, these established companies get their regular quotas and, in addition to these, they get people from 'outside the area', who have nothing to do with fishing to hold some of the smaller quota allocations that they cede to them. He goes on to say that even if they, as smaller fishermen, did not get the quotas, surely the big companies should have employed them to do the fishing instead of employing people from outside the area (Fieldwork Notes, 2011).

Dickie Meter has been an activist for over 30 years and has deep roots in Hout Bay. He was born and raised in Hangberg and is a fourth generation resident. He says he has 'a fair understanding of the background and the struggles for

---

20. The Sentinel is land above Hangberg and the harbour, which is largely owned by the Parks Board.

equality and justice in Hout Bay'. As far as this study is concerned, Dickie is one of the key players and belongs to a 'historical' political leadership of this community; he was the first mayor of the area during the transitional authority.

'I think the fundamental property for any social cohesion is equality. Very early on land has been a big question. While the "non-white" communities were in numbers more than the white communities, the "non-white" communities were living on only two per cent of the land. The situation has not changed much since then – the '"non-white" communities might now be living on three or four per cent of the land. And there is just no planning to change that. There's overcrowding in "non-white" communities and the privileges of whites in terms of space are being preserved. As long as that doesn't change I don't think there's any possibility for peaceful coexistence (Dickie was interviewed in Cape Town city centre. Fieldwork Notes, 2012).'

Pastor Jonty Dreyer was born and bred in Hout Bay. In 1970, his family was forcibly removed from a farm near Hangberg. He attended Sentinel Primary School and completed his matric outside Hout Bay. He worked for a local company for 22 years and in 2005 was appointed to take charge of the Hout Bay Museum. The motto of the museum is: 'If we understand the past, we will appreciate where we are.' He is concerned about what role the museum can play to bring people together (Fieldwork Notes, 2011).

Nomathemba Sotomela is the chairperson of the Sinethemba Civic Association in Imizamo Yethu. Sinethemba is a rival association to the South African National Civic Organisation (SANCO) and was formed by people who consider themselves the 'original residents' of Imizamo Yethu. This was a group of African and Coloured people who lived in plastic and iron makeshift shacks near the graveyard so as to be closer to their places of employment. Her husband was, for many years, a fisherman in the area until he succumbed to a stroke and is now cared for by Nomathemba at home. Recently she has been involved, together with four other women, in an initiative to summon the ward councillor for the area to come and meet with the community of Imizamo Yethu. At the time of the interview the ward councillor had not responded positively to this invitation (Fieldwork Notes, 2011).

Nolitha Mngomezulu identifies herself as 'the wife of a fisherman' (Fieldwork Notes, 2011). Her husband is a fisherman who, when there is work, often works away from home for months only to return with very little money to take care of his family. As a result, Nolitha, together with other 'wives of fishermen', has became involved in the associations of small fishing communities. They seem to be in the midst of all the attempts to form co-operatives by small fishermen so as to secure better fishing quota benefits. Often, as she tells us in the interview, this leads to 'cheating and deceit' by people they had trusted. 'There is no love at the home of the fisherman (Fieldwork Notes, 2011).'

The first interview was with Denis Goldberg, and the first issue he raised was the overcrowded living conditions in Hangberg, to where Coloured people were moved under the Group Areas Act from 1963 onwards. The current struggle over the land was sparked by the community building on the nature reserve. While the municipality reacts quickly to the residents building on the nature reserve, a company constructing the toll road on Chapman's Peak was allowed to build an office block on the nature reserve. This has sparked a protest movement against the construction of the toll road.

This fact alone sums up one of the key issues in this community – access to land and housing. And the struggle over land is intricately linked to the project of nation formation and social cohesion. The extent to which public policy deliberately pursues spatial and social development or continues to reinforce the spatial development patterns of the past, determines possibilities for accessing land not only for recreation but for housing (Fieldwork Notes, 2011).

LOCAL NARRATIVES: UNDERSTANDING NATION FORMATION AND SOCIAL COHESION

After introducing, and without directly asking the question 'What do you understand by nation formation and social cohesion?' an attempt was made to get a sense of the respondents' conceptual view of the nation building project in South Africa and how far it has progressed since 1994. The focus then shifted to discussions on how the nation building and social cohesion project figures in the community in question; and whether there was a shared sense of identity and a desire on the part of the community to live together, interact and share social and public spaces. This allowed the respondents to provide impromptu assessments as to whether or not social cohesion exists and whether it is possible to achieve it.

Everyone spoken to expressed a desire to see Hout Bay treated as a single community, away from the divisions of the past, and for all the residents to move towards some form of integration. Those with a background of political activism articulated this desire very strongly, whereas those who did not have a history of political activism related to this desire as a need to be treated equally in the allocation of resources and opportunities. All were agreed that at the present moment there is no form of social cohesion in Hout Bay as a whole.

Although remnants of social capital in the form of 'we look after each other here: if I don't have anything I can go to my neighbour for help' exists within the different communities, this is often undermined by the sheer struggle for daily survival. Donovan van der Heyden, a veteran activist working with small and traditional fishermen, talks of opportunities for tourism in Hangberg but is equally conscious that should he attempt to set up an initiative the community will pull him down. While it may be expected of people thrown together in a situation of poverty and desperation to pull together, often a situation of 'dog eat dog' prevails. In this situation, the preoccupation with daily survival seems to blind people to seeing a vision beyond the present; let alone acting to realise that vision.

Veteran activist Denis Goldberg is scathing at the lack of vision, especially of those in positions of power. According to him, failure to understand the imperatives of nation building and social cohesion will leave us trapped under apartheid.

> You must not treat Imizamo Yethu as a community; you must not treat Hangberg as a community; Hout Bay is a community. There is lots of land in Hout Bay. So why don't you build houses where people want them and build the schools and other facilities where, over the next generation or two, people can come together and not be continually in ghettoes – a white ghetto, a black ghetto, or a Coloured ghetto (Fieldwork notes, 2011).

Nomathemba Sotomela, another activist with a long history in the fight for the right to land in Hout Bay, is the chairperson of Sinethemba Civic Association, which considers itself as a representative of the original residents of Imizamo Yethu. She paints a picture of a big dent in community solidarity that used to prevail during the days when the community was fighting for a right to live in this area.

Besikade sixubile umthetho wethu singabantu beBala singabantu abaMnyama. Ngelaxesha langaphambili lepasi, babesithi abantu abaMnyama xa besokola bebaleka baqale abantu beBala bakhwazi besithi 'Hey! Die blok is rooi!' Kuqhawulwe ke ngabantu abanye babafihle babagcine. Sasingabantu abavanayo, till nangoku ke sisavana. Kodwa ke ngoku into ebuhlungu apha ekuhlaleni bona ke ngoku abakinazindawo njengokuba bebefanele ukuba ba settlishile ngoba ke ngabantu bokuqala esafikela kubo apha e Hout Bay kodwa abanye basahleli ezipavementini (Fieldwork notes, 2012).

[We were a mixed community, with Coloured and black people. During those days of pass laws, whenever black people were struggling to hide, Coloured people would warn them by shouting *'Hey! Die blok is rooi!'* [Hey, the block is red!] This would give black people time to run and hide, and some Coloured families would hide them. We were a united community. Even today we are united. But what is painful today is the fact that some of them have not got houses. As people who received us here, they also ought to have had houses by now. But some of them still live on the pavements.]

During this part of the interviews and conversation, the focus fell on specific factors and social dynamics that have an impact on, and could either promote or impede, nation formation and social cohesion. These include the following:

Spatial distribution: This relates to the extent to which the geography, physical layout of the area and patterns of settlement impact negatively or positively on social cohesion and interaction between different social, cultural and economic groups. Spatial distribution determines whether processes that develop shared values necessary for nation formation and social inclusion critical for social cohesion are impeded or facilitated. The question of how town and community planning to allow for allocation of housing, schools and recreational facilities has changed since 1994, if at all, and how has this impacted on nation formation and social cohesion, is central to this particular social dynamic.

The overwhelming view is that the current spatial distribution is not conducive to social integration. And there is an awareness of the capacity of the State to use its power to intervene in favour of settlement planning that promotes spatial integration and avoids the forms of spatial segregations of apartheid and its notion of separate development. In this regard, Denis Goldberg observes: 'Our spatial development retains the features of apartheid. The City of Cape Town builds houses in Delft, 40 kilometres from the city centre, whereas people are living in squatter camps in Gugulethu and elsewhere, only 20 kilometres away (Fieldwork Notes, 2012).'

This continuation of the development patterns of the past can be ascribed to a glaring lack of will and vision to design and construct inclusive settlements and a willingness to follow the segregationist imperative of the past. Goldberg again finds a disturbing tendency to avoid taking a stand and making hard choices on the part of local, metropolitan, provincial and national authorities:

> ... there you have landlords, gangster bosses, who have taken control of the land and use threats to demand protection money if you build houses. This is what I'm told; I've not done personal research. And so, instead of taking on the landlords and taking back the municipally-owned land, the Council is avoiding confrontation. Building at Delft, people can't afford the transport costs ... going to shacks nearer. And so you have the recycling of the edifice of apartheid, and the ways of thinking of apartheid (Fieldwork Notes, 2012).

One instance in which the policy choices of the City of Cape Town seem to have been tested and clarified involves the building of the school in Imizamo Yethu. Originally the portion of land on which the school was built was allocated for public amenities. On this, both civic associations agree. However, with a sudden and unexpected influx of people into the area, which increased the number of families from 455 at the time of the allocation to 3,900, a rethink of the development plans and priorities became necessary to accommodate the rapidly expanding local population. This resulted in polarisation with Sinethemba Civic Association opting to stick to the original plans while SANCO was keen to reopen the discussion. Sinethemba claims to represent the 455 'original residents', which explains their stance. The association appeared not to be concerned with the needs and rights of the new arrivals who, in its view, take away resources legitimately meant for the original residents.

Kenny Tokwe, himself an original resident of the area who, however, belongs to the rival civic SANCO, was instrumental in the development of a new vision. He was part of the Hout Bay Liaison Committee that brought key people together from the three communities that constitute Hout Bay – Imizamo Yethu, Hangberg and The Valley. He observed:

> We had identified some places to build a school. We wanted schools and sports fields to be used for integration and transformation. We did not want a school to be built in the black community, especially because here in Hout Bay we [the different communities] are divided by the main road. It would be nice to share and to have a good environment for our children to start knowing each other while they are still young (Fieldwork Notes, 2012).

However, the fortunes of these plans of a socially integrated community were tied up with those of the outcome of the provincial and local elections. Kenny Tokwe says that after the ANC lost the provincial and metropolitan elections in the last election and the DA ascended to power. 'the people in The Valley who are in charge now are no longer singing that song' (ibid.).

> Theirs is to push for more of our people to be evicted. Theirs is to make sure that every little piece of land is occupied by other things. They want to force on us our own schools, our own everything. They want to keep this separation forever – that Imizamo Yethu is for blacks, Hangberg is for Coloureds, and The Valley is for whites (Fieldwork Notes, 2012).

Social interaction: Since 1994 has there been more social interaction between different groups in the community? What has made this possible or difficult and is there a discernible outcome, either negative or positive? Are changes in social relations and interaction gradual and organic or are there specific interventions that have contributed to changes over the years?

Observations in the area yielded very few signs of social interaction between the different communities. This fact was borne out in the testimony of Roseline Booi and Donovan van der Heyden. Roseline says if a Coloured or a black person walks down the main street in The Valley, especially in residential areas, they are immediately seen as a potential criminal. And Donovan laments the fact that the community development worker for the ward has never, according to him, covered Hangeberg during his duties.

However, in all of this there is a small project called the Kronendal Music

Academy run by a young white woman. She is a graduate of the Music Department at UCT, a jazz musician who, according to Denis Goldberg, 'loves music, loves children, believes that through music the children of our divided community can be brought together'. As a result, Denis has become a patron of this project and helps to raise funds and provide instruments.

> *I've brought here hundreds of instruments from overseas. And others have donated as well, and raise money; and I do every year. And there are about 200 young people involved in the project now. Those who can pay for their lessons pay, and those who can't don't, those who can pay something, do. And they make music together. And music has its own language, its own way of communicating. And the music they make is beautiful. It's their self-confidence, their self-respect, their dignity. I am a musician, I have a teacher, I perform in public. And now because of our connection in Germany we're taking our jazz band to Germany on a tour. These young people aged fourteen ... [one has a] wonderful voice, [a]young singer, originally from here (Hangberg), but she lives with her mother who's a domestic worker down in the rich village, probably gives her nice quarters, but it helps her with her schooling. But such a voice, such talent! And she's got to knock them dead in Europe, I tell you. And a boy who plays keyboard, his mother is a drug addict. The director of the project, her name is Dwyn, invites the parents to come to a rehearsals [so] we can talk about the trip abroad. And he begs the director, this boy, not to invite his mother, in tears, he's seventeen but he's in tears. He doesn't want her to come and embarrass him or herself. So for him to go on a tour and play keyboard before an audience perhaps of hundreds or thousands, the self-image, the prestige, the dignity, is transforming. And I've watched these kids perform, it's remarkable. So that's my direct contribution to nation building in Hout Bay, to try and overcome the divisions of the past. I have to say that Western Cape Province Culture and Sports make some grants sometimes, and the National Arts Council as well, but it needs far more than I can provide myself* (Fieldwork Notes, 2012).

It will be interesting to watch how this project develops and whether the political intention to integrate becomes pronounced; or if it simply remains at the level of dealing with basic survival imperatives to get kids off the streets and give them music education and skills. Does it have a potential for bigger things? The project manager is not the only individual who occasionally crosses the township barriers to make a difference. According to Kenny Tokwe there are some good people in The Valley who have a heart, who are spending time coming to these communities trying to engage and help in various ways. Some have even taken to commenting about the plight of these communities in the local newspapers.

> *But they are being targeted by those who oppose. In various projects in this area I have to be careful not to mention my name. It's only when a project comes about that people can say we were helped by so and so. So those are the challenges. They don't want to see any development taking place. They want to do things for the people of Imizamo Yethu. They want to be seen as people who care about Imizamo Yethu. They want to tell the people of Imizamo Yethu how to think, where to stay, how to stay, how to do everything as if people are subhuman. Sometimes I speak to them straight, openly, and when there's meetings I tell them you know you are taking us as subhuman, we are not subhuman. Give us a chance. You don't involve us on many things you just think what will be good for us without even asking us as if you are building kennels for your dogs. I even said it in one of their meetings – you talk on our behalf, you think you are planning how to build kennels for your dogs* (Fieldwork Notes, 2012).

Political dynamics: To what extent does allegiance to political parties or a political tradition (historically and currently) impact on achieving social cohesion? Do the political dynamics in the community (formal and informal) contribute to the promotion or the breakdown of social cohesion?

In relation to political dynamics, power is central here. Access to power is a key dynamic in this community. And this access is the basis for further benefits in terms of access to resources and to the allocation of these resources. What is interesting in terms of nation formation and social cohesion is that, despite all the problems, there is allegiance to the leadership. They may disagree with it and they may complain about what the leadership does but eventually they show allegiance to the leadership. Is this some kind of deference to authority? A case in point: while we were interviewing Natasha Meter and Shamiega Wyngard they articulated a great sense of unhappiness with the leadership of the Peace and Mediation Forum (PMF). Natasha Meter says of the Peace and Mediation Forum: 'There was a court case and eventually they chose a mediator to come in and assist, and *dat was 'n hele deermekaar proses, hulle was nie demokratik ge elected hier in die community'* [that was a completely confused process, they were not democraticly elected in the community] (Fieldwork notes 2012). And she goes on to complain about poor service delivery and lack of visibility of the ward councillor.

> *Die flatse is gekrak, die mure is gekrak, die venster … The whole of Hout Bay, 98 persent van die mense was geserved with eviction notices. As jy toilet vra om reg te maak, dan moet jy vir weeks wag. En hoe is 'n geblokte toilet in jou huis? Is anklag jy kan mos niks maak nie. Die bore binne, die roof. So waar het ons rêrig gekom? Ons kry nie services nie. Die ruite van venster is ge privatised. Jy moet privately om iemand te kry om jou ruite reg te maak. So hoe ver het ons rêrig gekom? Ons ken nie onse eie ward councillor nie.*

[The flats have cracks, the walls have cracks, the windows … the whole of Hout Bay, 98 per cent of the people were served with eviction notices. If you want your toilet to be unblocked, you must wait for weeks. And how does it feel to live with a blocked toilet in your house? It's foul but you can do nothing. The boards inside, the roof … so how far did we really come? We don't get services. The windows have been privatised. You must get a private person to fix your window pane. So how far have we really come? We don't even know our own ward councillor.]

But then as soon as Kevin Davids of the Hangberg Peace and Mediation Forum (HPMF) comes around he is deferred to and his authority is clear to see. An interesting form of resistance is perhaps displayed in Natasha's action when, as soon as she sees Kevin coming up the stairs, she quickly runs inside the house to fetch a camera to record his inspection of the house next door (Fieldwork Notes 2012).

BRIEF ANALYSIS

At Imizamo Yethu a similar observation can be drawn from an interview with Nomathemba Sotomela and Nolitha Mngomezulu. While both are critical of the community's leadership, and as it became apparent towards the end of the interview this includes the community development worker as well as the ward councillor, they still find it difficult to contemplate alternatives outside of forming a committee of concerned women and attempting to make contact with the ward Councillor to speak to her as women to a woman.

In both cases they do not confront the given authority as not their real leader, or not in leadership for too long, or being invisible in the area. But they acknowledge the PMF, the ward Councillor and the community development worker (CDW) as having some level of authority. This is the sanctioned authority, sanctioned by the State. And while people in the community may be unhappy, they accept that the State has that level of authority. Even when they challenge it, they do so within the constraint of what the State imposes. They do not go outside of that.

Denis Goldberg: 'I have to say as a member of the ANC where we have one branch, named after Johnson Mayeke, who was in MK, he was 'taken out' in the SANDF after liberation, got into an argument with a white defence force member who shot him and he is now a paralysed quadriplegic. And he's got a wheelchair, finally donated by some comfortable person which he can operate with a little joystick. Otherwise, he was utterly dependent on help from others. So the branch is named after him.

It's very difficult to build one branch where in Imizamo Yethu the members insist it is their right in speaking isiXhosa, which means I and a few other whites around here can't really take part in a meeting. I get invited from time to time as an old veteran from the Rivonia Trial to come and talk. And I talk in English and I've taken to insisting on an interpreter. But the members from Hangberg, who are crucial to winning a city council seat, and they are Coloured almost hundred per cent, also can't understand. And so I say to the meeting: please let us learn the habit of translating. The answer is, learn our language. I understand the attitude, I understand the feeling, why should we learn your language. We have history and we have history where English has become the lingua franca so to speak. And if in the Western Cape in the ANC, the party of non-racism, we cannot find a way of accommodating the communication needs of all South African members of the ANC, we're in serious trouble. I personally believe it's going to take at least a generation to overcome because I believe the depth of the scarring in the psyche of people is very deep-seated. And it gets transmitted from grandparents to parents, to children and grandchildren. And it needs to be consciously combated, and we're not doing it. In part it's through using political connection for access to state resources at municipal and provincial and national level, to connections into business and so on (Fieldwork Notes, 2011).'

Kenny Tokwe: 'What is happening now is they are taking advantage of the government of the day now. Because most of them are whites and they are pro the government that is ruling in the Western Cape. So they are using the influence of the government to practise what they have in their minds. Because five years ago, when Nomaindia Mfeketo was the mayor of Cape Town and Ebrahim Rasool was the premier of the Western Cape, we were about to take the court interdict away. There were many discussions to stop the interdict and come up with plans for total integration. The ratepayers then also took those agreements to court supported by this handful of people called Sinethemba. They had money, and they had almost everything to go to court and get an interdict that the 16 hectares will not be touched. This forced the removal of many people in Imizamo Yethu to be outside of Hout Bay claiming that there's no land available in Hout Bay (Fieldwork Notes, 2011).'

Nomathemba Sotomela: *'Kulapho ke ngoku ndibona ukuba ubunye bungabikho kwii groups zemibutho ekhoyo. And imibutho ke ngoku iqhayisa omnye uthi ndiyiparty ethile, omnye ndiyiparty ethile. Kanti iparty eyalwela ukuba sibe kulendawo iyi one, yiparty ka Tat' u Mandela. Sathi zesikwazi ukukhululeka sakhululeka ngenxa yakhe* (Fieldwork Notes, 2012).'

[This is where I see that there is no unity between different groups of organisations. And organisations start to boast about the political parties they belong to. But there is only one party that fought for us to be here – the party of Tat'u Mandela. We only got freedom through him.]

Kenny Tokwe: 'When the Irish guy came and built houses in Imizamo Yethu, there was a lot of backlash. Even the present government of the DA used that incident to divide the people during their elections – taking pictures of nice houses in Imizamo Yethu claiming the ANC has built houses for the blacks and nothing for you in Hangberg. It really worked for them because they got lots of votes in the Coloured townships. Even in their pamphlets they were showing these two areas, claiming it's the ANC government that built these houses and not even mentioning it's the Irish donor who built the houses. They don't want to see any further developments in these communities because they want to use this as a political football when they have elections (Fieldwork Notes, 2012).'

Socio-economic disparities: Do issues of unemployment, poverty, access to social and welfare services and social class impact on social cohesion? What degree of social capital exists in the community and how does this contribute to social cohesion?

Over time there has been a level of impoverisation in both Hangberg and Imizamo Yethu as a result of the collapse of the fishing industry as a main job provider in the area. With the advent of democracy there was a growing awareness of the limitation of natural resources, including fishing. As a result, concerns about overfishing led to the regulation of fishing rights. While the Reconstruction and Development Programme (RDP) intended to benefit the small and traditional fishing communities, the current system of allocating quotas for fishing seems to benefit the big companies. And in the process, not only jobs have been lost but the fishermen have been left struggling for survival on the small quotas they receive as individuals. One response to this situation has been attempts to form co-operatives and by so doing pull together all the resources and reap the benefits of collective efforts.

In Imizamo Yethu there seems to be tension relating to allocation of housing and the exclusion of some of the 'original' residents as against the 'newcomers'. At least two respondents who happen to belong to the Sinethemba Civic Association of the 'original residents' suggest that newcomers get prioritised over the older residents and they suggest that this is because of the leadership in the area. They suggest information gets used to exclude and include. Access to jobs, for instance, is seen as closely linked to this control by the leadership of access to resources.

Denis Goldberg: 'And nation building requires a conscious effort; it requires that top leaders don't get involved in scandals; that they seriously do not have to have shares in companies and empowerment companies. And I personally think that the outsourcing element of black economic empowerment was a serious error on the part of my government, because what it's created is a small, wannabe elite. I worked as an advisor to the Minister of Water Affairs and Forestry at the time. The forestry sector, big companies, were expected and encouraged to outsource. So they used to have workers looking after their plantations, cleaning the forest floor, stripping off branches. And they provided the safety equipment and paid national minimum wages. Then they were encouraged to outsource, and it's actually a saving of money for the corporation: you don't need the personnel department and so on. But the new contractors are not interested in the safety of their workers, and certainly do not pay national minimum wages. And they do not care. The big companies can be brought before Court easily, the small contractors, you cannot go after them. And the officials who are meant to monitor them are themselves badly paid and badly trained and can easily be bribed. Again, I must insist this is not an ethnic thing or a racial thing, this is a socio-economic thing which you will find all over the world. But I live in South Africa (Fieldwork Notes, 2012).'

Jasmiena Davids: 'At the moment, poaching is so big that even children, when asked what they want to be when they are grown up, say poacher. The quota limits fishermen to a certain number of fishes per day – for instance two crayfishes a day; ten a week. But this is often not enough for families to live on. If they catch you with more than this quantity you pay a fine or go to jail. Poachers and smugglers are seen as the heroes and role models in the community. There's high unemployment in the area. These poachers compete for business and often end up fighting among themselves. But they have a steady market to supply – mostly foreigners ... We've got peace mediation trying to get everybody together (Fieldwork Notes, 2012).'

Migration: Does the presence of newcomers and foreigners impact on the level of social cohesion in the community? Are there indications of tension between 'insiders' and 'outsiders'?

Hout Bay has always been home to migrants of one sort or another. In Hangberg there used to be a single men's hostel close to the harbour for African migrant workers. Today this building is about to be converted into family units. Some residents spoken to complained of the smell of fish as a potential deterring factor for those who might want to move into these units.

Another group of migrants in Hangberg has been the Namibian fishermen. Some of them have been completely integrated into the community. Roseline Booi is the daughter of a Namibian who came to live here.

In Imizamo Yethu, there is also a community of Namibian migrants living there. And in recent years Malawians, Zimbabweans, Congolese and Somalis have made the informal settlement their home. This, in addition to the tension between the 'original residents' and the 'newcomers' in the form of those who came afterwards from mainly the Eastern Cape, has shaped the social life and struggles for survival in this tiny community. For instance, residents interviewed spoke of the impact of Somali *spaza* shops in outcompeting and driving out *spaza*[21] shops owned by local residents. The initial resistance to this phenomenon took the form of robbery of Somali businessmen. And this was often accompanied by expressions of xenophobia directed at all foreign nationals in the area. Today, most of the local businessmen have opted to rent their premises out to Somali shopkeepers, and in this way earn an income.

There is a high level of resentment directed at Malawian and Zimbabwean nationals for driving down wages and displacing local labour in the domestic sector. For instance, it is said that a Malawian domestic worker not only provides services in the kitchen but doubles up in the garden as well. And the employers in The Valley prefer these often highly-educated and docile workers who will not complain no matter what wages they are paid. This is a definite hindrance to social cohesion. However, as Denis Goldberg says, migration and urbanisation are nationwide, global phenomena:

I was very careful in criticising the way that the matter had been handled by the DA province and the City Council, to say but it's not just in Cape Town, this is a nationwide problem of people streaming in, of every municipality. And I drive along the Garden Route, every little town has people streaming in to [what] we used to call shanty towns, squatter camps, now we call them informal settlements because we don't want to be nasty to people. The whole of the peninsula is covered with squatter camps. According to [Helen] Zille something like 300 000 people a year are streaming in.

They come from all over the Eastern Cape, from the North, from countries outside South Africa as well. But mainly South Africans I believe. No city can keep up with that kind of influx. And using the word influx, influx control is impossible. That just goes back to apartheid. I mention this because we have this Hangberg fishing village. We also have Imizamo Yethu. We believe there are about 40 000 people there, and every square inch of ground either has a

21. Small businesses in townships selling all forms of household items.

brick built house and formal sanitation – running water and flush toilet
[with] people buil[ding] shanties in between, under trees… crowded. They
take electricity from the street poles, it's like spaghetti junction, the wires just
go everywhere, terribly dangerous for short-circuiting. And then there is now
the white village and the new rich valley going up towards Constantia Nek.
And they are seriously divided (Fieldwork Notes, 2012).

Role of institutions and organisations: How do the interventions and
actions of institutions and organisations impact on the willingness and
ability of the community to achieve social cohesion? Here focus is on the role
of government and state institutions (local, provincial and national levels),
NGOs and CBOs, formal and informal organisations and associations like
faith communities, stokvels, funeral societies and sports clubs and businesses
– both the formal and informal sectors.

Denis Goldberg: 'There are two residents' associations, essentially white, one
more reactionary than the other. Their attitude to development at Imizamo
Yethu, building homes for people, building of schools is: we don't want any
homes here. There is a plan, homes are being built. I personally believe not
enough houses, too many social facilities. Because the attitude of the
Council, and I've had a personal interview with [Helen] Zille about all of
this, is that town planning requires that a community has its facilities nearby.
Which means that if you have 30 000 or 40 000 people in Imizamo Yethu, you
must have the clinics, the administration, the social resources, the football
fields and the schools; everything must be there …'

CONCLUSION

There was a sense that there is a desire and an expectation that things could
be better, in terms of both nation building and social cohesion: that people
could work together not just in Hangberg and Imizamo Yethu, but in the
whole of Hout Bay. On the one hand, everyone seems to be suggesting that
that is the way it should be, but on the other hand, no one seems to be
putting in substantial effort to say this is how you do it.

People like Denis Goldberg, Kenny Tokwe and Dickie Meter are thinking
about that and are trying. However, solutions remain elusive. There are two
related problems – the one is spatial, in terms of how the place is designed
and how they continue to develop the place reinforces this kind of

separation. At this stage one cannot be sure whether this is a deliberate policy or if it is just the easiest thing to do. At a city level, it would appear that there is no evidence of a lot of thought having gone into how to create an integrated community in Hout Bay. At a community level, people are so preoccupied with daily survival that, despite their expectations and their hopes of building a better community, they are fundamentally focused on seeking economic opportunities, and so on, so that even if people are saying we want Hout Bay to become more integrated, they are not going to put much energy into bringing this about because they are too busy trying to figure out what they are going to eat and whether they can get a job.

Then is there is the Peace and Mediation Forum that is supposedly designed to act in the interests of the community; but because the individuals involved often benefit from it personally they are more likely to be indebted to the State. So rather than really helping to achieve cohesion and integration in the community, because of their close collaboration with the State, they reinforce the kind of separation that goes on among the three different communities.

Where movement is possible there is a potential for integration in Hout Bay because of the history – it is a fairly small community, it covers a small geographical area, there is not a lot of division that you find in other communities. This comes through in many of the conversations. Social problems predominate and one would expect that it would be easy to mobilise people around small projects but it is easy to get discouraged in the light of things appearing to go in the opposite direction. It is almost a situation of people knowing each other too well. And they are unable to go beyond where they are now. It is a small community: 'We know each other, we all have the same problems (Fieldwork Notes, 2012).' And yet, despite all of that, they are not really able to sit down and plot a way forward. There are all sorts of initiatives here and there, the city does this, the civic does that, and so on. It would be useful to explore further whether there have been initiatives to bring everyone together to talk about the future of Hout Bay. If there has not been, the question is who could do this? The 'old historical' (black) leadership of Hout Bay could do it but there are all sorts of suspicions surrounding them. The City seems either unclear or very clear about what it wants to achieve, which does not take matters to a higher level of intervention.

When talking to people, there is a sense that there are a lot of possibilities but no clear idea on how to break through the misery and powerlessness in which people are trapped. So if someone starts doing something they externalise it – that guy is doing something good for our community. There is not a sense of – we need to become part of it and get involved here. Hout Bay C.A.R.E.S. is a bit like that: community members and even leaders talk about Hout Bay C.A.R.E.S. as 'something there' (Fieldwork Notes, 2012). They are involved in it, they are doing something with Hout Bay C.A.R.E.S. but they don't own it. The same applies to the Peace and Mediation Forum.

APPENDIX 1

LIST OF INDIVIDUALS INTERVIEWED AND THEIR ORGANISATIONS:

Denis Goldberg: African National Congress

Kenny Tokwe: community development worker, City of Cape Town and South African National Civic Association (SANCO)

Zulfa October: Hout Bay Community Awareness, Rehabilitation and Education Services (C.A.R.E.S.)

Natasha Meter and **Shamiega Wyngard:** Hout Bay Civic Association

Dickie Meter: Hout Bay Civic Association and former councillor

David Africa: former resident and political analyst

Donovan van der Heyden: volunteer community activist working with traditional fishermen

Florince Clark: outreach worker at Hout Bay C.A.R.E.S.

Roseline Booi: outreach worker at Hout Bay C.A.R.E.S.

Phumla Madikizela: social worker for Hout Bay C.A.R.E.S. at Imizamo Yethu

Jasmiena Davids: resident and grandmother assisting her daughter to run a crèche from home

Nomathemba Sotomela: Sinethemba Civic Association

Nolitha Mngomezulu: Sinethemba Civic Association and fishing activist

CHAPTER SIX

FIETAS AND RELATED AREAS

Introduction

The chapter deals with the research carried out in the 'Fietas and Related Areas' case study. In addition to interviews and filed reports it also makes observations on some aspects of nation formation and social cohesion.

This chapter explains the method for the selection of the social agents and the analytical and subjective specific questions that guided the interactions with the subjects. The choice of subjects and subject localities, and the questions, derive from a particular framing of the study, which is expounded below.

FIETAS AND RELATED AREAS

'Fietas' is the name of the Pageview section of Vrededorp in Johannesburg. This was a popularly known nickname for the historically black-populated south section within the broader locality of Vrededorp in Johannesburg. Pageview lies about five kilometres west of the city centre and is a defined area of some 15 parallel streets from 11th Street to 26th Street. It offers a practical concept of aspects of social cohesion that is little, if at all, factored into studies of nation formation. In addition, Fietas offers a cohesive historical window into the first settlements for black people in Johannesburg through to the present townships of Johannesburg founded on the Group Areas Act.

Historically established under the Paul Kruger government in 1893, alongside 'Coolie Location' and 'Kaffir Location', for Indian and African people respectively, Fietas was established as a 'Malay Location'. By the time of its destruction in the mid-1970s it had become a community of diverse cultures living together in a close community criss-crossing race and class divides.

Fietas provided for homes, shops and recreational and entertainment facilities all within walking distance. This made for daily interaction between members of the diverse community and contributed to self-sufficient, integrated community life. Fietas can also be said to have boasted a profoundly integrated local economy wherein dressmakers, for example, working out of their living rooms, literally supplied the corner shop, which fostered social bonding on the streets as it were.

In these ways, Fietas, before its dismemberment primarily into three so-called 'non-white race-based' townships of greater Johannesburg, provides a historical case for the possibilities and prospects of nation formation and social cohesion in post-apartheid South Africa. The emergent townships were: Lenasia (Indians), Eldorado Park (Coloureds), and Soweto (Africans), particularly Orlando and Meadowlands.

'Coolie Location' was established in what is today's Newtown. Although established together with 'Kaffir Location' and 'Malay Location' as 'sanitary areas', presumably to safeguard the white population from 'contamination', it was an officially neglected slum.

Of the 3,000 inhabitants of the area only about half were of Indian descendent. Most were black Africans. The outbreak of bubonic plague in 1904 gave the authorities an excuse to raze the area to the ground and the residents of 'Coolie Location' were temporarily resettled to Klipspruit, which is today's Pimville in Soweto.

After a while these former residents of 'Coolie Location' moved to settle in 'Malay Location', one of the few areas in Johannesburg without restriction to black residential settlement, adding significantly to its multicultural development of Malay, Coloured, African, Indian and some Chinese inhabitants. It was a place not unlike District Six and Sophiatown because of its popularly known dynamism and vibrancy.

The community was integrated residentially and commercially and comprised African, Indian, Coloured, Malay and Chinese people of Hindu, Christian, Muslim and indigenous African faiths. There were workers, professionals, shopkeepers, sangomas[22] and artisans; there were mosques and churches. There were bioscopes[23], shebeens and corner cafes; alleyways, backyards and *stoeps*[24], and the internationally famous 14th Street bazaar.

Of Fietas, Peter Abrahams in his autobiography *Tell Freedom* (1954)[25]

---

22. Traditional doctors.
23. The South African name for a cinema.
24. Verandahs.
25. *Tell Freedom*, Faber and Faber, 1982.

captured its spirit thus: '… and from the streets and houses of Vrededorp, from the backyards and muddy alleys, a loud babble of shouting, laughing, cursing, voices rise, are swallowed by the limitless sky, and rise again in unending tumult. And through, and above, and under, all this is the deep throbbing hum of the city. It is everywhere at once without beginning, without end'.

A snapshot of the locality on any day may show children playing cricket, soccer and *kennetjie*[26] in the streets, watched from *stoeps*[27] by their families and neighbours; *langarm*[28] dancing at the Springbok Hall and *umqomboti*[29] drunk in the shebeens; busy barbers, cobblers, watchmakers and bazaars; the sounds of jazz, *kwela*[30] and *qawali*[31] – and a nickname for almost everyone.

Already well before the implementation of apartheid laws, black people in Vrededorp were subjected to discriminatory legislation. Under the 1927 Native Urban Areas Act and the 1934 Slums Act the removal of African people began from sections of Vrededorp. They were moved to Orlando East, pioneering what eventually grew to become the townships of Soweto. Very many African people, however, continued to live in Fietas.

In 1948, the National Party came to power on its now infamous apartheid ticket. In 1950 the Group Areas Act, by which separate 'racially' designated areas were established, became state policy.

As a consequence, Fietas, like other mixed urban settlements, was to be demolished; its inhabitants dispersed to the new segregated townships. This came to pass through the protracted and desultory implementation of the Group Areas Act from 1956 to 1977.

Testimonies by the displaced former residents of Fietas in Lenasia, Eldorado Park, Meadowlands, Orlando and Riverlea reveal that the historical impact of the Group Areas Act went beyond the bulldozing of homes and the resettlement of its residents. It disrupted the possibilities of the emergence of an integrated urban community and decimated a diverse and dynamic site of cultural interaction and exchange, replacing it with conditions for profound social and cultural alienation. In effect it ripped the social and cultural fabric of the community apart and uprooted people from a place that had become home.

The corrosive social effects of these violent displacements would inflict

---

26. A street game fashioned from sticks that includes elements of bat and ball games.
27. Verandahs.
28. A form of ballroom dancing.
29. Traditional beer.
30. Pennywhistle-based African jazz music.
31. A form of Indian music played with harmonium and tablas.

deep social wounds and resentments on generations of former inhabitants of the area and their descendants.

The effect of this was to consign the entire population to ethnic ghettoes that would assume a grand plan with the adoption of the Homeland Policy of the apartheid government in the 1960s. The former inhabitants of Fietas, once friends and neighbours, found themselves separated and insulated in their respective 'racially' conceived ethnic ghettoes. Over the years the gulfs would widen.

Rather than being an exaltation of the past, the subject is critical both in its historical and present manifestations but perhaps more significantly in its future-directedness; drawing, as the case study seeks to do, on past experiences and the fabric of those societies as resources for future reckonings.

As a case signifier, however, the subject canvasses more than just Pageview. It is an integrated historical and spatial interrogation of issues of social cohesion and nation formation that traverses:

- a genesis from the late 1800s Johannesburg settlements of 'Malay', 'Coolie' and 'Kaffir' Locations;
- the cosmopolitan development and experience of the Pageview/Vrededorp locality of at least the 1930s up to the late 1970s, and
- the subsequent race-based Group Areas Act period settlements of Lenasia, Eldorado Park and Soweto, to the present.

This demarcated historical perspective allows for the tracking of processes of social interaction and assimilation; national and local identity formation; and the making, constitution and destruction of integrated community – all of which speak to the questions of nation formation and social cohesion.

The latter, in particular that of the making, constitution and destruction of Fietas, is rich in its offerings of a practical concept of social cohesion that is little, if at all, factored into discourses of social cohesion.

While challenged by experiences of racial, class, religious and ethnic tensions and divides, the overwhelming subject narrative of Fietas proclaims it to have been richly integrated to the point of spawning a fused local identity including: its race, class, religious and ethnic identities; its multi-residential, commercial, social and recreational nature; its local economy; its spatial design that inadvertently encouraged community bonding.

In this the experience of Fietas, it is argued, provides a touchstone for a deeper concept of social cohesion – one that is brought into relief by the destruction of the locality and the experience of dislocation under the Group Areas Act of 1950 and other pre-apartheid legislation. While black, Coloured and Indian residents were moved to new townships on the periphery of the city, the small number of Chinese people who were seen as members of the Fietas community fell through the cracks. No separate Chinese areas were established by apartheid legislation. Chinese South Africans went on to be allowed to live in white-designated areas as long as the white residents did not object.[32]

Primary and secondary sourced subject interviews and primary field observations provided the basis for analysis. Primary research subjects were randomly sourced, often with interviewed subjects providing the follow-on leads to further subjects, but selected in general by them being resident in, or associated with, the following specific localities:

- Pageview
- Vrededorp
- Lenasia (in particular Extensions 8 and 9)
- Thembelihle Extension 9, Lenasia
- Eldorado Park (in particular Extension 1)
- Orlando East, Soweto
- Orlando West, Soweto
- Meadowlands, Soweto.

Thembelihle as a locality is of particular interest in that it is an informal settlement populated by black African residents in the midst of a locality in Lenasia that is primarily populated by South Africans of Indian descent. The dynamics of the relationship between these communities, contrastingly homogenised on race and class lines, is of interest to the challenges to, and prospects for, social integration.

While white subjects may be deemed to be under-represented in the study, an account was sourced from one white Afrikaner woman about life in an old white section of Vrededorp, with some relevance to the study.

---

32. Park, Yoon Jung (January, 2011). *Living In Between: The Chinese in South Africa.*

ACTORS' PERSPECTIVES, MEANINGS AND INTERPRETATIONS

That Fietas came to be an integrated community with a shared identity draws attention to the early history of Johannesburg and the historical processes that fed the development of shared local and national identities. Fietas, as has been described, had its antecedent populations in the officially established racial localities of 'Coolie Location', 'Malay Location', and 'Kaffir Location', which in the late 1880s likely lacked a sense of common identity among and between its peoples. While the officially defined racial localities may suggest a strict separation, this was not necessarily so in practise. In 'Coolie Location', for example, almost as many African people lived there as Indians. Processes such as the development of the economy, urbanisation, the role of political resistance movements and everyday processes of social interaction, mutual influence and assimilation may be projected to have fostered a sense of a common 'South Africanness' over time. These processes are flagged for further study as factors for social cohesion.

The everyday social interaction and mutual assimilation between people at the time and their impact on the development of shared ways of living is particularly interesting for defining aspects of South African culture. Period accounts of this, however, are hard to come by and, if contemporary accounts are anything to go by, would have been hard to define.

Belinda, a young woman in Eldorado Park, for example, said she lived 'the South African lifestyle' but was patently unable to articulate a definition of it. She said she did 'the normal things that South Africans do, sitting at home doing nothing, talking about other people, you know ...' (But it must be established that these processes as factors for cohesion are contradictory.[33])

Economic development, for example, while promoting some aspects of cohesion may also undermine others. As far back as the early twentieth century, Gandhi alluded to the loss of fraternity between people as a result of early Johannesburg's development:

> ...the citizens of Johannesburg do not walk but seem as if they run. No one has the leisure to look at anyone else, and everyone is apparently engrossed in thinking how to amass the maximum wealth in the minimum of time.[34]

---

33. Field notes, 2011.
34. Quoted in Itzkin, E. (2000) *Gandhi's Johannesburg: Birthplace of Satyagraha*. Wits University Press.

Being South African

All the subjects interviewed identified themselves as South African, however diversely this is held, interacting with racial, ethnic and other identities, sometimes fluidly and other times as static separate identities. Among the various ways in which this national identity was claimed and defined were: by birthplace; 'blood'; 'lifestyle'; the right to vote and the act of voting in national elections, and support for the national soccer and rugby teams.

One instance in which the diversity of South Africans found unified expression was in reaction to the influx of foreign nationals, seeing them as competitors for resources, an economic threat, unmindful of South African rules and regulations and responsible for crime. Among the so-called 'Coloured' and 'Indian' South Africans there is some vulnerability to the claim of a South African identity. Among the factors raised for this is the perceived privileging of black Africans by black economic empowerment and affirmative action policies. On the other hand, black Africans view the historical hierarchy of apartheid as a persisting disadvantage.

In another example, Rashid, an Indian resident in the mixed-race Extension 13 Lenasia, the site of controversial Housing Department demolitions of illegally built homes (many by black Africans), felt accused of being non-South African for not joining African neighbours in street protests against the demolitions.

'We always knew we are South Africans; we are born here, we are part of this place ...'[35] he felt challenged to assert. Black Africans in post-apartheid South Africa, it would seem, are rarely, if ever under pressure to defend their South Africanness – unless if suspected of being illegal foreigners by the police.

Rashid's view that the homes were built illegally and that it was wrong to break the law and to protest violently is indicative further of other general racialised differences among South Africans that are not to do with racial and ethnic identities per se. In this case it relates to historical differentiations in socio-economic conditions and generally different experiences and cultures, identities if you will, of social protest.

On the other hand, others, like Tiffany in Eldorado Park, often positively point to the way Africans 'stand together' in lamenting their condition. 'Coloureds look more down on each other: I'm ... better than her,' she says.[36]

---

35. Field notes, November 2012.
36. Field notes, August, 2012.

IDENTIFICATION WITH PLACE

One of the findings emerging from the fieldwork is that identification with place is a strong factor of the sense of identity that people may have. This is true not only of a country but of local places as well, right down to street level – and including the Group Areas localities to which communities had been uprooted. Many people carried the identities of their former places of residence into the new localities. (A case of carrying one's roots with one it would seem.)

Respondent Newone, unemployed and with an alcohol problem, in Extension 1 Eldorado Park says Eldorado Park (to which he and his family were forcibly relocated from Fietas) was a 'breeding ground for gangs ... different people were moved in from different areas and they went up against one another according to the area they were from. There was fighting because each group stuck together on their own ...'[37]

Later, as the residents got to know one another, the tensions disappeared and new ones arose as gangs in Extension 1 started to take on gangs from other Extensions in Eldorado Park.

Eventually, Newone grew to 'love Eldos', made 'new friends'[38] and developed an identity associated with his new place of residence.

For the younger generations, who did not have a prior experience of residence in pre-Group Areas locations, the new townships of their birth readily assumed a place in their sense of identity:

'We are all from Orlando West[39],' says Lerato, an artist who grew up on Vilakazi Street, now famous for being the street where the home of Nelson Mandela was situated. For Tiffany, *'Eldo's is my kasie'*[40]; although she aspires to have her own family home elsewhere than in Eldorado Park. Migration, whether driven and influenced by policy or not, is a feature of South African lives and new identities of place are continuously adopted.

The Ahmed Kathrada Foundation, for example, in community group dialogues it had organised as part of its mission to promote 'non-racialism', was struck by accounts of people's life journeys from one place to another – often because of poor living conditions and in search of suitable housing. For many, this was 'the fourth or fifth stop on their way to decent housing'.[41]

Even within a shared identity of place there may co-exist tensions related

---

37. Field notes, July 2012.
38. Popular name given to Eldorado Park.
39. Field notes, March 2012.
40. Vernacular term for 'location'. Field notes, August 2012.
41. Shan Bolton, CEO, Ahmed Kathrada Foundation.

to this; for example, as Newone described: tensions between residents of different Extensions, who all may cohere as residents of the same township.

These fractures also exist along lines of race, ethnicity, class and the like within the coherence held as South Africans. The case of Fietas is particularly instructive in this regard: in the multiple factors that contributed to a very strong sense of cohesion as a community, which simultaneously enjoyed multiple identities.

ON PRESENT-DAY FIETAS: PROSPECTS

Ntate Modimokwe: Pageview[42]
Ntate Modimokwane, 58 years old, observes that currently Fietas is different because some community places have been taken away; for example the historical sports field, Queen's Park Grounds, which is now a bus depot. The current Fietas has lost its former leadership and has no one speaking on its behalf. The Fietas Festival is a commemoration of the past: a nostalgic reflection on what was and what could have been. It stems from stored memories of Fietas that the organisers want to recapture and maybe re-live as a reflection of what the place represented for them whilst also trying to capture that which was lost as a result of the forced removals. Ntate sees the current Fietas as having too many wide open spaces (under unresolved land claims and unable to be developed) and does not understand why they were moved from there if there is this huge space. Homeless people are now using these open spaces as living areas.

Susan[43] and her husband: Vrededorp[44]
Susan is a historical white Afrikaner resident of Vrededorp: 'I don't know who stays here anymore – I do not know who to trust'. At one point there were complaints about 'illegals' (immigrants) moving in and corrupting the area. Similarly, the main complaints about the degradation of the area came back to problems with what had happened to the empty plots in the area (the result of what appears to be a demolition campaign in the early- and mid-1990s, though an explanation was not forthcoming) and the abandoned buildings – particularly the idea that outsiders were claiming them for use in informal businesses involving recycling (which causes debris to accumulate in the streets), mechanics (causing problems and scrapyards and taverns, etc.

42. Field notes, April 2012.
43. Not her real name.
44. Interview, June 2012.

and to living in often overcrowded spaces). These complaints are not only about outsiders coming in but also about them being a corrupting force in a formerly solely residential area.

At one point in the interview there was a brief but vitriolic discussion of the New Nation School, the darling of the city, and many NGOs and charities.[45] Susan and her husband pointed to the school as a major source of injustice for the children in the area saying that it is 'their school' but that they are forced to go to school in Brixton, which is a long way for them to walk and relatively expensive for them to bus to. They insist that the children who do go to that school are brought in from Soweto and that it is unfair.[46] Susan linked the 'loss' of this service to the removal of the local clinic to be consolidated with one in another area. Similar vitriol was reserved for the residents of the 'old "Perskor"[47] building' (the homeless shelter where Ntate Modimokwe lives), which has been occupied by homeless people and contains, in Susan's view, the sum total of all social ills possible in an urban space – it represents for her, and many others in the community (especially property owners) the major problems facing the area, and as she put it was one of the core concerns at all community meetings: 'Empty stands, Perskor building and illegal businesses, those are the three things that always come up'. These social ills include a reference to HIV, saying that it functions partly as a brothel and thus is a locus of the illness – this harkens back to the 'sanitation syndrome' described at the beginning of the chapter which refers to the way in which disease and sanitation are used to demand the removal of the urban poor to peripheries, in particular in the case of the invention of the South African township.

Susan's actual involvement is having organised a residents' association (which her husband interestingly feels, despite the prevalence of absentee landlords, should really be a property owners' association: simply being a resident does not provide an equal voice). This is born of a close relationship with, in particular, the pensioners, who have long relied on her to make phone calls for them, either to the police or to the municipality. This, she says, is partly because they are intimidated by the people who have settled near them (she says that all the major abuses take place in the vicinity of the pensioners' houses, though this was not obvious from the tour of the area, and might involve a slightly warped understanding of how informal business

---

45. It is a school specifically catering to homeless children and those in shelters.
46. No evidence was offered that there is a concerted effort to bring children from Soweto in to that school (field researcher).
47. An old established publishing company in South Africa.

people think of their businesses, that is, in terms of the enforcement of the law). Apart from this she attends all the local meetings of the South African National Civic Organisation (SANCO) branch for the councillor's feedback; and those of the ANC branch and those that take place in Pageview (apparently separate); and at all of which she claims to be very vocal. This she has been doing since the early '90s (having been employed before as a nurse), though there was repeated reference to the ways the community 'used to hang together before' and so it is possible that she got involved when she noted that this was no longer the case and that the area was changing.

Commentary on Susan's narrative

The gentrification of the area would drive up the rates payable and push much of the community out; possibly including Susan and her husband too. The thinking is that the area should be well maintained and looked after as are wealthier suburbs; but presumably that this should be for the benefit of existing property owners, isolated from the results of opening the area up to the market. This is just what this sort of neighbourhood was designed to be – a transitional space.

Susan talked about her vision for what could become of the area. Having said that it 'should be the elite', she said that why the area really needed to attain this was for 'the Indians to come back'. As she put it: 'They have the money to build; they can develop the area.' Her thinking is that the shops could reopen, and there could be legal businesses there and the result would be that there would be investment in the properties (thus assuming that the council would release the vacant land, something she had previously said they refused to do, essentially as a result of administrative atrophy). She said that 'if the Indians can come back, then I can stop, then I can die. Then everything will be fine'.

She found it 'easier to communicate with the Indians than with other groups'. I asked if this was a language issue, to which she responded that 'yes, some of them even speak some Afrikaans, but I just find it easier'. Language for her is not really the issue (though in reality this might be an interplay between race and class rather than simply one or the other).

BEYOND FIETAS: CONTEMPORARY PERSPECTIVES

Rasheed Subjee[48]: Lenasia

Subjee claims that he does not know who the leader of the ward in the area is, or who the representative is. Also, most of the people who voted for the ANC who stayed in informal houses thought they would get free houses.

He talks about Thomsville 'two rooms' in Lenasia Extension. It took the government a few more years before they built some more houses and shops. The first set of shops was by the administration building where they paid rent, water and lights. A sewerage system and the fixing of roads was done in 1968/69. The community was happy as it was progress. Today things have got worse: now nothing is done. Then they appreciated everything the government did. They applied and got houses because there were plenty.

He argues that although apartheid was bad, there was some good as people respected the law, hence low levels of crime. 'You felt safe and that you were not in a dark corner. It has lights because you can go to the cops ... nowadays ask someone if they feel that they will get 10 per cent of help from the police, that person will say not even one per cent. ... that time it was a bit bad, the truth is the truth you understand?'

None of their children received houses from the government. Rashid does not even know where they can apply. He says the younger family members will have to move to surrounding areas. All his nephews and nieces are scattered, implying the break-up of families.

Shadrack Motaung: Orlando West, Soweto[49]

One of the problems that affects social cohesion is the extent of corruption and nepotism, particularly at the governmental level (both provincial and national). Corruption for Shadrack, defined as when the few benefit from whom they know, is the biggest problem. He believes a nation is being built but questions what type, given that there are people in top positions who do not possess leadership qualities. He believes that politicians are not respectful, and are failing to build South Africa to be the best in the world.

Shadrack does acknowledge, however, a lot of improvement in the country: 'It's only a few people who mess up ... I do not identify with tenders being given to family or friends. Everybody has got to be afforded an equal opportunity. There has got to be transparency. Whatever happens has to happen through a process which is in place. I believe in things being done in

---

48. Field notes, November 2012.
49. Field notes, 2012.

such a manner like we are in church. Respect...'

Tiffany Jacobs: Eldorado Park[50]

Tiffany Jacobs believes that the current government should treat Coloured people as they do Africans. She believes that the government is racist. 'If you go to Soweto it looks really nice ... they can leave Standard 7 and get work ... if you do not know how to *kuluma*[51] you must just forget it ....' In Baragwanath[52] when she burned herself she went for a daily dressing: and they helped 'their people before they secured us. Why must one human being be treated differently from another?' she asks.

Tiffany wishes there were more schools or colleges to take in high school leavers. She was excited by a news report on *Morning Live*[53] that prospective school leavers would be attended to and absorbed into colleges. She feels that she is not a failure and can better herself through further studies.

Ntate Modimokwane: Pageview[54]

Ntate Modimokwane explains that lines of division are racial and are exacerbated by the City of Johannesburg in the house allocation. In the end, the homeless end up frustrating these people who have homes, which leads to invasions of houses like when Coloured people invaded houses in Fietas claiming that these were the houses from which they had been forcefully removed. 'People are feeling lost', having lost faith in the promises of housing that are given by the City of Johannesburg, which are not being fulfilled (Field notes, 2012).

Shan Bolton: Ahmed Kathrada Foundation[55]

'For Coloureds there was a sense of encroachment that their space was being taken over primarily by Africans: people flooding their schools, recreation centres and libraries.' These facilities were not understood as open to everybody, as Bolton states. 'It was a feeling of being under siege in some way.' Some of the Coloured people who had been more politically active blamed the municipalities for not providing enough services to both communities, bringing them into contestation and conflict around resources.

'People thought that unity could only be built around the tackling of a

---

50. Field notes, August 2012.
51. Zulu for 'talk'.
52. The largest hospital in South Africa.
53. South African Broadcasting Corporation morning television talk show.
54. Field notes, April 2012.
55. Interview, August 2012.

whole range of socio-economic issues in the area: facilities for kids were a major concern; drug addiction was a major concern for everybody; civic accountability of councillors, services in the area; poverty and unemployment across the board. Sessions where people could get to understand the different religions and cultural practises of people there in terms of different cultural days, heritage days and so forth … tackling issues of race and racism head-on did not come up at all.'

Doreen Roberts: Eldorado Park[56]
Doreen believes that social standing/class is the main differentiating factor in today's society.

Shadrack Motaung: Orlando West[57]
Shadrack, qualifying Doreen's point, says that class differences have changed people. They now look at one another through the prism of status and material wealth. 'Some people think they are better than others. They outsmart the rest. They are aloof. They are not at our level. They are high up there. You can look at the type of cars they are driving. It changes their humanity. They look down on those who do not have.' These class divisions have marked his community.

CONTRASTING PERSPECTIVES

Ntate Modimokwane[58] likens current living to watching a movie where people come together from all walks of life, and races, to watch. When the movie ends they all go their separate ways. For him, it's a brief getting together which is then shattered when the project is finished or completed, implying that the bonds that tie us together are not strong enough to keep us permanently together.

Shan Bolton reports that 'by and large it means we go to the mosque, we pray and then we move our separate ways.'[59] Again, the religious space is similar to that of residential or schooling: where people can come together as different races but still do not know how to understand and transcend issues of difference .

Junior Jacobs[60] says that previously in the training environment of the

---

56. Field notes, July 2012.
57. Field notes, July 2012.
58. Field notes, April 2012.
59. Interview, August 2012.
60. Field notes, March 2012.

South African Defence Force soldiers would not be mixed. The Indian battalion was trained in Lenasia, the Coloured battalion in Eersterivier in Cape Town and the black battalion in Kimberley. Only when it came to border duty did the soldiers mix. For border control they needed one another. If someone from the artillery had to protect Junior as a foot-soldier, he in turn had to protect the artillery soldier. Bushmen were present but the rest did not understand their language; 'another battalion would speak Tswana; another coming from Natal spoke Zulu; Griqua, Ovambos of "South-West"; Coloureds spoke "Dutch [Afrikaans]". All of you would be there in one front and had to protect one another ...' For Junior it was remarkable that despite their differences, including language, they all came to understand one another.

Trusting the State

Phindi Ncekana: Thembelihle[61]
One move saw the relocation of 3,000 people from Thembelihle to a formal settlement in Vlakfontein while others were removed to a new RDP settlement just east of Thembelihle that she calls 'Lehae'. Those people were immediately replaced, however, largely by people migrating to the city: some from other parts of Africa leading many residents to dub the area 'OAU'. Due to the further subdivision of stands, the area's population continued to grow: from 5,000 before the relocation to between 7,000 and 8,000 now. Interestingly, this relocation was the source of great conflict in the community when it was proposed, which resulted in some violence and intimidation on the part of people who did not want to move. This is partly explained by a general distrust of local government: many people refuse to believe that the area is really unsafe for building (despite subsidence already having set in in the north-western corner of the area).

Doreen Roberts: Eldorado Park[62]
Doreen Roberts feels that the government has not really supported them. She keeps hearing on the news what is being done by the government but never hears about anything happening in 'Eldos'. 'Eldos' used to fall under Soweto before demarcations took place; now they fall under the 'Deep South'. She claims that there is no development taking place in their area; she has attended meetings, was on ward committees and feels that they are going

---

61. Site and service township next door to Lenasia. Field notes, June 2012.
62. Field notes, July 2012.

nowhere. All that they can try to do is to improve where they live.

Des Jones[63]: Eldorado Park[64]

Des Jones points to what he regards as the differential development between Soweto and Eldorado Park. He says that Maponya Mall, Protea Gardens and Jabulani Mall are clear indicators of the kind of investment taking place in black communities. In the Eldorado Park commercial centre there are a couple of banks, a post office, a furniture store, a Shoprite supermarket and a few other stores. Maponya Mall has the movies, a McDonalds and even the parks are much better, including Dlamini Park, which has outdoor sports training facilities.

Nation Formation

Ntate Modimokwane[65] insists that nation formation can only become possible if people go back to the basics; and if we say how we should go forward as communities to find solutions for the problems that afflict them.

Phindi[66] mentions that active integration of her child's daily life into a different community at school is the method by which South Africa can become more socially cohesive; saying essentially that it is up to the younger generation in that they are already placed in social contact with people who are different from them.

Des Jones[67] asserts: 'My identity is South African ... I'm not sure whether I am Khoisan; I'm not sure but I'm still searching; I'm still searching for my true identity from the African soil. I know that I have British ancestry; I'm proud of it but somewhere along the line I did not reconnect with the Khoisan and all those other people. I'm now researching my life all over again to belong in this new South Africa. I know there is a place for me in this place. I want to belong to this South Africa. I'm alienated from the European lifestyle. I am proud of being a human being in the townships.'

Shan Bolton[68] says what became clear in the Ahmed Kathrada Foundation community dialogues is that culture and religion could be a new barrier. Interracial marriage was raised as an issue and people were asked what they would do were their children to marry across the colour line. One man said, 'I cannot allow it because it will be the end of the Zulu nation. If I allow my

---

63. Not his real name.
64. Field notes, 2012.
65. Field notes, April 2012.
66. Field notes, June 2012.
67. Field notes, July 2012.
68. Interview, August 2012.

daughters then it's the end of the Zulu nation; but if my son comes home with an Indian woman and she is prepared to accept all of the Zulu customs and starts to speak the language and all of that, I might consider it.'

Shan gave the example of Indian youth from Lenasia attending schools outside of the area or attending religious schools. Cricket teams and soccer teams are primarily organised along religious lines. Their social lives are also orientated along religious lines. The notion of an Indian community does not exist: 'there is a Muslim, a Hindu and a Christian community who have Indian roots. That fragmentation has not been clearly looked at and it exists across the country in a whole range of different ways.'

Victor Mokine[69] says that the high rates of violence against women and children and the growth of crime can be attributed to foreigners. But Victor acknowledges that in Sophiatown there was gender violence: 'the ordinary assault against women by gangsters: rape and so on.' He thinks that wrong influences from 'the North' have entered South African society. He believes that the Marikana miners are mixed with others who are prone to carrying assegais as the Tswana are generally known to be a peace-loving people and would never take on the police. He believes that *necklacing*[70] is particular to the Eastern Cape. A lot of miners who live in informal settlements are migrants from the Eastern Cape. The high level of poverty and corruption in the provinces is in the Eastern Cape. He does not want to say Xhosas are bad people but says they have a culture of violence.

Rashid Subjee[71] raised issues of race but the fundamental concerns were really around neighbours not understanding one another's religious, cultural and social practises. With funerals, for example, Africans have an extended ritual that includes an all-night vigil and singing, which was a new phenomenon for the Indian community. Some could not adjust and the police would be called in to stop the 'noise'. Africans were introduced to the practise of burying the dead in a short period of time. They also had to acclimatise to public events like the Hindu celebration of Diwali with its fireworks display and Eid (the breaking of the Muslim fast).

FACTORS PROMOTING EXCLUSION

Shan Bolton[72]

Shan says it was Indians (in Greenside, Johannesburg, a former white

---

69. Field notes, August 2012.
70. A brutal form of killing by placing a tyre around a person's neck and lighting it.
71. Field notes, November 2012.
72. Interview, August 2012.

suburb) who felt 'othered' by members of the white community in particular. They felt that they were regarded as foreign and that their religion was perceived as threatening and supportive of terrorism. Muslims and black people who attended Ahmed Kathrada Foundation dialogues thought whites to be extremely conservative and unwilling to share the space with anyone else.

African Muslims felt unaccepted by Indians in their communities and mosques. The sharing of common religious spaces was something people were grappling with, as Africans interacting with Indian Muslims felt a sense of inferiority, prejudice and being seen as 'different' when in places of prayer and worship.

At a workshop they attempted to explain the difficulty in converting to Islam in Soweto where it is seen by others as a minority religion. Indian Muslims, on the other hand, felt uncomfortable with expectations of support and expressed this rather as being badgered for charity.

Doreen Roberts[73]

Doreen does not like the term 'Coloured' inherited from the apartheid government. Since becoming involved in politics in 2000 she has engaged in a campaign to get the category 'Coloured' removed from all official forms. She feels that it is an obstacle to opportunity and progress and suggests that 'Coloured' should rather fall under 'black' with Zulu and Sotho instead of being a separate category. Having the term changed from Coloured to black would provide everyone with better economic opportunity as all would be categorised under one group.

Another issue for Doreen is that in the new democracy her age worked against her, whereas during apartheid, even though older, she would still be employable.

The injunction to speak an African language and to be from an obviously black cultural group is seen as further hindering access to economic opportunity: 'There may be freedom as in freedom to move around but not freedom in earning; jobs are still not accessible. As long as you have an English surname, your chance of getting jobs is so limited.' She states that Coloured youth are being asked if they can speak a black language. Given that the language in their community is Afrikaans and instruction at the schools is in English, how, she asks, are Coloured youth supposed to speak 'black language'? Doreen is concerned that the Afrikaans language and culture are going to be lost and with her community co-worker took a

---

73. Field notes, July 2012.

petition to a legislator, ' ... as Coloured people this is part of our culture and we feel that we are losing ....'

Identification with Place

Newone Daniels: Eldorado Park[74]
Newone, 65 years of age, unemployed and with an alcohol problem in Extension 1 Eldorado Park, says Eldorado Park to which they were forcibly relocated from Fietas was a 'breeding ground for gangs'. 'Different people were moved in from different areas and they went up against one another according to the area they were from. There was fighting because each group stuck together on their own. So if you were from Alex or Fietas or Kliptown with Kliptown ...'[75] Later as the residents got to know one another the tensions disappeared and new ones arose as gangs in one extension started to take on gangs from other extensions of Eldorado Park.

Tiffany Jacobs: Eldorado Park[76]
Tiffany is the last-born in a line of five children. She grew up in Eldorado Park where she has been living going on 20 years now. She describes 'Eldos' as her '*kasie*'. Everyone in Extension 1, she says, knows her as a 'people's person': sociable and outgoing. She sees herself having her own family and wants a house somewhere else, not in Eldorado Park.

Shan Bolton: Ahmed Kathrada Foundation[77]
Shan says that at two public meetings convened for the purpose of holding a conversation 20 participants were recruited. Initially there were only two Indians but that number grew to eight over the month of the programme. Facilitators used a methodology tracing points of origin and participants were surprised by the stories people told of where they had been born and how they had arrived in Lenasia. They had all travelled similar routes to get there and most had moved because of poor living and economic conditions. For many this was 'the fourth or fifth stop on their way to decent housing'.

Shadrack Motaung: Orlando West, Soweto[78]
Shadrack says he and his family went to live in rural Hammanskraal and also

---

74. Field notes, July 2012.
75. Field notes, March 2012.
76. Field notes, August 2012.
77. Interview, August 2012.
78. Field notes, July 2012.

went to stay with his grandfather in the North-West in Kgabalatsane. Eventually his mother moved to Johannesburg as a domestic worker and Shadrack went to stay with different members of his extended family because his mother had no home of her own. He stayed in Alexandra Township, Diepkloof and Sophiatown: 'It was a bit of a nomadic life.' This moving from place to place continued beyond his schooling years into his work life: for over 20 years he had lived with his extended family.

Hanif Patel: Lenasia[79]
Hanif referred to time spent in Lenasia South as an uncomfortable time because he could not form close relationships with his neighbours. This is because his neighbours were by and large from Durban and therefore seemed to have a fundamentally different culture – he felt he had too little in common with them to really integrate.

Belinda Daniels: Eldorado Park[80]
Belinda declares that she is a 'Coloured'. This is in part determined by her surname. What is her Coloured identity? 'It's difficult to explain that one ... how do you explain that ... can't we skip that one? I will say I am a Coloured, you are an African because your president is Zuma ... (ha, ha, ha) I wouldn't know ...' She is not sure of how 'Coloured' comes about; having both mother and father as Coloured 'means "mixed race" ... makes you Coloured or something ....'

CASE STUDY

The story of Thembelihle through the eyes of two community leaders

Mampi: Taxi owner, community activist and single mother[81]
Mampi first says that she is Zulu (both parents) and then corrects herself and says she is Swazi, her parents coming from Nelspruit to Johannesburg before she was born in 1954. She was one of three children and then one of two siblings passed away.

Mampi was born in Kliptown, grew up in Phiri (Soweto) and then moved to Dlamini (Soweto). She dreamt of being a lawyer one day but claimed she

---

79. Field notes, February 2012.
80. Field notes, August 2012.
81. Field notes, 2012.

had big problems that stopped her from proceeding. One of her problems was that she did did not pass her matriculation certificate. Mampi came to Thembelihle in 1988 from Soweto. She got land from the owner, 'Mr Steyn', who owned a brick factory (SA Block) in the area and provided the land for residential purposes. Others who moved to Thembelihle during this period came to farm. Mampi shares her story in a seating area outside her two-storey brick house. Chickens roam; cars and people move past on the wet dust road; some call to her.

In the 1980s residents liked the land because it was not a squatter camp; it was not crowded. They liked having shops in the surrounding Indian area of Lenasia and there was a bullet factory that created employment and paid a decent salary. There were also jobs in Vereeniging. After that she stopped formal employment and opened up her own tuck shop on her plot from where she sold liquor and groceries and became a community leader.

During the 1980s when she was young she was an 'activist'. During the apartheid era, she claims, the soldiers used to rape the people, 'the children'; and they raped and killed, including the young boys. Parents would collect bodies from Moroka police station with money, paying to have the body released. For Mampi, from the mid 1970s into the 80s Soweto was a place of strife, struggle and police brutality. She describes Thembelihle as being better: a place of peace where she could bring her two children and build a home, and now Thembelihle is that home.

Mampi's first house was in Section D Thembelihle, which she exchanged for land in Section N. It was 'said by the Indians' that the land in Thembelihle was dolomitic in 1992 and that is when negotiations around relocations from Thembelihle began.

Thembelihle residents were told at the time that they should move to Lenasia Extension 13. Some were happy to do so while others wanted to remain in Thembelihle. Only 50 people went to Extension 13 through an application process and most got houses. For others the option was to pay and receive a house after a two-year period. Mampi claims that people paid and did not get their houses. She further claims that the ward councillors promised houses and did not deliver. Today Mampi is a taxi owner, having bought a minivan and, as she asserts, she is just trying to serve the community.

As to her relationship with the Indian residents of Lenasia, Mampi has had limited interaction. In the 1980s Mampi's two elder children, both daughters, were under 10 years old. They resided in Eldorado Park with an uncle and were schooled at a mixed Indian school in the area. Mampi says that the children were not really accepted by the Indian community. In the mid-1990s, Mampi had financial problems and then went to work in Lenasia Extension 10 as a domestic worker. 'They gave me R6 for a lot of washing ... and you know you just wash from eight in the morning to two, and then for R6 for the day ....' This was in 1995. She did it for one day and never went back.

She recalls that during apartheid you called Indian employers '*Madam, Missus,* even to a child ... you mustn't just touch their plates; you mustn't use their toilets, but you wash the dishes; you just wash even the toilets, but you mustn't use the toilets, you must just go wherever, in the veld ....' Recently a woman told Mampi that 'they' (Indian employers) are just abusing her and that she gets R30 for the whole day for cleaning, looking after the dogs and doing the washing. She gets R800 per month after working for the family for more than 10 years.

Mampi is disillusioned by politicians. 'If you want the votes you just come to Thembelihle; the government just gets the votes from Thembelihle ....' Mampi proffers that she is a 'full' member of the ANC but is critical of some councillors who, according to her, are illegally selling houses in Thembelihle.

Thembelihle used to be a snake-ridden area until the residents cleaned it up. It was then, Mampi claims, that the Indian community asked for the Thembelihle inhabitants to be relocated to alternative land.

'This land was sold long ago by those Indians ... [to] those people who are selling ice cream.'

She says that Indians took themselves for Europeans and calls them lazy. She believes Indians to be racist, although '...others are more blacker than myself'. An indicator of racism, for her, is that in shops owned by Indians money is not exchanged by hand with black customers but is instead put on the counter. Mampi does admit that today things are better than in the past. 'It's better, but now they just hide ....'

A positive sign towards non-racialism would be changing the name from Lenasia. Mampi and others are calling for the entire area to be renamed 'Thembelihle Extension 1–13'. She says that the Indian community is against the idea as they understand the land of Lenasia to be theirs. There used to be an advertisement on a street board: 'At long last we found our brothers and sisters in our land, in Lenasia.' It hurts, because according to Mampi '... this is not their land; they did not even die for it; they did not even fight for it, but they just want that everything for them must just go easy, in our land'.

Mampi argues that multiracialism means fighting together. She wants equal development for both communities. 'You must be better; I must be better also. You must get electricity; I must get electricity also ...' Any improvement for the Indian community must also be undertaken for the Thembelihle community. Mampi does not feel the Indian community fights in solidarity with the Thembelihle community for their rights. There is no electricity in Thembelihle and so residents illegally tap into the street lights as a source of power, 'because we want a better place also ....' Getting arrested for electricity tapping she believes is wrong. Primer stoves, which provide light and warmth, are also a source of danger with shacks burning down and children consequentially dying.

When democracy arrived Mampi was very happy: 'We thought that maybe we would live like a king.' When asked what this means she says to live where race does not matter, and in multiracialism, to have no fear and not be suspicious of your neighbours. Yet this has largely not happened. For her the problem is that the ANC gives out money and the 'middle field are eating the money'. To deal with this matter she suggests that inspectors investigate the municipality and hold them accountable. She is angry about the Presidency hotline that was set up to help deal with complaints. She called several times and was put on hold and according to her nothing happened. She wanted to report a councillor for corruption.

For the future, what Mampi wants are basic services. 'If they do not give Thembelihle services, I mean they will just show us that they want us to fight with the Indians because we won't like to see other nations living better while we are suffering up to now ... we love them, then we must just live like them.' When asked how she feels about communities living in Bryanston and Sandton she responds, 'we just say they are living there because they have money.' Mampi targets Indians 'because of apartheid: they just want their things – to own the land as if it's theirs'. She wants the Indian community to stand up for the Thembelihle residents' rights on sanitation and build houses and act like brothers and sisters and fight for the Thembelihle residents living in the area. 'They isolate themselves because its Len/Asia. Now they just show us that they do not love us...'

Mampi says that she would not have a problem with Indians residing in Thembelihle. There are, according to her, 10 poor Indian residents. She would like her neighbours to live better lives, have their own houses, have nice streets – a better quality of life.

Despite all her other comments, Mampi says that she sees the Indian community of Lenasia as South African. She feels secure in her life 'because what they can do to me I will do to the Indians ... if they can just come and demolish ... we will do that [chase away the Indians] and go and stay that side ... we'll chase them because at least they've got land in India, their land, it's theirs, and we won't even go to that side (India)'.

At this point Edmund, Mampi's husband, who came and quietly sat in on the interview, interjects that an MEC from the Gauteng Province told the Thembelihle residents that they must move to Lehae. 'They are sent by the councillor to the Lenasia Municipality, which is controlled by Indians and they receive no assistance.' Whenever they ask for services they are told by an ANC councillor in Lenasia that they must leave Lenasia in order to get the services they request. The problem for them is that the ANC chooses councillors and not the community.

Edmund argues that the ANC is afraid of Indians because they have a lot of money: '... they are depending on them, they are rich ... Mandela was a good man because he was not depending on anybody ... he was not working for money, he was educated ... these people, they are here for money ... me, myself, I am very angry.' During 1976 he and others were fighting the system at school. 'I've got scars here, both knees, torn ligaments, because of the police, fighting for democracy. But today we are nothing. We are nothing ... If you talk too much they come in and arrest you, sometimes they shoot you ....'

Bhayiza Miya: Civic activist, businessman[82]
Bhayiza Miya has been a resident of Thembelihle for the past 17 years. He was born in Zola, and the family then moved to Dube in Soweto. From there his parents moved to Zuurberkom Community Farm for two years, and during that period Bhayiza moved to the Thembelihle informal settlement in Lenasia. That was in 1995.

By the time they moved to Zuurberkom (two kilometres from Lenasia) in 1990 Bhayiza was 23 years old. Bhayiza's parents had bought and sold the four-roomed apartheid government house in Dube and then bought the plot in Zuurberkom. White people moved from the area with the influx of Africans coming to reside in Zuurberkom so the Miya family got an eight-roomed house.

Bhayiza's father worked as a truck driver for over 30 years for a steel-making company up until his retirement. His mother worked as a supervisor at the Mariston Hotel in the city until she retired.

The Miya children knew Johannesburg Zoo, Pretoria Zoo, the Snake Park,

---

82. Field notes, November 2012.

Hartbeespoort Dam. They would cook and make provisions and then on a Sunday the whole family might visit the zoo. 'Those are the kinds of parents we had', Bhayiza says with pride.

Bhayiza only started to enjoy school in Dube when he was at secondary level. An elder brother had matriculated, and he was used as an example for the other siblings to exemplify. At a certain point Bhayiza had a problem with Afrikaans in Standard 8 and started missing school due to a harsh teacher who beat them. During her class she would tell them that if they were not trying they would be beaten up. He could not understand much Afrikaans so he and other pupils would leave the class. Then he took this as an opportunity to leave school entirely. He did not tell his parents about the challenges.

When he left school Bhayiza made it look like he was going to school every day. When they discovered that he was not attending school his parents insisted that he go to his mother's family in Lesotho to help with the family business. So Bhayiza relocated and learnt to speak Sotho and got his first job. Among their other businesses Bhayiza's mother's Lesotho family had a motel near the border gate for those travelling between South Africa and Lesotho which included a shop and a driving school. Bhayiza worked at the motel for two years but did not like it as he missed friends and playing soccer.

Soccer was a passion for Bhayiza and seemed an achievable dream. At a young age his friend Doctor Khumalo succeeded in entering professional soccer and this is what Bhayiza dreamt for himself. He tried out for three teams: 'Kaizer Chiefs, Pirates and Swallows' but did not make it.

He began to concentrate more on the business of the tuck shop he had set up. The business was lucrative and he ran it for three years. Then Bhayiza moved to Thembelihle where he says, '... there is nothing much for people to do to entertain themselves except alcohol.' In the 1990s, with the advent of democracy, certain economic freedoms came.

His father, Mr Miya, used to tell the children that the big eight-roomed house in Zuurberkom was the family house but that each child needed to get their own place – the family house was for holidays. Mr Miya did not want the siblings to fight amongst one another for the house. Ultimately, Bhayiza bought a place in Thembelihle for R600. 'What normally happens in these informal settlements is that you [the seller] go to the police station and do an affidavit and then that's it.' The affidavit is given to the buyer, and the buyer takes it to the councillor's office and then the buyer would go to SA Block[83] and the paperwork would be done.

---

83. The property owner.

Bhayiza started selling liquor. There was no electricity then but today they use electricity (albeit illegally). Fridays, Saturdays and Sundays are the busiest days, and Bhayiza would operate the business with his brother.

Bhayiza has four children with different mothers: two in Dube, the first of which he had at the age of eighteen. For Bhayiza, having his first child at that age was one of the most difficult things he could tell his parents. The mother of his first child was eventually accepted by the Miya family when the child was born. Today Bhayiza lives with his youngest, a four-year-old daughter, whilst the other children live with their mothers. He has three girls and a boy.

Developments since the advent of Democracy

Thembelihle was established in 1985, and by 1995, when Bhayiza moved there, there was a population in the thousands. Today, Bhayiza estimates that stands have grown in number from 3,500 to 7,000. With the advent of democracy came the prospect of economic freedom and Bhayiza was happy to have an ANC background because he saw that the freedom that was fought for manifested for him through ownership of a shop and being able to have his own business. This he understood as part of democracy. Indeed, democracy looked promising.

According to Bhayiza, since his arrival in Thembelihle up until the present there has been little interaction between the Thembelihle residents and the residents of Lenasia, except on the most functional basis. Bhayiza says that the majority of the Thembelihle inhabitants work as domestic servants and gardeners for the neighbouring Indian community. Thembelihle residents cross the road into the Indian community to get goods and some services and then return to the settlement. That is the extent of interaction.

In explaining the distant relationship, Bhayiza says that there were signs that the Indian community were not happy about Thembelihle since its inception as it was associated with a rise in crime: 'Since us coming here in Thembelihle, the crime has gone up.' He mentions burglary, house robbery and car theft as the main crimes. The person he claims who had interaction or a working relationship with the Indian community/business people is the current MMC for Housing/Thembelihle former councillor Dan Bovu.

It took some time for Bhayiza to develop his social consciousness. He was living in Thembelihle for a long time, not helping anyone just taking care of himself and his family. In 1997/1998 he became, as he describes, 'close to the community' because he got involved in social issues, specifically helping to register school kids into the local Lenasia schools. 'I could see the living conditions of people who did not have anything ... their living conditions were very bad.' For instance, in Thembelihle Bhayiza saw people fight over chicken skins. 'Being Muslim, they would throw away the chicken skins. People would fight over them and one guy was stabbed to death ... in some shacks, seeing what kids are eating, then you would tell yourself, "No, we haven't reached the democracy that I spoke about earlier."'

Some of the shacks have been occupied and managed by child-headed households and others by pensioners living with their unemployed children and grandchildren in a single shack, abused because their children want access to the grants.

Bhayiza believed that he would end up living in a formal dwelling through democracy. Most people living in Thembelihle believed that in five to ten years they would end up residing in a formal area. 'The majority of us were saying: at long last we will have our own houses to live in. The roofs we were fighting for were not shacks ....'

The reason for the poor conditions in which many Thembelihle residents live is, according to Bhayiza, twofold: the majority of the residents are working as gardeners/domestic workers for the adjacent Indian community by whom he believes they are underpaid and exploited. 'Our Indian community or neighbours are exploiting our people.' He says that domestic workers earn R6.50 an hour in an industry where they should be paid R20 an hour. The second issue is that since government's new laws for domestic and farm workers the employers 'have changed their strategy' so that domestic workers will instead work two times a week and at the end of the month their salary will be R400. 'So people are living from hand to mouth ... some people are paid with food and old clothes.'

Unemployment is a major factor and most people are engaged in 'piece work'[84]. There are no sports facilities that help keep youth away from liquor and drugs. People are selling drugs within the Indian community (drugs can be bought from people's houses) but not inside Thembelihle, although there is a growing number of Nyaope[85] users. Youths who are on Nyaope will steal anything that they can. 'They'll even rip off your gate and go and sell it.' Even vigilante justice, according to Bhayiza, 'people's justice' does not deter them. Alcohol is another problem.

Bhayiza has seen a marked change in crime from 1995 to the present. 'If

---

84. 'Piece work' means working ad hoc.
85. Nyaope is a cocktail of drugs with heroin and marijuana as the principal ingredients. Cocaine, HIV antiretroviral pills, and a powder found in plasma TVs are mixers.

you want to do any crime you should be doing it outside, not inside Thembelihle.' If you came with goods from outside Thembelihle people would buy the goods. 'Even if we are being chased by our Indian community coming into Thembelihle they would be protected by us in the camp.' The Thembelihle community saw criminals as Robin Hoods: stealing from those who have for people who do not.

'But now it's worse …! People are stealing now *inside* Thembelihle because now they are being shot at by our Indian neighbours. It's easier for them to steal here than to steal at other Extensions.' So in effect there used to be permissible crime but now because of the Indian community protecting itself with arms the way of doing crime has changed. 'We promoted something that at the end of the day was now killing the very same community that allowed it to happen.'

From his time in Dube, Bhayiza used to be a member of the ANC. When it seemed that no developmental change was coming to Thembelihle he left the ANC and in 2001, during a forced removal protest, joined a social movement called the Anti-Privatisation Forum (APF). This is where he learnt about issues confronted by women and children. The Thembelihle Crisis Committee was initiated.

During the 2001 forced removal protest residents of Thembelihle resisted plans to move them to Vlakfontein. As an ANC member, Bhayiza at first could not see why people were resisting the government. But Bhayiza himself did not want to move from Thembelihle because his children were closer to the schools, the clinic and other amenities. In Vlakfontein there was nothing except for what were called 'VIP' toilets[86].

He describes the incident that changed his life: He was on the side of the ANC during the protest. That day the police started to shoot rubber bullets and Bhayiza tried to mediate to get the community to stop throwing stones. It was not helping so he went to stand on the side with a journalist from *The Star* newspaper. Bhayiza claims that he was standing far away from the protest itself and was shot in the face and lost seven teeth. Bhayiza went to Baragawanath and when he came back he opened a case against the police and then he, in turn, was arrested. The police picked him up at one in the morning. They wanted to know about the case that he had opened. They were sent by the MEC of Safety to pick up Bhayiza to give a statement. When he arrived at the police station around five that morning, others had also been arrested for their involvement in the protest. The outcome was that the

---

86. Ventilated improved pit latrine.

police said that, despite his protestations of being an innocent bystander who was shot by the police, Bhayiza was implicating himself in the very statement that he was making. This is why he joined the Crisis Committee in that year, 2001, when some Thembelihle residents were to be forcefully removed to Vlakfontein.

Around Thembelihle Bhayiza says there are four primary schools and one secondary in the Indian area and all the children in Thembelihle attend these schools. There are clinics. There is a place where chicken pieces, fruit and vegetables and two litres of milk can be purchased for R5. Moving to Vlakfontein would mean losing access to all of this for Thembelihle residents. Additional transport money – R300 per child per month – is needed for children who had relocated and had to attend school in Lenasia. One girl's mother could no longer afford transport fare and the girl was raped walking to school. Most people want to live in Thembelihle because the employment, amenities, schools, shops, police station are in the area.

Bhayiza believes that 'where there is money the ANC leadership will be there; where there are tenders, where there are subcontractors, they will be there. But when there are issues and challenges that are facing the community they do not even attend [to the problems]...' He recalls how the Crisis Committee helped ANC leaders to get their children into schools since they knew the policy better than the ANC leaders and that this is a big concern. 'The ANC's main focus is tender, tender, and tender ...' If there are functions of the ANC in the area they are being catered for by the Indian community.

According to Bhayiza the Crisis Committee had evidence and received numerous allegations that some ANC comrades were, and are, selling stands in Thembelihle to 'people that are coming from outside'. He claims nothing has been done about the matter.

Bhayiza believes that in solidarity with other communities in Gauteng a social movement can be developed for issues confronted by informal settlements. He argues that the conditions for the Thembelihle inhabitants will only change through the residents themselves.

In 2006, Bhayiza converted to Islam through reading Islamic literature that his brother, a metro cop, used to bring around. 'It was closer to my culture the way I should be looking after my family ... you know, what my father taught me was intertwined with Islam, there was a link ...' He converted to Islam through a relationship with a Muslim woman. He laughs at the question of whether she was Indian and retorts that he cannot get an Indian woman. 'It's a crime.' His partner was black. 'When it comes to intermarriage with the Indians, it does not happen.'

Bhayiza attends the mosque in Lenasia. He states that as a Muslim he finds that the most cruel people are Muslims of Indian origin. He argues that Afrikaners/white people exploit and discriminate '... but Indians are worse. There are mothers that are being employed by them that are not allowed to use their toilets and ... go to the bush to relieve yourself. Your plate and spoon, they will be outside. You do not take it inside a Muslim house, you do not ...'. According to Bhayiza, Hindus and Christians within the Indian community seem to treat Africans better than Muslims. 'Coming to the mosque itself, even if you give a *salaam* to an Indian Muslim ... as Muslims when you meet you must greet ... when you say *salaam* as an African, as a black person, he [the Indian] will look the other direction [and say *salaam* quickly] or maybe even not responding to your *salaam*. But with me ... I do not greet them.' He goes into the mosque and stands next to the door, prays and then goes home.

A CITY RESPONSE

Zunaid Khan, Mayoral Committee, Johannesburg City Council[87]
Zunaid Khan's area of expertise is housing policy and research for the City of Johannesburg. Zunaid says that across national, provincial and local government in the respective housing departments, the policies that are at play are all geared towards integration and social cohesion on various levels: from typology of housing to various levels of tenure. The policy frameworks have gone a long way to ensuring that whatever delivery agenda is available at the local level, including large-scale projects, it has to gear itself towards social integration: what is referred to as a 'sustainable human settlement'.

The Integrated Residential Programme is thus one of the key housing programmes found in the national housing code. It is one of the largest programmes for the City of Johannesburg and is comprised of mixed-use development projects: rental, social housing, RDP, tenure types, gap market housing and fully-bonded homes. It includes access to social, health and educational facilities and works across various spheres of government to deliver in these areas. It also includes access to local economic development opportunities as that is a critical part of the housing delivery agenda. The idea is to redress the apartheid model (of dormitory-style townships) by

87. Field notes, December 2012.

creating small towns. The programmes within the national housing code are geared towards cities (as they are implementing agents) to ensure that social cohesion exists. Within that, the allocation process looks at people from a range of different backgrounds across a range of incomes, rather than race groups. 'The idea is to use the physical landscape to facilitate social cohesion.' The reason Zunaid uses the term 'facilitate' is because social cohesion cannot be forced. Irrespective of what is put physically into the ground, how people tend to use housing may not be as intended by the architect/designer.

In the urban environment the city has focused on mixed housing. Zunaid cites Cosmo City, Lufareng, Lehae and Pennyville as examples of social cohesion housing. The city's social housing institution, the Johannesburg Social Housing Company, has conducted a range of different projects across the city proper to try and integrate and provide access to affordable rental houses for a range of different communities. It has had relatively measured success with social cohesion as it also comes down to the dynamics between people. The city is made up of a tapestry of little enclaves and communities that congregate where they share an identity. Zunaid cites New York as an example and parallels Johannesburg. In Johannesburg there is the Somalian quarter on the western side, the Ethiopian quarter on eastern side, the Nigerians in one part of Berea and the Congolese in a section of Yeoville. It is not that they are segregated physically but they conglomerate in areas where they share an identity around religion, culture, even food. Fordsburg is another example of religion and food around which people cohere.

Zunaid spoke of a project where a social housing development was done in a largely middle- to upper-middle-income neighbourhood, and there were initial concerns regarding property values and a range of issues around social dynamics. But the neighbourhood went forward in partnership with the city and made a success of the project. Alexandra Township is another example where the city has made an effort with different housing typologies and access to different people to get people to co-exist. These initiatives form part of the city's programme to address social cohesion.

'As South Africans, for so long we have been segregated and to a large extent we remain so. It's going to take some time. Lenasia, Eldorado Park, Soweto, people in those neighbourhoods are looking for expansion and increase in supply in those areas; more of the same if you will. There is the example of how with some of the older person facilities people want to be segregated. As a post-apartheid democratic state that is just not feasible. It flies in the face of all the policy instruments we have, and the national mandate of delivering sustainable human settlements.'

ON THE SUBJECT OF SUSTAINABLE HUMAN SETTLEMENTS

According to Zunaid, sustainable human settlements have to be strategically located, cannot be racially exclusive, must be integrated and should include mixed tenure types and mixed typologies and be socially habitable with recreational facilities, amenities and social services – educational, healthcare and economic development services — creating, in effect, a microcosm of a small city.

For the city itself, he says the council has prioritised affordable housing and a range of different rentals so as to give people access to the opportunity of housing where there is access to major transportation hubs.

'Brickfields' in Newtown is an example. It is the first time in 20 years that the City of Johannesburg has built residential units inside its inner city. The idea was to offer accommodation to people needing to live close to transport hubs and better services because the statistics in South Africa showed that citizens were spending close to two thirds of their income on transportation. Where there is a transport hub and available land, city policy says the land should be maximised through the erection of social housing – a critical integration tool.

There is a social housing institution (not-for-profit company) called the Johannesburg Social Housing Company (JOSHCO) which is city-owned and administers projects, runs campaigns, advertises, makes lease agreements and manages the properties. JOSHCO benefits through land prioritised through the city's processes so that they can make land affordable. Pageview, Vrededorp and Fietas have been targeted for such urban development approved by the city.

However, says Zunaid, processes do take time as they run through a cluster-based system. With the Urban Development Framework having been approved, it will be incorporated into Johannesburg's greater development framework to say that 'in this area these are the controls and this is what the city is looking to do because it meets the objectives of the city'. The city had a 30-year time frame from 2010 encapsulated in the Growth and Development Strategy (GDS) and Vision for 2040. All programmes will cascade from this vision. There was an intensive two-year public engagement to determine where the city would like to see itself in 30 years. Out of that process the city has planned over three decades and does an assessment

(Integrated Development Plan [IDP]) every five years; and within that there is an urban development framework and regional spatial development framework that will include Region B (which includes Pageview, Vrededorp and Fietas), thus bringing them into that regional spatial framework. Once that has been done there can be approval on how the area as a whole will be developed.

Phuthadichaba in Alexandra Township was one of eight pilot projects in the city to provide transitional accommodation for homeless and relocated people. This was part of inner city regeneration, particularly around its major transportation hubs used by the homeless as residential space. They were then transferred to this facility as a place where they could be 'transformed'. They would enter on a six month basis at R50 a head. Accommodation, with a range of training programmes and skills development, would be provided to help individuals and families transition, following which they could access affordable rental in the city. Increases in tariffs, leading to a boycott by residents to pay rental, as well as the stipulated six-month time frame being too short a time for transition, saw the initiative falling apart.

ENVIRONMENTAL CHALLENGES IN THEMBELIHLE AND SPACES BETWEEN TOWNSHIPS

Zunaid was asked about the prospective building of the Trade Route Mall in Lenasia and not Thembelihle, purportedly situated on a large piece of dolomite. His response was that if the city were to develop it as a residential site it would not be able to house all the people living there at the moment. Capacity on dolomite is limited, especially for low cost/RDP housing because of the nature of the rock. Extensive engineering is required to ensure that the site and structures will not collapse because the area is prone to sink-holes.

The risks on these sites, he asserts, are excessive. Usually they make the best industrial, recreational retail centres. The retail centre can spread its footprint over a large base and is usually very light in structure. The developers are also able to pay for deep foundations for the structure to hold. This is not possible for the State, whose subsidy quantum is R56 000 per house.

If dolomite collapses, it runs the risk of killing 'quite a lot of people' as well as a 'collapse of infrastructure'. 'The city is liable for its residents and where it places their development and the long-term urban management that is required to manage the water tables as well as the cost ...' Lenasia has an ad hoc nature to its development because of the dolomite, which is often pocked by masses of open land.

'Toxicity of the soil is also an issue ... but South Africa, being what it is, it comes down to an issue of race. Things get racialised. As more information is made clear, and as community is engaged, there will be a better understanding. The issue is technical.'

'They are doing a project in Ruimsig on the western side of city where the majority are white and wealthy and there is small Thembelihle in proximity to the wealthy community. Ruimsig also wanted the Thembelihle community to be moved. We need to learn that we have to live side by side, otherwise we might as well go back to where we came from. We cannot ask for people to be removed as if [they are] landfill or garbage. These are people that we are talking about. We need communities to start partnering; we need them to start seeing each other as rightful beneficiaries of the Constitution together ....'

'The Ruimsig community also has legitimate fears around property prices, crime and safety. The informal settlement has been known to harbour criminals. Both have to come to the table instead of threatening one another.'

ON TENSIONS BETWEEN THEMBELIHLE AND LENASIA

In Thembelihle Zunaid is worried about the growing tensions between the local Indian community of Lenasia and the local African community residing in the area: 'Communities all over experience crime ... there is a problem if your neighbours live without while you live with. The goal is to see those who are more privileged and who are willing to be proactive about taking the development forward with the City to take up the cause for others. The community of Lenasia cannot be looking every day to get rid of Thembelihle, and in Thembilihle, if you are harbouring criminals then you are not fostering good relations.'

'This has come down to a need for an exercise in good neighbourliness ...' There is no one in the city of Johannesburg who can lay claim to being here for more than five generations, maximum. And new migrants are coming. 'We have no right to claim anything, any of us. Cities in the world are formed by migrants. You've got to find ways to co-exist.'

Zunaid is of the opinion that, relatively speaking, between Lenasia, 'Eldos' and Soweto people are asking for more development but often along racial lines. The City is in a difficult position, and as much as the State is trying to force things, on another level there is a real class distinction in South Africa. The community in Sandton has a huge potential for power and they do not use it; they do not work for the betterment of Alexandra (Alex), despite Alex residents working in Sandton. Enclaves of wealth cannot isolate themselves forever. Eventually it smacks one in the face that there is something wrong. Melrose Arch is another example of an enclave of wealth while five kilometres away others are living in abject poverty.

The Thembelihle resident's assertion that she will take the Indian's houses[88] is to be seen as an expression of frustration. People are losing hope because they are not seeing the benefits that they were once promised and that they were hoping for.

ON PROVIDING ACCESSIBLE HOUSING FOR ALL

Job security is 'getting very difficult. The Coloured community is one of the most marginalised communities in this country; the problem plays out in the housing crisis. They indicate that a large number of houses in Soweto were given. A lot of Coloured areas have flats and it is very difficult to have people own them …'

'The wealthier in this country are integrating better,' Zunaid surmises. 'They share schools and facilities and the wealthy blacks (living beside wealthy whites) in Ruimsig are also unhappy about the settlement nearby, saying "move them". So class distinctions are getting deeper and will be a lot more difficult to break down than the racial issues under the previous regime. The responsibility of the State is to stop this right now.'

Zunaid explains that typology of housing means different types of houses for different ranges of affordability for different people of any colour. The City is looking at models for poorer white, Indian and Coloured people who could qualify for RDP housing. These people, he said, need to get themselves onto the RDP house database. Previously the State provided the RDP house as the only option, but the problem is that it created another kind of exclusivity – of poor people living with other poor: segregated and ghettoised. For this reason the State realised the need to integrate housing, so varying ranges have been put within people's reach.

'We need to provide housing for people to aspire towards – something that citizens can realistically strive for.' 'The gap between a Michelangelo

---

88. Referring to 'Mampi'.

(Sandton) apartment', Zunaid says, 'to a shack in "Alex" is unbridgeable. The idea of mixed-use housing is to say that one may be living in affordable rental housing today, but there is the option of gap housing, which is subsidised and a 'bit better' than an RDP house; and beyond that there is the option of the fully-bonded house – all being within the same proximity, although not next door to one another. Related to this are the banking requirements that housing be put into "zones"[89].'

'Luforeng, on the western edge of the City between Soweto and Lenasia is a case in point. The City is trying to bring the regions together under one project. For example, recreational spaces are integrated – parks, sports areas, schools and retail community nodes. The Project has 25 000 houses. It has a fully-dedicated economic development plan. One part of the site has dolomite so it has been used for agro industry and food security projects. All the land portions have been identified for usage; one section for light industry has access to their places of employment and also access to major sources of transportation. The City learnt its lessons from Pennyville and Cosmo City[90]. So Luforeng has been designed like a little city with access to everything for people living there. It is an all-in-one project where residents can aspire and transition. Luforeng is clearly aligned with the City's land acquisitions strategy.'

ON HOW ETHNICITY AND POWER PLAYS AFFECT COHESION

Dan Bovu: MMC for Housing Johannesburg City Council[91]

When Dan Bovu moved to Thembelihle it had 4,500 sites. These he said have been subdivided over the years.

Dan was an activist and was at the 'forefront of the struggle'. When he and other activists had demanded to be housed they were informed that where Thembelihle is located there is dolomite. They did not trust what the apartheid regime was saying. A study was conducted and Dan and his fellow residents participated. Boreholes were drilled and Zone 4 in section F was

---

89. Zunaid's reference to banking requirements raises an important point about banking loan policies working against the objectives of social cohesion; working against class integration, for example, by their categorisation of localities in terms of property values that provide for particular class categories of people.

90. Pennyville provided a housing mix of semi-detached units, multi-storey, walk-up units, social rental family apartments, and open market rental stock. One of the lessons learned from Pennyville was the ratio between subsidised versus non-subsidised, according to Ben Pierre Malherbe, CEO of Calgro M3, which partnered with the City of Johannesburg in developing the 100ha Pennyville into an integrated housing estate. The 'integrated spread' was wrong as there were more subsidy beneficiaries than ratepayers. 'We took prime land and gave it to those who were getting it free.' At Pennyville the prime land was allocated to fully subsidised government housing. This was at the time that the Breaking New Ground concept was promulgated and the development was converted to allow inclusion of rental units. (Interview: Zunaid Khan, 2012)

91. Field notes, 2012.

identified as dangerous because a drill pipe got lost and went straight down into what appeared to be a chasm.

They returned to the committee with the results and wondered how they were going to interpret these results to the people. According to Mbovu they took a decision not to tell the people of Thembelihle. Mbovu then said: 'I am not going to be party to that because we will not be able to respond in the long run when residents question why are we are not developing … it's better we tell them now; if they say we're useless let them say so.' That, he says, is what split the group along political and interest lines. Operation Masakane for the Homeless (OMHLE), of which Dan was a member, is the other group that was no longer interested in reporting to the committee. When they broke off Dan remained within the ANC and community structures. Every year they went to the election of the community leadership and Dan would win the leadership election. But troubles were brewing, '… people said, "no, Indians had bought me; I took some money". All those stories were very big, but I'm happy because we managed to tell people.'

A further instance where Dan describes the interplay of power and ethnicity and cohesion is to be found in another personal story: In 1994, before the first democratic elections, the ANC was appointing representatives and Dan was appointed to be a councillor for a year in the south-west of Johannesburg. At that time there were 11 councillors. Dan has served the South-West since 1994 and is currently southern MMC. In 1997/98 a new area was opened up called Vlakfontein under the City's Mayibuye Programme[92]. It was a 'site and service' area. Dan and the community leadership refused to move because the site was too far away. He argued for a location within 25 kilometres of Johannesburg. This, then, was how similarly named Vlakfontein was identified, five kilometres away from Lenasia, and an agreement was reached in 1998 to develop it. During 2000, 1,500 people were relocated there. In the middle of this relocation Lehae became available, one kilometre from Thembelihle. In 2002, Dan recommended Lehae instead of Vlakfontein, stopped moving people and the allocation of sites in Lehae started in 2006. The opposition parties, viz. The

---

92. The key delivery milestone in this programme is the approval of a general plan for each project area by the Surveyor General's office, which approval means that the project area is ready for the installation of essential services. The result of such a programme is a legally proclaimed residential area and security of tenure, through the issuing of title deeds for each beneficiary. Undeveloped pieces of land (greenfields) are formalised and townships are established and proclaimed before the transfer of title deeds to beneficiaries commences. The process of formalisation and title deed transfers predominantly applies in areas where informal settlements already exist. This is commonly referred to as an 'upgrade', and can either be in situ or roll-over upgrades, or a combination of both. Essential services such as water reticulation, sewer reticulation, roads and storm water infrastructures are installed in both greenfield and upgrade projects. The end product in this regard is a water and sewer connection for each stand. (www.joburg-archive.co.za/city_vision/annualreport2002…/chapter10)

Crisis Committee, the PAC, The Landless People's Movement, rejected the idea because Dan said he had suggested it 'for no other reason'.

ON PROSPECTS FOR COHESION: TEMBELIHLE AND LENASIA EXTENSION 9 AND 10

Community views

Phindi Ncekana (Ward 9)[93]

Phindi Ncekana (community activist) has witnessed 'quite serious violence' in Thembelihle in the past regarding influence over the people there and the site rental that they have paid. Unrest began around 1990 when the newly arriving residents from elsewhere rebelled against the control of what was then a tent camp by the so-called Ma Russia (the Russians) gangsters who had started it. One of the reasons for this was ethnic prejudice against the idea of being under the 'authority of Sotho people'. Another was that the control of the Ma Russia was associated with the control of (brick factory) Corobrick, and thus the paying of a R15 site rental and a 20c 'Easy Loo'[94] toilet usage fee (for cleaning and maintenance) levied on every use. Eventually a committee was elected to replace the Ma Russia, which was in turn challenged by a group of Xhosa migrants who did not feel that they could be at the mercy of 'boys' who had not undergone initiation[95], not to mention women who traditionally do not speak for the family and therefore should not have been heard. These struggles resulted in violence and death, and ended with what appeared to be a form of power-sharing arrangement. Interestingly, this arrangement was partly necessitated by the activism of the women in the area. The settlement was (and Phindi says she thinks still is) a majority female population with many single-parent households. Thus, they refused to be sidelined by the men fighting for control and arranged for a certain number of positions to be held by women in the elected council.[96]

The second spate of violent conflict was a long-standing disagreement between Masibambane, a local civic organisation and the local SANCO branch. Phindi could not really explain the divisions between the two, other

---

93. Interview, 17 June 2012.
94. Portable toilets that are hired out.
95. The ceremony that transitions youth to manhood.
96. The reason for the number of single-parent households is not clear, though Phindi suggests that men essentially run away when things get too difficult. It should be noted, though, that many informal settlements in the East Rand are associated with the families of miners, etc. who were living in the compounds but brought their families to live close by, among other things.

than to say that they were competing for 'power' over the residents in the area and that the conflict thus was really a continuation of the conflict that removed the Ma Russia from control and pitted the Xhosas against the elected council. Again violence and killings took place; this was solved by an election. The Electoral Commission (IEC) was asked to conduct the election in 2005 after the local government elections for the official civic organisation of the settlement, under the conditions of which the losing party would disband and seek no further influence. SANCO won that election but Masibambane claimed it was unfair. Masibambane thus dissolved, but only for many of the leaders to form the Operation Khanyisa Movement (OKM), a rival civic organisation, later.

Phindi says that local doctors, business people (including chemists) and activists have played a strong part in giving access to services for the community: they pressured an unwilling clinic in (Lenasia) Extension 5 to accept patients from the neighbouring settlement, they provided drugs for the clinic in the shack settlement and they set up a weekly tent clinic where doctors attended to serious cases. Other help she could remember came in the form of charity with winter clothes drives, families bringing large pots of food to feed the hungry, help with school fees for struggling families, a nearby chicken farm and a butchery delivering offcuts. This took much of the tension out of the borderline existence of many in the tent, and then shack, settlement as one would not have to worry about going to bed hungry or freezing in winter.

Having said this, Phindi was quick to say that 'most of them [the Indian residents] were very prejudiced against the Thembelihle residents' and, as such, when the community started to balloon in 1990 and after, many of those living in the areas adjacent to it began to feel more threatened and eventually moved to other parts of Lenasia (and later to other parts of the city) if they could afford it. Many of these were the teachers and students at the local schools. Others, however, used the expanding population as an opportunity to start small shops and did very well.

She says that living with people who have different cultures and norms is necessary to understanding them, to accepting those differences, and that this means 'using her example' that she does not think Indian people rude any longer. 'When they do not greet you and chat to you when they see you, that is just the way they do things: they are different from us.'

Hanif Patel: Lenasia Resident[97]

Hanif, aged 55, speaks of spaces left by families leaving the area for the suburbs and how they are gradually being filled (especially in the case of Extension 13) by black African, 'Coloured' and recent Indian immigrants. He says that there exists some discomfort in the rest of the community about some of these developments, including xenophobia levelled against the Indian immigrant shop owners for their success. On the back of this and his general sense of the mood in Lenasia he pointed to Tembelihle informal settlement and said that he felt that if, hypothetically, the Tembelihle community were to be given housing in Lenasia, his feeling was that the Lenasia community would be very angry.

Russel Abrahams: Lenasia resident[98]

During the late 1990s there was an influx of people into established Lenasia neighbourhoods and informal settlements. Lenasia is made up of a number of localities. Black people moved into Extension 10 near Thembelihle; those who started buying were professionals, police, nurses, etc. Later, some professional people moved into Extension 13 as well as ordinary working people. Even though democracy had been established, it took a while to get mixed racial communities right.

When houses were built in Extension 13 it was with the idea that Indian people would occupy them. Blacks and Coloureds objected and said that now that there was democracy houses could not be allocated according to racial groupings. Although there was a list, as well as an application process, people saw the process was taking too long so they got impatient and there were house invasions, breaking the locks and taking occupation.

The other area people moved into was Lenasia South, with a lot more professionals and a far more integrated community. Zakariyya Park and Mixon Manor used to be only Indian, but as informal settlements developed in the southern part of the area Indian people began moving out and so houses became vacant and then black people bought the houses. In those areas, Russell claims, you have a pretty strong mix.

A pastor from Zakariyya Park told Russell that he is leaving his church because he does not have a single Indian member, only black people. His ministry focus has been changing and he is no longer much of a teacher and has joined another bible school. In Lenasia 'proper', like Extension 1, no black people have moved in as it is too expensive – so if black people have one or

97. Field notes, February 2012.
98. Interview, November 2012.

two million rand, they would rather buy in Sandton than Lenasia.

The way forward, the pastor said, was to invite leaders from the camp. They had a series of meetings and saw a real possibility from the religious grouping in the area to help move things forward.

Rashid Subjee: Lenasia[99]

Rashid tells how his brother 'Baba' was canvassing for the ANC and took his own car and collected old people, or those who could not walk, to go and register to vote. Baba lives across from the Thembelihle informal settlement and used to give residents water.

Rashid says that during the demonstrations against the demolition of homes, his brother was stoned by youngsters. Parents and older children stood by and screamed at the demolitions. Rashid understands that they are upset about their homes being broken down. However, some do not respect the law and defy the 'cops'.

Ahmed Kathrada, he said, encouraged people to greet one another to bridge the racism between Indians and blacks, and this is why Rashid greeted a woman protester. He recounts the encounter:

> *A black woman walked past (Rashid greeted) and said, 'You Indians are just standing and looking.' I said, 'What must we do?' She said, 'You must be happy.' 'What must we be happy about?' I asked. 'We don't like all this, violence and that, how can we be happy?' She said, 'Yah but you must come and help us.' I asked, 'Do what? Come break our streets, burn tyres, throw rocks, fight with the police? We respect the law ... this is what the previous government did and it took them about 20 years to make this a little town for us people that were sent here ... and why must we break our own things; why must I break the stop street if I'm going to use it?'*

Rashid told the woman that he did not want an argument with her and said that she made it a racial matter. He says it makes him very unhappy that they are staying in these circumstances: 'We had peace in the previous [apartheid] government. Because how can a person come, and you're standing there by your gate, and defy you like that, looking for an argument ... the most sadness for us is that people breaking the stuff that you are going to use, and you're thinking, will they do that to the schools now and prevent the children from going to school? ... we negotiate, we go through the right channels. That is

---

99. Field notes, November 2012.

how life must be ....' He is worried that the violence could lead to the burning down of schools. 'We believe that a march will be a peaceful march ...' Rashid says that some Indians bought houses illegally and others have just taken the land and say someone sold it to them. They should check deeds and plan if they want to build. 'How does it get passed if the stand doesn't belong to you?'

CONCLUSION

There are rich development policy implications arising from the Fietas case that the imperative of social cohesion motivates, not least in respect of integrated mixed-use development, local economic development, and spatial, streetscape and housing design.

The local state seemingly validates the historical experience of places like Fietas in terms of housing developments that are integrated across race and class to promote social cohesion, as in Penyville and Cosmo City, for example. Yet, it is questionable whether what arguably may be the litmus test of cohesion is resulting: the individual and collective sense of caring and sharing, of meaning and belonging that the historical residents of Fietas attest to of their relationships with one another.

The experience of dislocation by the Group Areas Act serves to raise this sharply as an object of social cohesion relating to a sense of 'wholeness' that individuals feel in relation to themselves, family, friends, community, space, livelihood and history. In all of these senses the impact of the forced removals was profoundly rupturing.

Significant as the local integration of people and space and mixed use are to the promotion of social cohesion, the change in the macro context since the days of old Fietas is pertinent. Despite the cultural and other distinctions and differences among and between black communities and the racial distinctions in the application of colonial and apartheid laws, black people in general shared a broadly common experience of racially-based exclusion and underdevelopment. These circumstances, enforced across race and class, ironically somewhat contributed to interdependency, communality and cohesive community in the context of anti-apartheid resistance.

The nature of post-apartheid society's development under the influence of self-centredness as a dominant value system and its increasing social differentiation seem to mitigate the object of social cohesion. This raises the significance of 'equity' as a factor of social cohesion and a question as to how an open, democratic society that spawns distinctly varied social circumstances among its peoples may be truly bonded. It would seem that cohesion prevails discretely and according to the commonality of circumstances of distinct social classes and groups.

However, there seem to be greater possibilities for interaction, and hence the building of relationships between people in poorer and working-class communities, and in general among black communities, than among the middle and upper classes, especially within the white community. This may be a factor of spatial dynamics (smaller, closer homes and narrower streets in poor areas), sensibilities (concepts of privacy), communalism (including use of public transport), and so on.

It would not be erroneous, either, to generalise that many more poor black people either walk or use public transport than drive between places as a result of apartheid legacies and resource constraints. This too lends itself to possibilities for greater interaction between peoples.

Crime has had a devastating impact on the prospects for social cohesion. Whatever its drivers, including inequality, it has created a sense of siege with suspicions held between people and a general fear of social and spatial openness. No doubt it has impacted too on the possibilities for interaction across apartheid's social and geographical divides and feeds racial and class prejudice.

That people in some communities can rattle off the names and occupations of others in their neighbourhood is revealing of an integrated community. This may be true not only of poor and working-class communities, but it would not be inaccurate to surmise that such knowledge of one's neighbours is less likely in a middle-class former 'whites only' suburb. The suburban experience is generally described as one of greater isolation. It seems that even in middle-class cluster developments, while there may be similar lifestyles and formal interaction on communal matters to do with body corporates, there is very little informal interaction. Chipkin (2012), in his essay on the 'middle classing' in Roodepoort ('Middle Classing in Roodepoort: Capitalism and Social Change in South Africa'), supports this view. He writes of upper-income townhouse complexes that seem to embody Benedict Anderson's thesis of 'imagined communities' (p.70). This, he says, is because the 'measure of social solidarity or "social cohesion" [in these sites] is not represented by the physical relations between neighbours or within communities ... despite their racial diversity, townhouse complexes are not places of non-racial conviviality ...' (ibid. p.69–70).

The opposite holds true, even in Thembelihle, constituted more recently by people of diverse histories and backgrounds. Dan Bovu, now the MMC for Housing in the Johannesburg City Council, says he used to know his neighbour better than he does where he now stays, in a 'better' part of Vlakfontein. When he gets home there is quietness, but in Thembelihle there was a lot of social activity: 'everything was open and people would greet'. He misses the community and 'vibe' of Thembelihle, he says.

The Fietas case points to an experience of cohesion despite distinctions, tensions, and even tensions of race, religion and class. It is an argument against any conception that cohesion is necessarily attendant on socio-economic development.

Racial, ethnic and class-based distinction and interaction coexisted with diffused margins between peoples in a melting pot of embracing identity. This dialectic between 'fixed' and 'fluid' senses of self is instructive for concepts of inclusive identity, like national identity.

The concepts of nation formation and social cohesion should therefore not imply sameness and homogeneity. They accommodate nuance and tension and contradiction, rather than a belief for the absence of such.

Fietas, of course, was not made up only of distinctly defined groups of people. Many families were racially, culturally and ethnically mixed. There were families consisting of Muslims, Christians, Hindus and Tamils, and respondents from these families said they were respected without attempts to try to change their identity.

The experience of mixed families in intimate relation probably best proves the possibility for fused identities. This is an ideal of non-racial South Africanism: something to consciously strive for, and which should form the driving basis of policy. In this respect, the continued racial categorisation of peoples post-apartheid in the interest of historical redress should be critically evaluated, at least in the medium-term, for an unintended consequence of promoting immutable racial identities.

No single and authoritative account stands for how that section of Vrededorp, from 26th Street south to 11th Street, which was the official racial divide between black and white, got its nickname 'Fietas'.

One account by an Afrikaner woman who had relations in Vrededorp has it that 'Fietas' is an Afrikaner slang term for something 'disagreeable' or 'unpleasant' – and that this was applied to the black section of Vrededorp by the white Afrikaner residents who lived north of 11th Street.[100]

---

100. Informal conversation with Ronelle, 2010.

Fietas may indeed be described to have been an inner city slum. It was generally poor, and boisterous multitudes crowded small decrepit homes, backyards and alleyways dotted by shebeens that spilled drunken patrons onto dirty narrow streets. However, it was a dynamic locality of residence, recreation, trade, entertainment and diverse cultural observance and ceremony that subverted the meaning of 'Fietas' as 'disagreeable' or 'unpleasant' – if indeed this was the slang term of disparagement – to become universally adopted by its people as a positive identity of endearment consistent with their lived experience.

ANNEXURE 1

List of individuals interviewed and their organisations:

Ntate Modimokwane: homeless security guard
Zwelakhe Zulu: elder
Susan: housewife and community worker
Husband to Susan
Hanif Patel: unemployed paraplegic
Rasool Patel: retired dressmaker
Russel Abrahams: pastor
Rashid Subjee: former Sophiatown resident
Victor Mokine: former Sophiatown resident and heritage tour guide
Amos Motale: sports administrator
Mrs Mophosho: unknown
Derrick Thema: former journalist
Satch Tata Jalamba: taverner
Junior Jacobs: unemployed community worker
Tiffany Jacobs: drug-addicted youth
Newone Daniels: unemployed alcoholic
Des Jones: community worker, businessman, academic
Belinda Daniels: unemployed youth
Doreen Roberts: unemployed community worker
Lerato: dyslexic artist
Shadrack Motaung: heritage tour guide
Shan Bolton: CEO, Ahmed Kathrada Foundation
Phindi Ncekana: community activist
Bhayiza Miya: community organiser
Thembelihle community activist who wishes to remain anonymous
Councillor Dan Bovu: MMC: Housing
Zunaid Khan: Member of the Mayoral Committee

CHAPTER SEVEN

LOCAL PERSPECTIVES IN THE NORTHERN CAPE AND KWAZULU-NATAL

Introduction

The following chapter is made up of a series of perspectives and narratives of community actors in the Northern Cape and KwaZulu-Natal. They come out of conversations held in 2012 in both provinces. The purpose was to reflect on nascent and emerging trends regarding the coming together of diverse peoples and cultures around shared community values and a sense of being. These reflections thus are constitutive and active parts of a larger whole that includes social, political, economic and historical aspects based not only on key principles of the democratic project but also on practises of equality in diversity.

The sites of conversation were:

- The provincial capital of Kimberley and the small urban settlement of Ritchie, south of Kimberley. Both are located in the Sol Plaatje Municipality, Northern Cape.
- Cato Crest, Umlazi and Chatsworth in the Ethekwini Municipality (Durban), KwaZulu-Natal.

The voices that speak in the chapter come from a wide variety of sectors: local government, the business sector, the church, the unions, the arts sector, the not-for-profit sector, the media and the national political arena.

NORTHERN CAPE: CONTESTATION AROUND RESOURCES

Terry Matthews
Community Works Programme and learning co-ordinator

There is a critical rural-urban dynamic that is coupled with difficulties facing national flagship projects like the Richtersveld Communal Property Association land restoration victory in their claim against Alexcor Trans Hex diamond fields, as well as major conflicts in the Asbestos Relief Trust. 'These rural cases demonstrate a major population shift to urban areas due to increasing poverty inequality caused by poor leadership, lack of social organisation and social cohesion. Conflict is rife and corruption reigns supreme.' Terry's insights into the plight of the rural people also highlighted the impact of declining mining activity in Kleinzee; emerging resource conflicts in the copper belt – Sishen, Okiep, Carolusberg, Komaggas; an unresolved relationship issue between land, identity, forms of social organisation and the impact of the apartheid Coloured reserves; the shaping of people's national consciousness and identity (local and national) through labour organisation on the mines; the impact of land struggles and evictions of the Bosluis Basters from Eksteenfontein; and the role of the 'Uhuru Group'[101] in fomenting dissent and 'undermining social cohesion' in the Richtersveld, due to a concerted business effort to usurp the Richtersveld claimants' newly-gained mineral rights.

Lulu Johnson
Member of Parliament

Nation formation and social cohesion 'cannot be divorced from the Reconstruction and Development Programme (RDP), which laid the national basis to align rights-based industries like agriculture, forestry and fishing, noting short-, medium- and long-term goals for employment creation, sustainable livelihoods and equitable economic participation for black people (ownership and otherwise) in the "commanding heights" of the economy. This must lead to benefits for … individuals, households and communities. Since 1993, the RDP has aimed in the medium- to long-term to transform the South African economy, and as such the enhancement of a South African nation! The exploitation of women and blacks in … the

---

101. A reference to the Nama Council, which is financially backed by Uhuru Communications.

fishing industry undermines the object and foundation of the RDP. A new fishing regime must be implemented in 2013 which will deal effectively with controversial practises like fronting, exploitation of BEE groups by the major fishing companies, as well as those officials involved in the perpetuation of these maligned practises. The nation building project must benefit economic lives, therefore we must connect mining/mineral rights, farming, forestry, fishing to the economic integration of the country and its citizens – black and white!'

Lulu is sure in his assertion that South Africa is not 'a nation … regardless of the concept of the Rainbow Nation'. The country is 'seeking and building a nation … [an] objective and outcome [that] is intrinsically linked to economic participation and benefits to all – regardless of race, colour or creed'. It is these issues, he says, that 'are testing our people's patience to the limit'.

Linking poverty, natural resource management and the environment, Lulu offers a detailed analysis of the role (certain) scientists play in promoting ecosystem protection (fisheries) at high social cost and working against building sustainable livelihoods at the grass roots. Scientific assertions (to protect and to conserve) set against poor communities' desperation to access sustainable livelihoods mitigate against achieving the nation building project and its objectives. Contradictions and fault lines, Lulu says, relate to the country's educational structure as well as the curriculum. The current system that is in place, he says, builds the individual 'who is not part of the whole' with narrow career and materialistic interests coupled with very little focus on 'national pride and patriotism'.

PROGRESSIVE TRADITIONS AND THE UNION MOVEMENT

Papi Tau
Member of the National Council of Provinces

'… Kimberley used to be a national hub for the non-racial sports movement during the struggle. It produced national leadership for both the SACOS[102] and the SARU[103] nationally. Non-racial sport is a foundation for the nation building and social cohesion project in this country. Therefore, more must be done to accelerate integration of people … we failed, we did not do enough and we must critique ourselves for being too soft on reconciliation. As a

---

102. South African Council on Sport.
103. South African Rugby Union.

former trade unionist, let me point to another good example: If we adopted a much more aggressive approach towards early childhood development in 1994 this process of social cohesion and nation building would have been accelerated. Where and how did we miss it?'

Papi then reflects on the current role of trade unions in nation formation and social cohesion: 'The shop floor struggles of workers for better wages and working conditions cannot be separated from the community service delivery struggles. They are essential parts of a broader political evolution in this country. There is a great need to return to progressive trade unionism. Focused worker education programmes in unions are critical. For example, the NUM[104] had one of the best political education programmes among unions in this country. This lesson is ignored or overlooked and constitutes a serious mistake. How many shop stewards today are actively involved in their community struggles? Unions must move back to their roots, back to active and conscious efforts to uplift communities where they work and where they live – reconstruct, build and de-racialise society, he says.

Job Moshou
Trade Unionist

Job is of the opinion that shop stewards and union leaders should improve their leadership and technical skills. They should stop wanting (demanding) things. They must give to society and build the nation by providing leadership and getting involved in community struggles. Collective effort is required, he asserts, 'Not a quick, fast buck – like manna from heaven, which will eventually kill the organisation because resolutions are not followed through with rigour. Selfishness and chasing wins is now the major focus and mantra.' Currently, he says, there is no feedback to members, no consultation; there is position mongering and the suppression of criticism leading to new practises in the union to govern and rule by means of threatening adversaries with suspension. Provincial secretaries, he says, have adopted new corporate management styles of company CEOs. Membership declines because of internal tensions; and union policies, rules, procedures and democratic practises stifle union growth and development. 'Why is there no growth in Kimberley? No skills and leadership development! Industry and economic development are stagnant making people dependent of the welfare system. Departments are not meeting their targets and the general work ethic among

---

104. National Union of Mineworkers.

officials is at its lowest. Some departments' employee profiles take on tribal and racial stereotypes. Senior officials are not contributing to their communities. People are not talking community languages but instead emphasise themselves (me) and not us or we. The individuals reign supreme.' Job says further that a general lack of concern is displayed for skills transfer and a greater concern placed on money. 'Everyone in the community becomes pawns to be used, and no one sees the pain of others. Those who study get no employment and our politics discard and ignore (marginalise) expertise, competence and ability.'

IMPACT OF GOVERNMENT POLICY

Garth Damerell
Community radio broadcaster

Garth speaks of how government is biased towards the print media while overlooking the needs of community radio stations in their communication campaigns. Community radio stations – just like the print media – have to create/generate sustainable income/revenue, he says. The lack of support of the community airwaves and the barriers that have been built up over the years between government and community radio, not only work to the detriment of the stations financially, but remove a vital communication instrument for government with the result that this available resource is not being optimised to its full potential.

Bongiwe Mbinqo-Gigaba
Member of the Provincial Legislature

... we still don't reach our target of integrating disabled people into our staff establishment. Currently we are sitting at 0.007 per cent (a far cry from even one per cent, which is still below the national target). People feel left behind, hence we need to do rigourous oversight. Our performance in maths and science is declining. The SKA[105] Project is not factored into our strategic plan as a department. Service delivery backlogs for school restrooms, operating budgets and school infrastructure – these things need to happen, otherwise there's negative impacts and serious consequences which will follow. We need to

---

105. Square Kilometre Array.

understand each other and solve problems. This requires lots of work and dedication. However, there are positives: a gradual maturity of co-operative governance, political stability and continuity ...

Allen Grootboom
Member of the Provincial Legislature

Dr Grootboom believes that the nation formation and social cohesion project in South Africa is 'on track – we are a rainbow nation'. The major issues and concerns are serious emerging divisions which he articulates as employment equity; the ANC's cadre deployment (the country is unable to address skills shortages because cadre deployment advances and promotes cronies and patronage and the exclusion of skilled individuals); the protection of corrupt cadres and perpetual corrupt practises in governance in the Northern Cape in particular; the inability to act and prosecute perpetrators who have political connections (the more you steal the more you are protected) which erodes the nation building project and further demotivates and erodes trust; non-attendance at school, dropping out and setbacks to equity goals; lack of career guidance, rote learning and lack of discipline; lack of access to work opportunities for the youth and 'role models' who display attitudes of 'I don't care' to society, and over-politicised education. As an example of this, Grootboom cites the rejection of a proposal to locate the new university in Upington instead of Kimberley....

Philip Vorster
Councillor, Kimberley

'The entire Frances Baard District and Sol Plaatje Municipality suffer from potholes by design! This is tearing communities apart. We do not only need a moral regeneration campaign, but the complete regeneration of the twenty-year-old apartheid bulk infrastructure system in this area. Municipal officials abandoned basic maintenance programmes which built this internationally known city. Municipal systems are collapsing all over the province as far as Namakwa, Siyanda John Taolo Gaetsewe, Pixley ka Seme. Waste dumping is a common sight, no upkeep of roads ... five workers died in Homevale during a mundane maintenance procedure at a sewer plant. Their health and safety was compromised because training and skills development in the municipality is neglected ... our children are leaving this province in droves because there is no future for them … and those that qualify somewhere else never return but prefer to settle somewhere else. Poor service delivery of municipal services dislocates communities. It also destabilises otherwise normal functioning families and further leads to tragic consequences for the city and this province. This water crisis impacts on children who are supposed to write final exams…'.

Die Volksblad – case of Pieta Serfontein[106]

'… This weekend, a local businessman and owner of Hancor Dairy donated 64 000 litres of water to locals after the city was hit the second time by a collapsed water supply. The businessman, Pieta Serfontein, supplied the water by means of tank containers from his farms Tierfontein and Kameelfontein in the Boshof District. On Saturday people arrived in their thousands to fill various containers and bottles after news spread like a wildfire in the townships. Serfontein said he had already distributed 42 000 litres free to people at the time of writing. Many people cannot afford to buy bottled water from the shops (he passionately states). During the week I have to cart water to the dairy plant but decided on Saturday to avail water to our citizens because the factory did not require any supplies over the weekend. Serfontein expressed a special concern about the poor communities who needed and collected the water at the factory. This is our service to our community who supported us and in this way I can plough back to the community as a sign of appreciation and gratitude for their loyal support.'

Shaun Atlee
Former offender

'I am very fortunate as a juvenile offender to get this job (at NICRO)[107] because upon release it is very difficult to adjust. Reintegration into society is difficult. It takes discipline: in my case, gym-school-home. The community do not adjust or accommodate you. Stigma and labels pursue you forever. Even if you passed your ABET[108] programme, gained hard technical skills in carpentry, building, welding, craft, you will not find a job or support or resources or access to government services. Here we teach ex-convicts not to blame society but to move forward in this long process of reintegration.

---

106. Excerpt of an article, 12 November 2012: author's translation.
107. South African National Institute for Crime Prevention and the Reintegration of Offenders.
108. Adult Basic Education and Training.

Qualifications do not matter because stigma and labels continue. They do not have a lack of ideas but face a lack of support. For the youth it is all about money (*skroppetjie*). Most of my clients are youth and under 35. They always re-offend. I have very few clients over 40. We need advanced skills programmes for the youth. The department doesn't want to take risks or take chances to drive initiatives in designing products, clothes, etc. This is what the youth want to do. They want to kill time. They prefer voluntary labour-based projects but the Department of Correction's infrastructure for these projects and initiatives is limited. Youngsters don't want to go to school or do anything beyond the call of duty; therefore we need to go beyond the level of artisan training. We depend on the Department of Labour to absorb or place ex-convicts, or the Department of Correctional Services to rehabilitate – but prisoner rehabilitation is not a pipeline, just a pure dream which will be made real with hard skills ... That is my experience and reality.'

KwaZulu-Natal: Conversations on local urban socio-cultural activism

Phindani Nene
Entrepreneur

Phindani Nene has been an entrepreneur since 1988 and does not take kindly to being described as a black economic empowerment (BEE) product since he first took the plunge before BEE was conceived. Since 2003 to date, Phindani has been associated with the now defunct National First Division soccer team, Durban Stars FC.

In the early 1980s he taught at Phambili High School, a progressive independent institution started by the likes of struggle veterans Fatima Meer and Florence Mkhize. Based in central Durban, the school catered mainly for United Democratic Front-aligned learner activists displaced by political violence in nearby townships and squatter camps. In his student days at the University of Natal in Durban a few years earlier, and in line with his Black Consciousness activism, Phindani was a weekend tutor at Umbumbulu High School as part of the Black Student Study Project.

In early August 2012, Phindani was to host the annual Durban Stars Corporate Challenge to be held at Amanzimtoti south of Durban. Now in its sixth year, the event is popular for promoting a multiplicity of sports and healthy lifestyles in the corporate sector. Participants at the event included parastatal organisations and major private companies from KwaZulu-Natal, Gauteng and Western Cape. The event seems to be a good example of social cohesion in action.

Phindani is currently consulting for the Ethekwini Municipality on soccer development. He is clear that the government and corporate sectors can do much more to promote sports among ordinary South Africans. He says that soccer development in South Africa urgently needs major improvements and that the government has to take a lead and not leave it to soccer administrators; and that further, when developing sports amenities the government has to prioritise townships and other black areas.

A former Black Consciousness Movement (BCM) and United Democratic Front (UDF) activist who used to work in central Durban, Phindani believes that '…the legacy of racism in South Africa still continues in various ways and persists'.

However, all actors involved in the process of transformation need to recognise that for the different races to socially interact, all racial groups must embrace non-racialism as a way of life. 'Equally, we need to create policies that will espouse the values of non-racialism more explicitly. In this case, the city's authorities must act accordingly, to what the constitution prescribes …'

Abel Msane
Photographer

Abel Msane has been an independent photographer since the mid-70s. He is self-taught and continues to lives in Umlazi Township south of Durban. Abel is known as one of those warm and brave community/social photographers people grew to respect, not only for his photographic talents but mainly for his positive spirit towards life and the courage of raising two boys as a single father and seeing to their education right into tertiary level.

The studio out of which he now works is called Mazidlekhaya and is in the centre of Durban near the city hall. His services include taking photographs for graduation ceremonies, ID cards, family weddings and digital photo processing. Business, however, is not good. Despite having had some modest successes in recent years, including being commissioned to provide the official photographic facility for the World Parks Congress and the KwaZulu-Natal Premier Awards, both held at the Albert Luthuli International

Convention Centre in Durban, Abel is desperately trying to improve his business fortunes.

Abel's take on his situation is that poor access to capital by emerging black entrepreneurs makes it hard for their businesses to be sustainable. He notices the reluctance by leading black business individuals to mentor and support their small counterparts and says this does not bode well for the building of an impactful black entrepreneurial class. General racial mistrust between Indians and Africans in Durban continues to have negative effects on small African entrepreneurs like him. Stringent government tender requirements often increase the odds for emerging entrepreneurs like Abel as they often lack administrative capacity to fulfil tender obligations.

'My experiences in terms of business are that the majority of black people are excluded from the economy because big business and government are reluctant to involve them in the local economy. There can be no social cohesion when you have so many poor people without jobs and when black people are excluded from the local economy.'

Abel also alludes to what he perceives as mistrust between Africans and Indians with regard to commercial business. The perception is that Indians are dominating the commercial industries. Africans feel marginalised. This, according to Abel, negatively affects social interaction and social solidarity and must be attended to by the State.

Abel cited numerous observations he has made with regard to social interactions when doing his photography. These range from the historical perceptions that white people have about Zulu people, the way other South African ethnic groups are treated as outsiders, and how these factors have affected social relations between different racial groups. Key to some of these was the inferior way women are treated by men.

Raphael Vilakazi
Opera singer

Famous Durban baritone and head of a small music company, Kwantu Opera, Raphael Vilakazi has had a promising career in the arts, particularly in the 1990s. He has featured in numerous international operas in South Africa and abroad and is an alumni of the Southern African Music Rights Organisation Bursary Fund, being the recipient of the fund's bursaries.

Also often described as 'a music clinician', he was the co-founder and Deputy CEO of Opera Africa, the opera company that pioneered the production of sterling operatic works inspired by legendary music icons such as Princess Magogo kaDinuzulu at the turn of the millennium.

With a performer's diploma from Technikon Natal and being an Academy of Music graduate, in 1989 he became a full-time member of the NAPAC[109] singers, performing in numerous musicals and opera productions.

Vilakazi, who also attended the Ethekwini Municipality's social cohesion workshop, is critical of how certain influential individuals and music companies enjoy almost lifetime financial support from local government while many others are not given an equal chance. No matter how noble nation formation and social cohesion may be, he says, when individuals feel that their livelihoods are threatened, these ideals become irrelevant. In the arts and culture sphere, 'often local government does not have transparent policies for awarding contracts and financial support' and budget constraints in local government make it hard for a genuinely fair distribution of financial resources.

Peter McKenzie
Photographer

Peter McKenzie is a South African with a wide range of experiences in community and arts and culture work. He has worked in many social organisations and regards himself as an activist. Peter is a social actor/local community leader and is originally from Durban but has resided in other parts of South Africa. Having been out of the city for a long time, he argues, places him at a good advantage to see and understand the social spaces in his city.

He is currently working as a photographic teacher in Durban at a photographic school, whose main objective is to teach the art of photography to young people from townships like KwaMashu, Chatsworth and surrounding areas.

Peter also works with an organisation called Dala, a multi-disciplinary social movement that works with street vendors and foreign nationals who are selling goods on the street pavements and are 'car guards'. According to him, street vendors working on the pavements are the best people to observe how people interact racially in Durban. This is so because they themselves suffer discrimination in various ways (i.e. socially, economically, politically, and by the authorities in power in the city). Hence their work with them as an NGO is crucial in understanding how they survive in a city racially

---

109. Natal Performing Arts Council.

polarised such as Durban.

Peter explained that the way the State plans, allocates resources and seeks to change the legacy of apartheid within the various sites selected is an ongoing problem for the province. In his view, nothing much has really changed since 1994 in terms of racial integration with regard to planning and development. The beaches are evidence of this. Indians, Coloureds and Africans always gather as groups in separate spaces.

In Peter's view, the problem is not in socially interacting at the beach but rather where people live. People still live in separate areas according to the old 'notorious Group Areas Act'. This, to him, informs their social way of behaviour in social spaces like the beach. Hence there is no social interaction, no social integration and no cultural understanding of the other by the other racial groups.

> ... *our observations as people who worked in the streets, as Dala indicates to us, that even in town, on the pavements you see this separation. A video programme we have done, shooting people randomly, shows very clearly what I am referring to. That is, even on the pavement people do not look at each other's faces or communicate as different races ...*

On the subject of historical violence in the province, Peter pointed out that the historical violence that started in the 1980s between the African National Congress and the Inkatha Freedom Party continues to build mistrust within the areas under study. According to Peter, this has implications for how people interact socially, and thus it has implications for social cohesion in the context especially of the urban-rural divide. This view also gains support among different church organisations and church activists interviewed.

Mdu
Car Guard

Mdu is Senegalese by origin, residing in Durban. He also works with Dala. His primary role at Dala is to interface and work with the foreign nationals residing in and around Ethekwini (Durban).

According to Mdu, foreign nationals are the most discriminated against in the city. This is so because as people from other countries they suffer harassment by the local authorities; racially as blacks they suffer discrimination and their language disabilities (unable to speak Zulu and English properly) further place them in difficulties to survive.

Mdu says that the issue of foreign nationals for the province and the City is a serious one. 'In my work with Dala over the years I have observed that the people who are more accommodating to foreign nationals are "car guards" from South Africa who are working with car guards from countries outside South Africa. They all have something in common and accommodate each other in work and social life.'

The key actors whom Mdu notices have a problem with foreign nationals seem to be state actors and middle-class locals. To the state actors, Mdu explains, foreign nationals are a burden and must be removed from the streets. They are constantly accused of vandalism and are seen as intruders, criminals and drug traffickers. All these factors create enormous problems for a foreign national wanting to survive within the city space, especially those of them who do not have higher levels of education. To the middle-class locals there are old labels like 'jobs stealers', '*Makwerekwere*', and 'drug lords' that are attached to them. When cars park in the city centre Mdu notices that a local middle-class person will rather give money to a local than to a person who speaks a foreign language or has a foreign accent.

Sarah Daignon
French Embassy

Sarah originally comes from France and is currently working for Alliance Francaise in Durban as the executive director. She had worked on a project on the Durban Botanical Gardens, the main objective of which was to examine the past, present and future identity of the Botanical Gardens as a botanical public space (hence a vehicle for developing social cohesion within the city). According to Sarah, we need to take into account the history of botanical gardens in South Africa. The gardens as public spaces have long been excluding the majority of the city's population.

'The botanical gardens in South Africa have always been exclusive of the other races. Thus, when other races are socially excluded from public spaces they are bound to react negatively. In this sense, botanical gardens, when they continue to exclude others, are an impediment to social cohesion.'

Thembinkosi Ngcobo
Manager Ethekwini Municipality

Local government official Thembinkosi says progress with regard to building social cohesion programmes for the municipality and the province is taking place and there is a lot of enthusiasm from the public on this theme. He feels, however, that the State needs to intervene more effectively in this process, which means, among other things, 'developing better programmes that will encourage racial integration' and 'support the sport and cultural initiatives we, as the municipality, have put in place'.

'Equally, we need state officials that will embrace and understand this process at all levels of government. That means ... attend a choral musical initiative organised by choral musical groups, which is not necessarily my musical taste. We are here to serve and listen to every racial [and] ethnic group's initiatives that seek to build a social[ly] cohesive society'. Thembinkosi believes that arts, culture and sports are all initiatives that seek to promote social cohesion in society. 'However, as you know, historically, in both the domain of sports and culture, we have different racial groups in the country that subscribe on a racial basis to one or other form of these domains.' He ends by saying, 'the municipality needs to work faster and try to create a mechanism that will get our cultural and sports facilities to be used by all racial groups.'

Annexure 1

Northern Cape
Terry Matthews: consultant for the Community Work Programme and learning co-ordinator for the Seriti Institute
Lulu Johnson: National Chair, Portfolio Committee on Agriculture, Forestry and Fisheries
Papi Tau: House Chairperson: Oversight and Institutional Support – National Council of Provinces
Bongiwe Mbinqo-Gigaba: Member of the Provincial Legislature and Chairperson of the Portfolio Committee on Education & Recreation
Allen Grootboom: Member of the Portfolio committee on Education & Recreation
Phillip Vorster: Councillor (DA) Sol Plaatje Municipality
Shaun Atlee: Fieldworker, NICRO, Kimberley
Job Moshou: Chief Shop Steward: National Education, Health and Allied Workers' Union in the Office of the Premier
Garth Damerell: Manager: Teemaneng Stereo, community radio station

Annexure 2

KwaZulu-Natal
Phindani Nene: Entrepreneur and organiser of the annual Durban Stars Corporate Challenge
Abel Msane: Photographer and photographic shop owner
Raphael Vilakazi: Opera singer
Peter McKenzie: Photographer and activist
Sarah Daignon: French Embassy
Thembinkosi Ngcobo: Manager: Ethekwini Municipality, sports and recreation department
Mdu: Car guard

CHAPTER EIGHT

CONCLUSION

As set out in the introduction, this project sought to investigate the relationship between the social processes of nation formation and social cohesion in South Africa in theoretical and historical terms, as well as through four case studies. Both the theorisation and the case studies are a snapshot of specific approaches and experiences and do not claim to cover the totality of the conceptualisations and debates on, and the manifestations of, the processes of nation formation and social cohesion within society. The aim is to surface these issues as part of the contribution to the discourse on this vexed subject.

For instance, three lacunae in the study need to be acknowledged, which we hope researchers will address in further studies:

- The practical absence of the voice of white South Africans. The works of Melissa Steyn (*Whiteness Just Isn't What It Used To Be: White Identity in a Changing South Africa*, 2001) or Christi van der Westhuizen (*White Power and the Rise and Fall of the National Party*, 2008) alert us to the varying ways in which South African white identity is being reformulated. Given the social stratification it has undergone, as well as the differences in outlook between those who come from English- or Afrikaans-speaking backgrounds and then the political choices being made within such communities, there can be no doubt that much work needs to be done on 'whiteness'.
- The absence of the explicit voice of the youth. The tumultuous events of 2010 to 2012, described as the Arab Spring, and the leading role played by the youth in those and other uprisings around the world got many a

nation scurrying to examine the position and attitudes of their youth. While some took the sanguine attitude that South Africa's Arab Spring had happened a few decades ago, others have highlighted the dire socio-economic conditions our youth find themselves in.

• And what about the voice of business, at whose feet we lay so many societal ills? Apart from entrepreneurs such as Richard Vilakazi, we need to get a sense of how the better-off in our society see themselves in relation to the South African nation or in contributing to social cohesion. The movements to create nations in the eighteenth and nineteenth centuries were the work of the bourgeoisie as they tried to remove the shackles of anciens régimes. Does the South African bourgeoisie see the need for the nation to emerge, or does it feel that regional and global markets make such quixotic notions unnecessary?

As the reader would have seen in the case studies, one cannot but be struck by the deep despair many South Africans express about the fortunes of our 20-year-old democracy, leading us to revisit the question asked at the beginning of our study: Has there been a 'regression of the liberating ideas'[110] that were dominant in the years of struggle? In looking at the prospects of the South African nation through the hopes and aspirations of its people we have to distinguish between the national mood of this moment (part of which may reflect the pace of progress rather than the lack of progress as such) and the protracted process to attain nation formation and social cohesion. Faced with a myriad difficulties – problems in governance, economic development and demographic changes – the tendency may be to focus on the negative of the national mood instead of the beauty of the unfolding nation formation process.

But the reality is that national identity does not fill the leaks in the roof, the potholes in the road; nor does it fill empty stomachs. It may fill us with pride if our national team performs well, but such is the nature of the South African nation that it all depends on who is the 'us' and which national team we are talking about. There is no doubt that even among the elite, one part would rather watch football while others would be more energetic about the national cricket or rugby teams.

The study confirms the persistence of the historical patterns of exclusion of the majority of the population. This disturbing aspect of post-apartheid South Africa calls for further reflection on the *nature* of nation formation

---

110. Chapter 2, p.18.

and the question of national identity in the context of South Africa's cultural diversity. Further, this reflection must take into consideration the objective of the national liberation project – to overlay racial and ethnic identity categories with an inclusive South African national identity. This objective is meant to render the designations 'blacks' and 'whites' irrelevant in favour of an inclusive national identity while acknowledging diversity. How attainable is this, given the race-obsessed ethnic engineering of the past and the cautious transition to democracy?

It could be argued that an inclusive national identity has been constitutionally attained at one level and qualified, if not exactly contradicted, at another. More specifically, in the light of the questions and challenges raised in the chapters on nation formation and social cohesion, as well as in some of the findings in the case studies which confirm the persistence of race-based exclusions and inequalities across several indicators, the process of nation formation and social cohesion, it seems, requires further theorisation.

We will be doing not just the people of Imizano Yethu a huge disservice if we do not address the deep concerns and mistrust of other races, their disillusionment with cronyism, as well as the persistence of crime and corruption. Whites visiting their areas are assumed to be looking for drugs. Their children are growing up with an anti-establishment gene in their DNA, aspiring to become the poachers and gangsters they so admire in their townships. Kids playing in the shadow of a spaghetti junction of illegal electrical connections grow up thinking that it is natural to steal, poach and live life illegally. The limits to this anti-establishment attitude are shown in the experience of Thembelihle, when the criminals who were being protected by its residents started turning against the community itself.

With reference to this, Bentley and Habib (2008) point to several forms of national identity constructions operative in different societies. They refer to the 'nativist' (p.350) form, which relates to the essentialist manifestation of nationalism discussed in Chapters Two and Three, in which fixed and closed national identities based on 'race' are extant. In addition, there is a 'multicultural' form of national identity that accommodates diverse, separated cultures within a national state characterised by domination rather than equality. Although these forms of national identity are not explicitly applied to South Africa, they are both considered as potentially dangerous if adopted as national policy in the country. What is advocated is a form of cosmopolitan national identity in which different cultures are embraced and identity is not fixed but dynamic and constantly changing in response to social and economic changes and in interaction with other cultures. It is not clear how cosmopolitan and multicultural national identities differ and the extent to which cosmopolitan identities, strictly speaking, are not national but transnational identities which cannot be fostered nationally. This notwithstanding, the alternatives outlined by Bentley and Habib (ibid.) are pertinent to this study insofar as they point towards the need for context-specific strategies of nation formation at a time of intensified interchanges between national and global developments.

This would suggest that clear conceptual distinctions are made between cultural, economic and political identities and their practical impact on each other in the processes of nation formation and social cohesion in South Africa. Mahmood Mamdani (2001) is helpful in this regard. He points out that economic identities are 'a consequence of the development of markets' (p.622). This means economic factors determine not only the social form of the State but also shape national identities in class terms. Accordingly, modern nation states, be they capitalist, socialist or postcolonial societies, have assumed class-refracted identities relative to class domination. On the other hand, cultural identities are viewed 'as the consequences of the development of communities that have a common language and meaning' (ibid.). The reference to 'meaning' stands in contrast to the economic principles of exchange and monetary value to signify a sense of being. Political identities, on the other hand, 'need to be understood specifically as a consequence of the history of state formation within the modern state, [and they are] inscribed in law and legally enforced' (ibid.).

These distinctions enable two related insights posited by the theoretical and historical chapters on nationalism and social cohesion and corroborated, however scattered, by the case studies. First, the process of nation formation in South Africa historically involved a movement to construct a trans-ethnic national political identity. From the point of view of the majority this was initially conceived in inclusive African terms and later extended to fully embrace non-racialism. Arriving with the collapse of the bipolar order of the Cold War, to which the colonial and racial form of capitalism in South Africa was integral and seemingly impelled to underplay the class dimension during the political transition, it is precisely this multi-class African nationalist political project that is now showing signs of internal tensions and contradictions along class lines based on the continued economic exclusion of the majority of South Africans. The stark inequalities laid bare in Chapter Four that reveal the barriers preventing higher levels of social cohesion are pertinent here. In other words, the construction and consolidation of a non-racial national identity in South Africa has to negotiate political, economic and cultural factors and translate these into tangible forms of equality in relation to what Manackanjan terms the 'specific peculiarities of every context' (1967, p.63).

Accordingly, Neville Alexander's conclusion (1986) that insistence on 'the principle of "one language, one nation", is not a universally valid definition' (p.67) unable to account for alternative processes, atypical trajectories and different forms of nation-state constructions is being historically confirmed. While the methodology used in this study privileges local circumstances, the relation between local identity and national identity presents an important dynamic. As one respondent from Fietas said: 'You carry your roots with you'. Yet another respondent observes that 'cities are formed by migrants' – alerting us to the potential for identities to be continuously shifting, buffeted by experiences with neighbours as much as with national leaders.

The monolithic cultural model is thus inappropriate for South Africa, given its diverse population. As a postcolonial state there has been a sufficient level of unity derived from the juridical equality bestowed on all South Africans, regardless of linguistic, cultural and religious differences, within a geographically unified country, furnished with all the institutions that constitute a legitimate national state. This thus constitutes the *national political identity* of South Africa.

What about the toxic attitude towards migrants, especially African and South Asian immigrants? As Mdu the Senegalese car guard points out, there are all kinds of stereotypes attached to those who speak with a foreign accent – drug dealer, criminal, etc. Areas where migrants from other parts of Africa concentrate are anachronistically labelled 'OAU'. Mdu is emblematic of several million people who have been attracted to the opportunities South Africa provides. The average South African is more likely to hit the empathy button when they hear of migrants dying to get to the European heartland, or the plight of Hispanics in the US, yet we are conflicted when it comes to those migrants who live in our midst, who – even though they may have a legal status – have to live in the shadows lest they become the victims of various acts of discrimination or even another outbreak of mass lynching.

However, the greatest challenge facing society remains the eradication of historical and emerging inequalities. These inequalities – material, social and cultural – are discussed in Chapter Four and in the field reports of the four cases studies in Chapters Five, Six and Seven. There can be no more heartbreaking description than the picture of residents of Thembelihle fighting over the skins of chickens discarded by their neighbours in Lenasia. And how can South African society become so inured to gender-based violence that one of the female respondents talks of 'the ordinary assault against women by gangsters: rape and so on'[111]?

In relation to the Lenasia/Thembelihle dynamic, the Ahmed Kathrada Foundation is doing admirable work in improving understanding between different races. But it is clear that for the poorest in our society there seems to be no pot of gold at the end of the rainbow. In its stead there is hand-to-hand combat for survival. Similarly, the 'Coloured' identity – replete with its centuries old complexities – continues to bedevil discourse on the South African national identity. Mampi captures one part of the dilemma when she says, 'Afrikaans is part of their culture' – a notion that will surprise a fair sprinkling of those labelled 'Coloured', not only those from KwaZulu-Natal whose language may not be Afrikaans but also across the board, given the historical hierarchy of racial discrimination and neglect, even among Afrikaans speakers.

The issue of race relations has many dimensions, including an appreciation of contributions made in the struggle against apartheid: issues such as intermarriage and the simple courtesy of greeting people on the street.

In the light of this, it is clear the future development of South African society depends on the peeling off of fear and mistrust of 'the other' and the cultivation of a deeper sense of belonging and inclusion. This can only come about as historical, ethnic, cultural, linguistic, educational, religious, social, economic and spatial inequalities identified by the development indicators in the study are progressively eliminated at all levels of society.

The study confirms that nation formation and social cohesion cannot be divorced from the economic and material needs and realities of a society. To promote a sense of belonging and the further crystallisation of a durable overarching national identity capable of living with diversity requires bold interventions aimed at fundamental economic transformation, higher levels of employment, universal access to quality education, safety and security, equitable service provision and social support for the vulnerable to underpin the intangible factors and processes that constitute social and cultural life in South Africa.

This research alerts us to the many and varied examples of civic-

111. Chapter 7, p.160.

mindedness that still persist. Denis of Hout Bay contributes to the development of young musicians; Bhayiza of Thembelihle ploughs his personal wealth into soccer development. Mampi in Thembelihle says that 'some Indians are blacker than myself' in terms of their philanthropic contributions. While black entrepreneurs provide many examples of generosity, a number of them prefer not to be seen as beneficiaries of the government's black economic empowerment policy. This is especially true of those who were in business before the first democratic elections in 1994.

It needs to be emphasised that the modern phases of nation formation in South Africa did not commence in 1994 with the transition to democracy. As Mzala (1998, p.14) explains, it goes back to the early emergence of a national aspiration among colonised Africans in this country to establish a unified and non-racial democratic state. Netshitenzhe (1997) points out that a national consciousness developed and intensified in the active struggle for liberation during the twentieth century.

The democratic breakthrough of 1994, however, did not and could not sweep away the deep divisions, exclusions and inequalities historically imposed by law and enforced administratively and through coercion on South African society. All South Africans, categorised in negative terms as non-Europeans at the time of the formation of the (national colonial) Union of South Africa, and as 'non-whites' during apartheid, were, in a sense, 'denationalised'. Chapter Three underscores the point that under these dispensations, political oppression and economic exploitation were applied differentially between the colonised, with the African population bearing the full brunt of exclusion and oppression. This strategy was aimed at fragmenting resistance and preventing national coalescence and mutual solidarity among the majority of South Africans to safeguard minority rule.

It was done by dividing the population along racially construed identities of Europeans, Africans, Indians and Coloureds with further ethnic subdivisions made among Africans to erect a systematic order of segregation. Within this framework a segregated spatial dispensation was imposed and consolidated during the course of the twentieth century. In 1994 the racial order was abolished, insofar as the legal differentiation between whites as fully recognised national citizens on the one hand, and blacks as ethnic non-nationals relegated to ethnic enclaves on the other, came to a juridical end. In its place a unified national state was established.

However, one of the distinctive divisive features of the colonial and apartheid state was surprisingly retained. This was the native administrative dispensation, which under apartheid became the Bantu administration system.

Thus, Mamdani (2001) correctly observes that during the struggle for national liberation, which aspired to the attainment of a 'trans-ethnic' (p.662) national identity, this dispensation (and its institutions, the colonial Native Reserves, later Bantustans and Group Areas) was rejected and opposed as colonialist and racist. However, the new democratic dispensation retained aspects of the native administration system and renamed it the Traditional Authorities Dispensation to create a dual constitutional order, structured along the old lines of the colonial and apartheid orders, minus the racism. This prompts Mamdani, (ibid.) to ask whether South Africa at present constitutes a form of 'non-racial apartheid' (p.662) in respect of this dual system of national governance, partly inherited from the past and modified, but structurally related. This structural continuation from the colonial and apartheid legacies into democratic South Africa is directly relevant to the democratic and trans-ethnic reconstruction of South Africa posited by the struggle for a national democratic dispensation stripped of the ethnic identity markers.

In this context, the words of Schoeman and Lekgoathi (*Mapungubwe Reconsidered*, MISTRA, 2013), regarding the fluidity of ethnic identity bear repetition:

> *In the pre-colonial era, ethnicity was negotiable and reconfigurable and this flexibility continued, to a limited extent, even as the colonial and/or apartheid states were attempting to construct rigid ethnic boundaries through various forms of social engineering, such as the Native Affairs' Department project of classifying each and every African in South Africa into a 'tribe'. ...African societies did not live in static, homogeneous, self-contained ethnic units but existed in extremely fluid, porous and heterogeneous entities connected to shifting boundaries that allowed for individuals and groups to move in and out and back and forth across these boundaries (p.41).*

Does this mean that, 'for the nation to live, the tribe must die' as some activists have argued?[112] Naturally, unity in diversity should apply to the multiplicity of languages and cultures, even within the African community. Yet, if the legitimate reassertion of the languages and cultures that

---

112. *African Communist No. 89*, Second Quarter, 1982.

colonialism sought to obliterate is not consciously counterbalanced by the quest for the unity that the anti-colonial struggle represented, it could become a source of national fragmentation. Given their numbers and their critical role in the national liberation struggle and the postcolonial dispensation, such centrifugal tendencies among the African people would most certainly profoundly undermine the totality of the project of nation formation and social cohesion.

While considerable progress has been made over the last two decades in efforts to reconstruct South African society as an inclusive, non-racial democracy (founded on the equality of all its members), consolidating these efforts calls for co-ordinated national and subnational development programmes with the objective of creating cohesive communities and a society based on justice and inclusivity. To achieve this, Pallo Jordan (1997) asserts that 'no quarter [should be given to] racial discrimination in schooling, in employment, housing and recreation' (p.8) and deracialisation should be positively and vigorously pursued.

In doing so a number of areas call for co-ordinated attention. This is premised on the understanding that the formation of a united nation and the attainment of social cohesion depend, critically, on a sense of belonging that is related to material conditions of life and an overarching common identity that recognises diversity. In this regard, among others, the following areas can be identified, as indicative of the kind of interventions required:

VISION AND ITS PURSUIT

• Critical in this regard is socio-political compacting. The political transition of the 1990s was a seminal moment in South Africa's history that ushered in a legitimate democratic state underpinned by formal political equality as enshrined in the country's constitution. For the first time since the 'racial union' of the early twentieth century, South Africa formally became an inclusive nation state built on an inclusive political compact. Though the Constitution enshrines socio-economic and other generations of rights, these have yet to be attained for the majority, while the well-off live in the insecurity of material comfort. It is therefore critical to ensure that South Africans embrace and act out a common socio-economic vision, which many would argueß is contained in the National Development Plan. In brief, this vision calls for the attainment of decent conditions of life for all.

- Pursuing a common vision requires new forms of civic-mindedness and enhanced citizen activism. At the generic level leaders of various sectors of society and their constituencies should be prepared to contribute to, and to sacrifice for, the realisation of the common interest. At a micro-level, this can take different forms such as a conscious effort by all to take the initiative in endeavouring to better their conditions: professionals going back to their schools to run tutorials, undertaking maintenance work in their neighbourhoods and generally getting involved in the securing of their communities.
- The NDP cogently argues for a capable developmental state that is able to meet its obligations to society. This requires an appropriate socio-political outlook and value system, capacity to win over and provide leadership to society and state structures and systems that ensure consistent implementation of programmes to improve people's conditions. Further, the public services at all levels need to be re-orientated towards direct and sustained partnerships with civic society in matters related to social cohesion at a sub-national level, informed by an understanding of the relationship of this task to nation formation.

DECENT STANDARD OF LIVING

- A genuine sense of belonging – which is fundamental to both nation formation and social cohesion – is, to a large extent, dependent on whether the material conditions of all South Africans, especially the poor, are in fact improving. While it can be argued that poverty, as such, does not determine the existence or otherwise of national unity and social cohesion, a variety of research material, including the case studies cited in this work, does illustrate that 'relative poverty' or inequality is a critical inhibitor to unity and cohesion.

  At the same time, some minimal level of unity and cohesion – undergirded at least by a common vision and common aspirations – is required for a united pursuit of such a vision. In other words, nation formation and social cohesion are both cause and effect. A decent standard of living would include, among others:

- the absorption of the majority of the population into economic activity as employees, employers and the self-employed;
- improvements in the quality, reliability and timeous provision of services

in local communities with a special focus on rapid improvements in neglected areas;

- access to assets such as housing and acceleration of land redistribution coupled with resources, skills and capacities to grow the farming population;
- reducing the cost of living of especially the poor, particularly with regard to basic foodstuffs, transport and administered prices such as municipal rates and costs of basic services;
- quality primary and general health care services, and
- To 'free the potential of each person', as the Constitution enjoins, requires appropriate focus on the quality of education across all the levels, ensuring that such education prepares young South Africans for the world of work and active citizenship.

BUILDING A COMMON HUMANITY AND ELIMINATING SOCIAL BARRIERS

- The foundation of the social relations expounded in the Constitution is human self-worth, respect for others and empathy for the most vulnerable in society. This should inform the content of the education system and broader civic education.
- Eliminating spatial and physical barriers on which racial segregation was founded is also critical to promoting nation formation and social cohesion. This is aptly illustrated in the case study on Fietas in Chapter Six. As such, in order to facilitate racial, ethnic, class and immigrant interaction a systematic and orderly dismantling and reconstruction of South Africa's living spaces is required.
- Building relations across racial and ethnic lines should also include the promotion of multi-lingualism, which must incorporate understanding of cultures and the encouragement of friendships outside the classroom and the workplace.
- It is subject to debate whether the current provincial dispensation – with some of the provinces carved virtually along 'neat' ethnic lines – is appropriate for nation formation. Are there other ways in which geo-cultural integration can be promoted?

VALUE SYSTEM

- Human self-worth, respect for others and empathy for the most vulnerable in society are, as indicated above, among the core values that should define relations in society. This should inspire the fashioning of individual interactions at the micro-level between individuals and within geographic communities; and at the macro-level between employers and the employed, between educators and learners, between those who wield state power and authority, and the 'ordinary citizens' and so on.
- Linked to the above should be targeted campaigns and programmes that combat the habit of (negatively) 'othering' those who are not South African.
- Combating the manifestations and tendencies towards corruption in the public and private domains and discouraging approaches to self-advancement that are inspired by a 'dog-eat-dog' mindset would contribute not only to the promotion of the legitimacy and authority of the State, but also to the sustainability of the whole political and economic edifice of the South African nation state.
- Both the public and private sectors at all levels should consciously and convincingly be seen to pursue non-racialism, inclusivity, corrective action and skills development.
- The fostering of the nation's value system should also be reflected in how South Africans observe designated national (holi)days: there is need to redesign the observation of these days to promote both political and cultural inclusivity.
- This also applies to activities such as sport, which have great potential to promote nation formation and social cohesion.

Various longitudinal studies are conducted to gauge the extent to which South Africa is making progress in attaining national unity and social cohesion. Within the context of the enhancement of the place and role of humanities and social sciences – and in transdisciplinary partnership with other relevant fields – a concerted and systematic effort should be made to develop a set of indicators that can be used as a local, provincial and national barometer of progress (or the lack of it) in this regard. We do hope that the treatment of these issues in this study will make a modest contribution to such an effort.

The proposals identified in this section derive in the main from the content of this study. At one level are issues pertaining to material conditions, and at the other, matters to do with value systems, social outlook and identity. All these should co-articulate in the long journey towards genuine South African nationhood and social cohesion.

BIBLIOGRAPHY

Abugre, C., 2011. The Financial Crisis and Social Development in Africa: An Opportunity for Strategic Change. Tunis: CODA Conference on the Impact of the Financial Crisis on Africa.

African National Congress, 1997. *Strategy and Tactics Document*. Available: http://www.anc.org.za/docs.php?t=Strategy%20Tactics [Accessed 19 November 2013].

African Peer Review Mechanism, 2010. Second Report on the Implementation of South Africa's APRM Programme of Action.

Alexander, Neville, 1986. 'Approaches to the National Question in South Africa', *Transformation*, Volume 1:1.

Anderson, B., 1983. *Imagined Communities: Reflection on the Origin and Spread of Nationalism*. London: Verso.

Anderson, B., 1993. Nationalism. In Krieger, J. (ed.) *The Oxford Companion to Politics of the World*. New York and Oxford: Oxford University Press.

Atkinson, A. B. and Marlier, E., 2011. *Analysing and Measuring Social Inclusion in a Global Context*. New York: United Nations: Department of Economic and Social Affairs.

Balibar, Etienne and Wallerstein, Immanuel, 1991. *Race, Nation, Class: Ambiguous Identities*. London and New York: Verso.

Bentley, Kristina and Habib, Adam (eds.), 2008. *Racial Redress and Citizenship in South Africa*. Cape Town: HSRC Press.

Bernard, P., 1999. *Social Cohesion: A Critique*. Ottawa: Canadian Policy Research Networks.

Bhabha, H. (ed.), 1990. *Nation and Narration*. London and New York: Routledge.

Biko, Steve, 1978. *I Write What I Like*. London: Heinemann.

Biswas, Shampa, 2002. 'W(h)ither the Nation State? National and State Identity in the Face of Fragmentation and Globalization'. In *Global Society*, Volume 16, No. 2.

Bourdieu, P., 1977. *Outline of a Theory of Practice*. Cambridge: Cambridge University Press.

Bunting, Brian, 1992. 'Lionel Forman and the National Question'. In *African Communist*. Fourth Quarter.

Cabral, Amilcar, 1980. *Unity in Struggle*. London: Heinemann.

Carrim, Yunus, 1994. 'Changing Ethnic, Racial and National Identities of Indian South Africans' [Unpublished paper].

1997a. 'The National Question in Post-apartheid South Africa' [Unpublished paper].

1997b. 'Africanism and Non-racialism'. *The Natal Witness*, 13 July.

1997c. 'The National Question in Post-apartheid South Africa: Reconciling Multiple Identities'. In *African Communist*, Third Quarter.

Cavaye, J. (2002). *Understanding Community Development*. Toowoomba: Cavaye Community Development.

Chatterjee, P., 1986. *Nationalist Thought and the Colonial World*. London: Zed Books.

1993. *The Nation and its Fragments: Colonial and Postcolonial Histories*. Princeton: Princeton University Press.

1996. 'Whose Imagined Community?' In Gopal, B. (ed.), *Mapping the Nation*. London: Verso, 198–213.

Chidester, D., Dexter, P. and James, W., 2003. *What Holds Us Together?* Cape Town: HSRC Press.

Chipkin, Ivor, 2009. *Do South Africans Exist? Nationalism, Democracy and the Identity of 'The People'.* Johannesburg: Wits University Press.

2012. *Middle Classing in Roodepoort: Capitalism and Social Change in South Africa.* Public Affairs Research Institute Long Essays, Number 2. Johannesburg.

Clarke, W. S., 2001. 'Sub-Saharan Africa'. In *Encyclopedia of Nationalism*. San Diego: Academic Press.

Cloete, P. and Kotze, F., 2009. Concept Paper on Social Cohesion/Inclusion in Local Integrated Development Plans. Department of Social Development: Pretoria.

Cobley, A., 1990. *Class and Consciousness: The Black Petty Bourgeoisie in South Africa 1924 to 1950.* Connecticut: Greenwood Press.

Constitution of the Republic of South Africa, 1996. Preamble.

Cronin, Jeremy, 1986. 'National Democratic Struggle and the Question of Transformation'. In *Transformation*, Volume 1:2.

Davenport, T. R. H., 1991. *South Africa: A Modern History*. London: Macmillan.

Department of Arts and Culture, 2009. Assessment of the Promotion of Identity and Social Cohesion in Selected Cities in KwaZulu-Natal. Pretoria.

2010. Baseline Information Document on Social Cohesion Version 5.

2010. Delivery Agreement for Outcome 12. Ministry of Public Service and Administration and the Ministry of Arts and Culture, 2010. Pretoria.

2012. Declaration and Programme of Action of the National Social Cohesion and Nation Building Summit. Available: https://www.dac.gov.za/social-cohesion [Accessed 15 March 2012].

2012. *!Ke E: /Xarra //Ke: Creating a Caring and Proud Society: A National Strategy for Developing an Inclusive and a Cohesive South African Society.* Pretoria.

Department of Provincial and Local Government, 2011. *Integrated Development Plan for Local Government*. Pretoria.

Department of Social Development, 2012. *A Pocket Guide to Social Development*. Pretoria.

Department of Trade and Industry, 2001. *Industrial Policy Action Plan 2*. Pretoria.

Desai, Ashwin, 2002. *We Are the Poors*, New York: Monthly Review.

Dexter, P., 1999. Tayob A. and Weiße W. (eds.) *Religion and Politics in South Africa: From Apartheid to Democracy, Vol. 1*, New York and Berlin: Waxmann.

Duncan, N. and De la Rey, Cheryl, 2000. 'Racism: A Psychological Perspective'. In *National Conference on Racism*. Johannesburg: SAHRC.

Ebrahim, Hassan, 1998. *The Soul of a Nation: Constitution-making in South A.frica*. Cape Town: Oxford University Press.

Emery, E. and Flora, C., 2006. 'Spiraling-Up: Mapping Community Transformation with Community Capitals Framework'. In *Community Development: Journal of the Community Development Society* 27(1).

Ergan, R., 1996. *Herder and the Foundations of German Nationalism*. New York: Octagon.

Fanon, Frantz, 1990. *The Wretched of the Earth*. Harmondsworth: Penguin.

Filatova, I. 1997. 'The Rainbow Against the African Sky or African Hegemony in a Multi-Cultural Context'. In *Transformation*. Number 34.

Fine, R. and D. Davis, 1988. *Beyond Apartheid: Labour and Liberation in South Africa*. Johannesburg: Raven.

Foucault, M., 1977. *Language, Counter-Memory, Practice: Selected Essays and Interviews*. Oxford: Basil Blackwell.

Gellner, E., 1983. *Nations and Nationalism*. Oxford: Basil Blackwell.

Gender Commission of South Africa, 2011. *Ten Top Stumbling Blocks That Remain in the Way of Women's Empowerment in South Africa*. Johannesburg.

Gerwel, Jakes, 2000. *National Conference on Racism*. Johannesburg: SAHRC.

Good Governance Learning Network, 2011. 'Recognising Community Voice and Dissatisfaction: A Civil Society Perspective on Local Governance in South Africa'. Cape Town [Unpublished Report].

Greenfeld, L., 2001. 'Etymology, Definitions, Types'. In *Encyclopedia of Nationalism*. San Diego: Academic Press.

Greenstein, Ran, 1994. 'The Study of South African Society: Towards a New Agenda for Comparative Historical Inquiry'. *Journal of Southern African Studies*. Volume 20 (4).

1995. *Genealogies of Conflict: Class, Identity and State in Palestine/Israel and South Africa*. London: Wesleyan University Press.

Guha, Ranajit, 1988. 'On Some Aspects of the Historiography of Colonial India'. In Guha, R. and Spivak, G. C. (eds.), *Selected Subaltern Studies*, New York: Oxford University Press, pp.35–44.

Guibernau, M., 1996. *Nationalisms: The Nation-State and Nationalism in the Twentieth Century*. Oxford: Polity.

Halisi, C. R. D., 1988. *Dividing Lines: Black Political Thought and the Politics of Liberation in South Africa*. Dissertion: Thesis (Ph.D.). Los Angeles: University of California.

Hermer, M., 1978. *The Passing of Pageview*. Johannesburg: Ravan.

Hroch, Miroslav, 1985. *Social Preconditions of National Revival in Europe: A Comparative Analysis of the Composition of Patriotic Groups Among the Smaller European Nations*. Cambridge: Cambridge University Press.

2000. 'Real and Constructed: The Nature of the Nation'. In Hall, J. (ed.), *The State of the Nation: Ernest Gellner and the Theory of Nationalism*. Cambridge: Cambridge University Press.

2006. 'Modernisation as Factors of Nation Formation'. In Delanty, G. and Kumar, K. (ed.), *The SAGE Handbook of Nations and Nationalism*. London and California: SAGE Publications.

HSRC, 2004. 'Social Cohesion and Social Justice in South Africa': A report prepared for the Department of Arts and Culture by the Social Cohesion and Integration Research Programme, Pretoria.

HSRC, 2008. *Citizenship, Violence and Xenophobia in South Africa: Perceptions from South African Communities*. Pretoria: HSRC Press.

Hudson, P., 1986. 'The Freedom Charter and the Theory of National Democratic Revolution'. In *Transformation*. Volume 1 (1).

Itzkin, E., 2000. *Gandhi's Johannesburg: Birthplace of Satyagraha*. Johannesburg: Wits University Press/Museum Africa.

Jansen, Jonathan, 14 April 2010. 'We Need to See Ourselves as Occupying a Common Planet' [internet]. Available at www.timeslive.co.za [Accessed 21 November 2010].

Jenson, Jane, 1998. *Mapping Social Cohesion: The State of Canadian Research*. Ottawa: Canadian Policy Research Networks.
2010. *Defining and Measuring Social Cohesion*. Commonwealth Secretariat and United Nations Research Institute for Social Development.

Jordan, Pallo, 1988. 'The South African Liberation Movement and the Making of a New Nation'. In (ed.) M. van Diepen, *The National Question in South Africa*, Amsterdam: Brill.
1997. 'The National Question in Post-1994 South Africa'. Available: http://www.anc.org/anc_docs [Accessed 6 November 2013] 2000. Interview with author.
1997. Discussion Paper on the Preparation of ANC 50th National Congress. Cape Town. 2000. Interview with author.

Karis, T. and Carter, G., 1972. *From Protest to Challenge: A Documentary History of African Politics in South Africa 1882–1964*. Stanford University, California: Hoover Institution Press.

Kedourie, E., 1977. *Nationalism*. London: Hutchinson.

King, E., 2009. *Interventions to Promote Social Cohesion in Sub-Saharan Africa*. New York: International Initiative for Impact Evaluation.

Kohli, M., 1981. 'Biography: Account, Text, Method'. In D. Bertaux (ed.) *Biography and Society: The Life History Approach in the Social Sciences*. London and California: SAGE Publications.

Kohn, H., 1964. *The Idea of Nationalism: A Study of Its Origins and Background*. New York: Macmillan.

Landau, L. B., 2011. *Exorcising the Demon Within: Xenophobia, Violence, and Statecraft in Contemporary South Africa*. Johannesburg: Wits University Press.

Larrain, Jorge, 1994. *Ideology and Cultural Identity: Modernity and the Third World Presence*. Oxford: Polity.

Lemelle, S., 1992. *Pan-Africanism for Beginners*. New York: Writers and Readers Publishing.

Lenin, V., 1977. *Imperialism: The Highest Stage of Capitalism*. Moscow: Progress Publishers.
1977. 'The Socialist Revolution and the The Right of Nations to Self-Determination'. In *Collected Works*. Moscow: Progress Publishers.

Long, N. and Long, A. (eds.), 1992. *Battlefields of Knowledge: The Interlocking of Theory and Practice in Social Research and Development*. Routledge: London and New York.

Mamdani, Mahmood, 2001. 'Beyond Settler and Native Political Identities: Overcoming the Colonial Legacies'. *Comparative Studies in Society and History*. Volume 43(4) 651–664.

Manackanjan, M., 1967. 'Keine Nation Ohne: "Nationale Staatlickheid"' In *Ost-Probleme* (9(2) p.60–63).

Mapungubwe Institute for Strategic Reflection, 2013. *Mapungubwe Reconsidered: Exploring Beyond the Rise and Decline of the Mapungubwe State*. Johannesburg: MISTRA.

Mathole, M., nd. *The Genesis of the Interfaith Movement in South Africa* [online]. Available: www.anc.org.za/caucus/show.php?ID=1649 [Accessed 19 November 2010].

Matthew Goniwe School of Leadership and Governance, 2009. 'Social Cohesion: A South African Perspective'. Johannesburg [Unpublished report].

Mbeki, T., 1998. *Africa: The Time Has Come*. Cape Town/Johannesburg: Tafelberg/Mafube.
1999. Prologue. In *African Renaissance*, Cape Town/Johannesburg: Tafelberg/Mafube.
2000a. 'Statement of the NEC of the African National Congress on the Occasion of its 88th Anniversary'. Available: http://www.anc.org.za/show.php?id=60 [Accessed 15 November 2013].
2000b. Address by President Thabo Mbeki at the Opening of Parliament, 4 February. Available: http://www.gov.za/speeches/2000/000204451p1001.htm [Accessed 15 November 2013].
2000c. Opening of the National Conference on Racism in South African. In *National Conference on Racism*. Johannesburg: SAHRC. Available: http://www.dfa.gov.za/docs/speeches/2000/mbek0831.htm

Meli, F., 1988. 'South Africa and the Rise of African Nationalism'. In Van Diepen, M. (ed.), *The National Question in South Africa*, Amsterdam: Brill.

Meli, F., 1988. *South Africa Belongs to Us: A History of the ANC*. Harare: Zimbabwe Publishing House.

Michaud, G., 1978. *Identités collectives et relations interculturelles*. Edition 5. Paris: Editions Complexe.

Mnguni, P., Ndletyana, M. and Teffo, J. L., 2010. *Social Cohesion Colloquium Report*. Pretoria: Department of Education.

Moore, Margaret, 2006. 'Nationalism and Political Philosophy'. In Delanty, G. and Kumar, K. (eds.), *The SAGE Handbook of Nations and Nationalism*. London and California: SAGE Publications.

Motyl. A. H., 1992. *Nationalism: Fundamental Themes. Vol. 1*, San Diego, San Francisco, New York, Boston, London, Sydney and Tokyo: Academic.

Mouffe, Chantal, 1992. *Dimensions of Radical Democracy: Pluralism, Citizenship, Community*. London and New York: Verso.

Mzala, 1988. 'Revolutionary Theory on the National Question in South Africa'. In M. Van Diepen (ed.), 1988. *The National Question in South Africa*. London and New Jersey: Zed Books.

National Development Plan: *Vision for 2030, 2011*. South Africa: The Presidency.

National Youth Commission, 2009–2014. *National Youth Policy*. Pretoria.

Netshitenzhe, J., 1997. *Nation Formation and Nation Building: Theses on the National Question in South Africa* [manuscript] MISTRA Archive.

Neuberger, Benjamin, 2006. 'African Nationalism'. In Delanty, G. and Kumar, K., *The SAGE Handbook of Nations and Nationalism*. London and California: SAGE Publications.

Nkondo, G. M., 2007. 'Ubuntu as Public Policy in South Africa: A Conceptual Framework'. In *International Journal of African Renaissance Studies*, 2, 88–100.

Nkrumah, Kwame, 1976. *I Speak of Freedom: A Statement of African Ideology*. London: Panaf Books.

Nyawuza [Brian Bunting], 1990. 'Left, Right on the Road to the Black Republic', *African Communist* 123, 54–55.

Odendaal, Andre, 1984. *Vukani Bantu! The Beginning of Black Protest Politics in South Africa to 1912*. Cape Town: David Philip.

Offe, C., 2006. 'Political Disaffection as an Outcome of Institutional Practices'. In M. Torcal and J. Montero (eds.), *Political Disaffection in Contemporary Democracies: Social Capital, Institutions and Politics*. London: Routledge.

Oliphant, A. W., Delius, P. and Melzer, L. (eds.), 2004. *Democracy X: Marking the Present/Representing the Past*. Pretoria and Leiden: Unisa Press and Brill.

Oliphant A. W., 2004. 'Fabrications and the Question of a National South African Literature'. In the *Journal of Literary Studies*. Volume 20, June, pp.5–24.

Pahad, E., 1988. Indians And The Struggle Against Apartheid. In M. Van Diepen (ed.), *The National Question in South Africa*. Amsterdam: Brill.

Parliamentary Portfolio Committee on Arts and Culture, 2010. Moral Regeneration Movement: Annual Report. Cape Town.

Pillay, U., October 2010. Powerpoint Presentation. Leiden: African Studies Centre.

Pityana, Barney, 2000. National Conference on Racism. Johannesburg: SAHRC.

Plamenatz, J., 1976. 'Two Types of Nationalism'. In Eugene Kamenka (ed.), *Nationalism: The Nature and Evolution of An Idea*. London: Edward Arnold, pp.23–36.

Potekhin, I. I., 1986. In P. Hudson, 1986. 'The Freedom Charter and the Theory of National Democratic Revolution'. *Transformation*. Vol. 1(1).

Potter, J. and Wetherill, M., 1987. *Discourse and Social Psychology: Beyond Attitudes and Behaviour*. London and California: SAGE Publications.

Ramose, M. B., 2004. 'The Philosophy of Ubuntu and Ubuntu as a Philosophy'. In: P. H. Coetzee and A. P. J. Le Roux (eds.), *Philosophy from Africa: A Text with Readings*. Oxford: Oxford University Press.

Ramutsindela, M. F., 1997. 'National Identity in South Africa: The Search for Harmony', *Geojournal*. Vol. 43(1).

Reddy, T., 1995. *Hegemony and Resistance: The Construction of Subaltern Subject as Other in South Africa* (Ph.D.). University of Washington.

Renan, E., 1990. 'What is a Nation?' In H. Bhabha (ed.), *Nation and Narration*. London and New York: Routledge.

Report on the SAHRC Investigation into Issues of Rule of Law, Justice and Impunity Arising Out of 2008 Public Violence against Non-Nationals, 2010. Johannesburg: South African Human Rights Commission.

Rogers, G., Gore, C. and Figueiredo, J. B. (eds.), *Social Exclusion: Rhetoric, Reality, Responses*. Geneva: International Labour Organisation. pp. 42–56.

Rotberg, R., 1966. 'African Nationalism: Concept or Confusion?' In *The Journal of Modern African Studies* Vol. 4(1) pp.33–46.

Rutherford, Jonathan, 1990. *Identity: Community, Culture, Difference*. London: Lawrence and Wishart.

Silver, H., 1995. 'Reconceptualising Social Disadvantage: Three Paradigms of Social Exclusion'. In *Social: Rhetoric, Reality, Response* edited by Gerry Rodgers, Charles Gore and Jose Figueiredo. Geneva: International Labour Organisation.

Simons, H. J. and Simons, R.E., 1969. *Class and Colour in South Africa 1850–1950*. London: Penguin Books.

Slovo, Joe, 1988. 'The Working Class and Nation-building'. In: M. van Diepen (ed.), *The National Question in South Africa*. Amsterdam: Brill.

Smith, Anthony, 2006. 'Ethnicity and Nationalism'. In: G. Delanty and K. Kumar (ed.), *The SAGE Handbook of Nations and Nationalism*. London and California: SAGE Publications.

Social Cohesion Implementation Framework. Presentation to the Forum of South African Director Generals [Unpublished].

Soske, J., *et al.*, 2012. One Hundred Years of the ANC: Debating Struggle History After Apartheid'. In: A. Lissoni, J. Soske, N. Erlank, N. Nieftagodien and O. Badsha (eds.), 2012. *One Hundred Years of the ANC: Liberation Histories and Democracy Today*. Johannesburg: Wits University Press.

South African Democracy Education Trust, 2006. *The Road to Democracy in South Africa*. Volume 2 [1970–1980]. Pretoria: Unisa Press.

South African Government Communication and Information System, 2010. Statement by the Minister of the Department of Public Service and Administration Following the Signing of Delivery Agreement for Outcome 12. Pretoria.

South African Institute of Race Relations, 2012. *South Africa Survey 2010–2011*. Johannesburg.

Spectator, 1982. 'The Mozambican Revolution and the National Question: For the Nation to Live, the Tribe Must Die, *African Communist*, No. 89, Second Quarter. London and Leipzig: South African Communist Party.

Stalin, J., 1954. 'Marxism and the National and Colonial Question'. In *Works Volume 2*. Moscow: Foreign Languages Publishing House.

Statistics South Africa, 2010. Millennium Development Goals, Country Report, 2012. *South Africa National Statistics*, 2010–2011. Pretoria.

Struwig, J., Benjamin, R., Gordon, S., Davids, Y. D., Sithole, M. M., Weir-Smith, G. and Mokhele, T., 2013. 'Towards a Social Cohesion Barometer for South Africa'. In: U. Pillay, G. Hagg, and F. Nyamnjoh (eds.), *State of the Nation: South Africa 2012–2013*. Cape Town: HSRC Press.

Tambo, A., (ed.) 1987. *Preparing for Power: Oliver Tambo Speaks*. London: Heinemann.

Tazi, N., (ed.) 2004. *Keywords: Identity*. USA: Other Press / Cape Town: Double Storey.

The Presidency, 2009. *A Nation in the Making: A Discussion Document on Macro-Social Trends in South Africa*. 2009.

  2010. *Guide to the Outcomes Approach*. Pretoria.

United Nations, 1995. The Copenhagen Declaration and Programme of Action of the World Summit for Social Development. '

Vahed, G. and Desai, A., 2010. Identity and Belonging in Post-Apartheid South Africa: The Case of Indian South Africans'. *Journal of Social Science*, 25(1–2–3): 1–12.

Vincent, Andrew, 2002. *Nationalism and Particularity*. Cambridge: Cambridge University Press.

Woddis, Jack, *Africa: The Roots of Revolt*. Citadel, 1962.

INDEX

www.ingramcontent.com/pod-product-compliance
Lightning Source LLC
Chambersburg PA
CBHW032131020426
42334CB00016B/1118